Essential Readings On
Stress and Coping among Parents of
Deaf and Hearing-Impaired Children

Also from Richard Altschuler & Associates, Inc.

Law and Society
Jurisprudence and Subculture in Conflict and Accommodation
by Stanford M. Lyman

Essential Readings On Political Terrorism
Analyses of Problems and Prospects for the 21st Century
Edited by Harvey W. Kushner

The Gay & Lesbian Marriage & Family Reader
Analyses of Problems and Prospects for the 21st Century
Edited by Jennifer M. Lehmann

Essential Readings On Jewish Identities, Lifestyles & Beliefs
Analyses of the Personal and Social Diversity of Jews by Modern Scholars
Edited by Stanford M. Lyman

The Living Legacy of Marx, Durkheim & Weber, Volume 1
Applications and Analyses of Classical Sociological Theory by Modern Social Scientists
Edited by Richard Altschuler

The Living Legacy of Marx, Durkheim & Weber, Volume 2
Applications and Analyses of Classical Sociological Theory by Modern Social Scientists
Edited by Richard Altschuler

Triumph In Exile
A Novel Based on the Life of Madame de Staël,
The Woman Who Challenged Napoleon
by Victoria D. Schmidt

From the Couch to the Jungle
The Story of My Life as a Multicultural Psychiatrist
by Thomas L. Chiu

Copani
An Evaluation Study of the Career Impact of a High School Arts Program on Graduates
by Victor E. Negron

Essential Readings On Stress and Coping among Parents of Deaf and Hearing-Impaired Children

**Edited, with a Foreword, by
Idalia Mapp**

Gordian Knot Books

A Division of Richard Altschuler & Associates, Inc.

Distributed by The University of Nebraska Press, Lincoln, Nebraska

Library of Congress Control Number: 20041070942

ISBN 1-884092-61-6

Distributed by University of Nebraska Press,
Lincoln, Nebraska

Cover Design: Josh Garfield

Printed in the United States of America

Dedication

To my husband, John Milligan, whose continuous support and encouragement have uplifted and strengthened me throughout our relationship and my academic career. To all the parents and families of deaf and hearing-impaired children who have dedicated their lives to caring for, nurturing, and meeting the needs of their children.

Contents

Editor's Foreword

Idalia Mapp

Parents look forward to having a child who is healthy (five fingers and toes, no neurological problems, and with all the physical attributes of a human being). Some children, however, are born with genetic or congenital hearing loss; and on occasion, due to illnesses such as meningitis, a child might lose his or her hearing at a relatively early age in life.

A parent's reaction to his or her child's hearing loss may vary, but many mothers and fathers react with shock and disbelief. The disappointment of having a "less than perfect" child drives some parents to mourn the child's hearing loss, the way in which they might grieve the death of a child. In addition, in the midst of dealing with the natural development of a child—as well as with the process of parent-child bonding and relationship formation—these parents are often confronted with having to meet their child's additional hearing needs, such as audiological evaluation appointments, hearing aid fittings, and speech and communication classes, among many others.

The parents' time and attention are not limited to their child's hearing needs, of course; they also are confronted with struggling to understand the nature of the hearing loss and the numerous emotions they are experiencing, which were brought on by the stressful news of learning that they have a deaf or hearing-impaired child.

Dealing with this news can be sudden and, at times, surprising; it may also add stress to daily life events. This is not an easy task for parents to deal with, and thus forces many mothers and fathers to search for untapped strengths and internal resources, as well as to seek support from both family and external sources.

In general, parents cope with their child's hearing loss differently. While working at a school for the deaf and completing my dissertation for a Ph.D. in Social Work at New York University, I had the opportunity to interview many parents of deaf and hearing-impaired children. To my surprise, some spoke of the joy, responsibility and dedication they felt for what they considered a gift from God—to be chosen for a such special task as caring for and raising a child with a hearing loss; other parents, in contrast, viewed their child's hearing loss as the cross they would have to bear with pride and honor.

The majority of parents, however, shared the grief and pain of having a less than perfect child. Some blamed their partners while others were struck by guilt and made repeated attempts to review their life—especially during the pregnancy—in an attempt to pinpoint what they did wrong and understand if their punishment was merited. One parent, whom I would describe as well educated and sophisticated, expressed the profound sentiment that a parent may learn to cope with a child's deafness, but the idea that one reaches the point of acceptance is false, because acceptance is never attained.

This book was developed foremost to address issues related to the many stresses confronted by parents with a deaf or hearing-impaired child, by bringing together a rich collection of authoritative articles in one convenient volume. The purpose of this book is to help parents, as well as students and professionals, better understand the stressful emotions parents experience and the different measures they use as individuals, both to cope with their feelings and meet the complex needs of their children.

Idalia Mapp, Ph.D.
New York, July 2004

Stress and Coping in Families with Deaf Children

Terri Feher-Prout

Abstract: *More than 90% of deaf children are born to hearing parents who experience stress, not only in response to the initial diagnosis, but also in adapting to the unique needs of their deaf child. This article is a selective literature review summarizing information from three fields in order to broaden our understanding of family adaptation to deafness. Discussion includes (1) psychology's model of individual stress and coping, (2) family science's model of family stress management, and (3) literature on family adjustment to disability. The last part of the article traces the development of professionals' understanding of the reciprocal influences between deaf children and their families and describes recent research indicating that the impact of deafness on families is complex and variable. The final conclusion is that adoption of a family stress and coping paradigm would inform discussion of current issues in deafness, such as cochlear implants and bilingualism/biculturalism.*

"Oh, yes, hearing parents go through the stages of grief-shock, anger, denial and all that. I learned about it in one of my courses." Nowadays individuals training to be professionals in the field of deafness are routinely taught the stages of mourning. That hearing families experience grief in reaction to the diagnosis of deafness seems obvious enough. Nonetheless, prior to the 1970s, very little was understood about a family's adjustment to hearing loss in a child. In the last few decades, researchers and practitioners have made great strides in understanding the impact of a deaf child on a family, but professionals are only just beginning to appreciate the diversity and complexity in families' responses to deafness.

More than 90% of children with severe to profound hearing losses are born to normally hearing families (Moores, 1987). The realization that a child is deaf causes stress in families who have had little contact with deaf persons and know little about the implications of deafness. In addition to coping with the shock of the initial diagnosis, families must acquire an understanding of a substantial and complex body of knowledge. Parents are often swamped with information on amplification devices, sign language, educational methods, school placements, and legal issues, all of which demand comprehension to assure appropriate critical decisions about the deaf child's future (Meadow, 1980).

Professionals need to understand how families adjust to a deaf child for two reasons. First, federal law requires that intervention with deaf infants and preschoolers be family-focused. Thus, planning and implementing educational programming for infants and preschoolers demand an understanding of family processes. Second, research indicates that competence, achievement, and adjustment in both preschool and school-aged children are related to successful family adjustment (Bodner-Johnson, 1986; Greenberg, 1983).

The purpose of this article is not to report new research, but rather to bring together three separate strands of literature in order to broaden our understanding of family adjustment to a deaf child. The first strand includes information about individual stress and coping from the field of psychology. The second strand involves literature from the field of family stress management. The third strand includes information on family adjustment to a child with a disability as well as literature on family adjustment to deafness, in particular. In the final section of the article, I consider implications for future research and practice in the field of deafness.

Stress and Coping: A Psychological Perspective

Psychologists' interest in how individuals cope with stress has grown significantly in the past 20 to 30 years. Currently, most psychologists use the cognitive model of stress and coping that was developed by Folkman, Schaefer, and Lazarus (1979). Coping is defined as "the changing thoughts and acts that an individual uses to manage the external and/or internal demands of a specific person-environment transaction that is appraised as stressful" (Folkman, 1992, p. 34). Coping is conceptualized as an ongoing process that consists of a series of appraisals and responses to the stressful event. There are three types of appraisal: (1) primary, in which the person evaluates the significance of the event for his or her well-being, (2) secondary, in which the person evaluates the event with respect to available options and resources, and (3) reappraisal, which occurs as new information (from within and without) is received and processed.

Psychologists consider a person's appraisal of an event as stressful to be essential to the coping process. Because individuals vary in their perception of events, what one person views as stressful, another may view as inconsequential. The diagnosis of deafness presents an illustrative example of how events can be interpreted differently. Hearing parents almost always appraise the diagnosis of deafness in a child as highly stressful, whereas deaf parents typically accept or even welcome deafness in their children (Moores, 1987). Moreover, appraisal of available options and resources varies according to the hearing status and experience of parents. Obviously, deaf parents have a lifetime of experience coping with hearing loss and consequently have access to resources unfamiliar to hearing parents.

Once an event is evaluated as stressful, individuals respond with coping processes. Coping processes consist of information search, direct action, inhibition of action, and intrapsychic (thought) processes, all of which vary over time. Coping processes serve two functions or purposes: the regulation of emotion and the adjustment of the person-environment relationship. Thus, coping behaviors are described in the literature as primarily "emotion-focused" or "problem-focused." For example, parents of a newly identified deaf infant often seek out other parents with children who are deaf in order to validate and manage their feelings toward their child's deafness. This is an example of "emotion-focused" coping. On the other hand, parents also request literature on hearing loss as well as ask numerous questions about communication and educational options. This is an example of "problem-focused" coping. Obviously, a coping strategy can serve a dual purpose. For instance, persons can read information both to find a solution and to lessen distress. But, most strategies are used primarily for one purpose or the other.

Coping behavior necessitates the use of four kinds of resources, according to Folkman et al. (1979): (1) health/energy/morale, (2) problem-solving skills, (3) utilitarian resources (economic status, educational programs, etc.), and (4) general and specific beliefs (self-efficacy, belief in God, etc.). With regard to deafness, a family's resources might include past experience with disability, access to parent support groups, familiarity with legal and educational processes, and so on.

In summary, coping consists of, first, appraising the stressor (for example, hearing loss) and the available resources (support groups, educational programs, etc.) and, second, choosing behaviors to regulate emotions or solve problems. Folkman and her associates stress that this process is always dynamic and sometimes unconscious.

Folkman et al. (1979) suggest "goodness-of-fit" as a basis for evaluating the effectiveness of coping behaviors. According to the "goodness-of-fit" model, coping effectiveness depends on an appropriate fit between (1) reality and appraisal, (2) appraisal and coping, (3) coping strategies and task demands and constraints, and (4) coping strategies and one's other agendas (i.e., goals, commitments, and beliefs). A "poor fit" can occur at any one of these points and result in ineffective coping. For example, parents may demonstrate a poor fit between reality and appraisal if they believe that a deaf child's speech is intelligible to unfamiliar listeners in spite of much evidence that it is not. In addition, goodness-of-fit requires a match between coping strategies and task demands and constraints. For instance, denial and withdrawal may be effective strategies in regulating the intense emotions that occur in reaction to the initial diagnosis of deafness, but may prove to be maladaptive strategies if maintained an extended length of time. Finally, there is sometimes a poor fit between coping strategies and individuals' other agendas. For example, parents may commit to developing fluency in sign language and later find this commitment difficult to maintain as job and family responsibilities compete for time and attention.

As a final note about effective coping, the fact that hearing loss is a highly ambiguous stressor tends to exacerbate the stress experienced by hearing parents. Confusing information and contradictory opinions overwhelm parents who are attempting to appraise the impact of deafness and the appropriateness of various coping strategies. Although parents may seek to diminish this ambiguity by asking questions (information search), professionals often have to answer parents' requests for a specific description of a child's future abilities with vague generalizations and a qualified "I don't know." Moreover, the expansion of choices in the last few decades with regard to communication options, educational placements, and technological devices has served to increase, rather than decrease, the ambiguity of the implications of hearing loss (Gregory, 1995).

In summary, because hearing loss in a child is experienced as stress by hearing parents, the dynamics of the situation can be understood using the stress and coping model proposed by Folkman et al. Although there has been some disagreement over the specifics of the model suggested by Folkman et al., the model has been used in numerous research studies and its general aspects have been supported empirically. Additional distinctions have been made between emotion-focused and problem-focused coping, and Folkman (1992) concedes that two categories are probably too few, but that eight or more are too many. In addition, researchers have attempted to clarify under what conditions coping resources, such as social networks, are beneficial or detrimental. Nevertheless, the cognitive model of coping proposed by Folkman et al. (1979) has stood the test of time and proved very useful in understanding how individuals react to stressful events, such as the diagnosis of hearing loss in a child.

Family Stress Management

While psychologists have been studying how individuals react to stress, another group of researchers, family scientists, has examined how families manage stress. Family stress theory and research began in the 1930s when Reuben Hill developed his ABC-X model of family stress management. Before describing Hill's ABC-X model, a definition of "family" and a description of family processes are necessary. According to Boss (1988), a "family is a continuing system of interacting personalities bound together by shared rituals and rules even more than biology" (p. 12).

Two important terms in this definition are "system" and "rules." Family theorists believe that the family is a system, a whole greater than the sum of its parts. In other words, one cannot predict the characteristics and behavior of a system, in this case the family, simply by looking at the characteristics and behavior of its components, the family members. "Families have a structure, symbolic as well as real; they have boundaries to maintain; instrumental and expressive functions must be performed to ensure the family's growth and survival" (Boss, 1988, p. 16). A family has "rules" to fulfill its functions and ensure its growth and survival. Under normal stress-free conditions, a family's rules consist of implicit understandings about "who does what when." In addition, families share perceptions and meanings about everyday events and about larger issues such as the value of life, the efficacy or futility of human action, and the justice or injustice of the world.

According to Burr and Klein (1994), families usually interact with little difficulty, transforming inputs (energy, time) into outputs (meaning, affection) with ease. "Family stress occurs when feedback indicates the family does not have the requisite variety of rules to transform comfortably inputs into outputs that meet desirable standards" (Burr & Klein, 1994, p. 34). For example, in the first months after parents learn that their child is deaf or hard of hearing, they may experience stress because they lack "rules" about how to communicate effectively with a child who has a hearing loss. Furthermore, stress may lead to crisis if family members fail to perform roles, make decisions, and care for each other. In crisis, the focus shifts from family to individual survival (Boss, 1988). According to Reuben Hill's ABC-X model, the degree of family stress/crisis is the outcome (X) of a provoking event or stressor (A), the family's resources or strengths (B), and the meaning attached to the event by the family (C),that is, $A+B+C = X$.

Family theorists have refined Hill's model in a number of ways. Researchers have examined the stages that families experience as they attempt to cope with stress. The most common pattern is referred to as the "roller coaster" model in which the initial period of stress or crisis is followed by a period of disorganization and acute coping, which is followed by a recovery period and a new level or reorganization and normal functioning. Use of the roller coaster model led to the concept of "stress pile-up," a situation in which families face additional stressors before reaching a level of reorganization and normal functioning.

When faced with stress, families adopt strategies in order to cope and reach a new level of functioning. Family coping strategies resemble individual coping strategies in that they are defined as "the active processes and behaviors families actually try to do to help them manage, adapt, or deal with the stressful situation" (Burr & Klein, 1994, p. 129). Additionally, family theorists organize coping strategies into categories similar to those employed by psychologists studying individual coping (i.e., cognitive, emotional, community, etc). However, Burr and Klein (1994) add an interesting note to the study of coping strategies by suggesting that families progress through a developmental sequence in which level I coping strategies are adopted initially, followed by level II strategies if level I strategies fail, and finally level III strategies in the event that level II strategies are unsuccessful.

Level I strategies refer to attempts to change family rules, for example, reassigning household responsibilities. Level II strategies refer to deeper changes, that is, rules about rules. An example of a level II change is adjusting the intent and purpose of household routines. Finally, level III strategies refer to changes in a family's paradigm, its basic values and beliefs.

With regard to deafness, families often adopt level I coping strategies. They adjust family rules as they adapt to the demands of absorbing complex information about hearing loss, learning new communication strategies, and managing the educational and legal bureaucracy. Families use level II strategies as well. An example of the use of a level II strategy might be altering the purpose of household routines from that of maintaining order to that of providing practice in communication skills. And finally, many families faced with adjusting to a deaf or hard-of-hearing child immediately find themselves adopting level III strategies, as they begin to question the meaning and purpose behind life's unexpected events.

Families and Children with Disabilities

Professionals who work with families who have children with disabilities have found it useful to conceptualize the family as a system attempting to manage the stress imposed by the child's disability. As Seligman (1991) points out, "A disability in one family member affects the entire system and in turn affects the disabled person" (p. 27). Seligman describes the family in terms of its structure and function and makes a number of points about how disability can influence the family system and vice versa. For instance, family structure is defined by membership characteristics (single parent, extended family, etc.); cultural style (beliefs, customs, etc.); and ideological style, which is based on cultural style but is more specific to the individual family. As an example, Seligman says that culturally based beliefs affect the manner in which families adapt to a child with a disability. Cultural beliefs can influence if and how family members seek help, as well as the extent to which members trust the advice of various professionals.

Families are defined not only by their structure but also by their interaction or function. Seligman posits four components to interaction: subsystems (marital, parental, sibling, etc.), cohesion and adaptability, communication, and other functions such as economic, domestic, recreational. Obviously, there are a number of ways in which a child's disability can affect a family's interaction. The quality of parents' marital relationship may influence how the child's disability is managed, and, conversely, the strain of dealing daily with disability may affect the parents' marriage. In addition, a family's adaptability is a factor in how daily stresses are managed. As family members adjust to the needs of a child with a disability, changes in roles may be necessary. For example, fathers and siblings may be asked to accept greater caretaking responsibility.

As a final note, Seligman reminds us that families exist in a larger context both in terms of time and space. Families have a life cycle—a beginning, middle, and end-that interacts with the changes imposed by disability. Moreover, families live within a larger community and within a larger culture. Messages from friends, neighbors, health care workers, the mass media, and the political system have a major impact on the family. In fact, an ecological view reminds us that, "In understanding and helping families with disabled children, one cannot only focus on the child, nor the child and the mother, nor the dynamics occurring within the family. Rather, it is becoming increasingly crucial to examine the family within the context of larger social, economic, and political realities" (Seligman, 1991, p. 41).

Although Seligman's challenge to examine the family within the context of larger social, economic, and political realities may seem overwhelming, Gallimore, Weisner, Kaufman, and Bernheimer (1989) have constructed an ecocultural theory of family accommodation to a child with developmental delay. According to their scheme, families strive to create sustainable everyday routines with their developmentally delayed children. These daily routines or activity settings, as the authors call them, not only accommodate broader economic and social forces, but also afford families the opportunity to construct and communicate themes or meanings associated with their own particular goals and values. Thus, Gallimore et al. stress the importance of both meaning and context in examining a family's efforts to cope with a child with a disability.

Seligman (1991) and others (e.g., Quittner, 1990; Wikler, 1986) who have sought to understand the impact of disability on a family have noted that the stress experienced by families with disabled children is chronic, rather than acute. Both the individual stress and coping paradigm developed by Folkman et al. and the family stress model developed by Hill were first used to explain reactions to acute stress. Nonetheless, Wikler (1986) points out that a number of researchers have used Hill's ABC-X model, either explicitly or implicitly, to study families of children with mental retardation.

According to Wikler (1986), family stress theory can be used to organize and understand a large number of studies on families with children with mental retardation. According to Hill's model, the stressor (mental retardation) interacts with the family's resources (B) and the family's perceptions (C) to produce family stress/crisis (X). Thus, resources (B) and perceptions (C) are factors that mediate or buffer the stressful event (A) and the outcome (X). Wikler points out that most studies on families and mental retardation have ignored mediating factors and simply reported on the impact of a child with mental retardation on family functioning.

Nonetheless, a number of studies have focused on mediating factors (B) and (C) without using the conceptual framework provided by Hill's model. According to Wikler, the influence of family resources on the amount of family distress has been examined more often than the relationship between family perceptions and distress. And, of the large number of resources available to families, social class and social support have been the two resources most studied. In general, higher social class and better social support have been shown to mitigate the impact of mental retardation. However, the complex relationships among variables resist generalization.

Wikler (1986) mentions two studies that explicitly used Hill's ABC-X model to examine the impact of mental retardation on family functioning. In the first study, the researcher found the stressor (A), rearing a developmentally delayed child, when interacting with family resources (B) and family perceptions (C), to be significantly correlated with amount of family distress (X). According to Wikler, when variables B and C were removed from the analysis, there was no significant correlation between A and X. In the second study, the researcher used the ABC-X model to explore whether mental retardation had a different impact on families at different points across the life cycle. Transition periods (for example, the onset of puberty) were found more stressful than nontransition periods.

Families and Deafness: Historical Perspectives

Although the above discussion is but a brief glance at the literature dealing with families and disability, it suggests that a family stress paradigm is useful in understanding how families adapt to children with disabilities. While most professionals in the field of deafness would agree that normally hearing parents experience great stress in rearing a deaf child, until the 1970s, little notice was given to the interaction between deaf children and their families. Beforehand, writers typically focused on the detrimental effects of deafness on all aspects of development (Levine, 1967; Myklebust, 1964). Families were hardly mentioned, and when they were, writers usually noted that deafness had devastating effects on the family that only served to compound the deaf child's problems.

In the 1970s, writers began to pay attention to the impact of a deaf child on the family and, conversely, the influence of the family on the child. Several writers concentrated almost exclusively on the initial period of mourning experienced by parents in reaction to the diagnosis of deafness (Luterman, 1979; Mindel & Vernon, 1974; Moses, 1985). In one of the earliest books on the deaf child and his family, Mindel and Vernon (1974) discussed at length parents' reactions to the discovery of their child's deafness. These reactions included the stages of mourning human beings experience in response to significant loss, that is, denial, rationalization, shock, guilt, anger, helplessness, and acceptance. According to the authors, "If the parents fail to resolve their feelings of grief, anger, guilt, and helplessness, they will be forced to remain arrested in the earliest stages of their psychological reactions to the child's deafness . . . . [T]he parents' early reactions related to the discovery of deafness and their resolution of these feelings toward the child influence all future decisions" (Mindel & Vernon, 1974, p. 22).

The realization that parents of children with disabilities experience grief and that mourning is a normal stage in parents' adjustment to a deaf child was an important addition to our knowledge. But, because interactions between deaf children and their families are necessarily complex and everchanging, writers' interest in family dynamics expanded beyond the initial mourning period experienced by parents. Two important contributions to our understanding of families and deafness were made by Schlesinger and Meadow (1972) and Gregory (1976). Gregory interviewed 122 mothers of young deaf children in Great Britain and drew conclusions groundbreaking at the time. First, Gregory stressed the great diversity in parents' responses to deafness. Second, she suggested that some commonly held beliefs about deaf children and their families were simply not true. One was that mothers were unreasonably overprotective of deaf children, and another was that parents allowed deaf children to unnecessarily restrict their social lives. Third, Gregory concluded that global prescriptions for deaf children and their families only created problems, and she questioned whether integration into the hearing world was a reasonable goal in all cases.

Also in the 1970s, Schlesinger and Meadow (1972) introduced the idea that deafness affected a child's development because it inhibited communication between the child and the family. As evidence, the authors pointed to the superior performance of deaf children with deaf parents (who generally communicated with their children from birth through Sign Language) on tasks requiring social maturity and independence. Although the superior performance of deaf children with deaf parents had been noted by researchers prior to the 1970s, there had been little discussion of the factors responsible for this difference (see Altshuler, 1974). Schlesinger and Meadow pointed out that deaf parents not only communicated with their children from birth, but tended to take the diagnosis of deafness in stride. In addition, deaf children with deaf parents benefited from their parents' personal knowledge of how to cope with being deaf in a hearing world. Thus, the authors suggested that the quality of communication and interaction between the deaf child and the family was a factor that mediated the impact of deafness on the child.

At the end of the decade, Meadow (1980) articulated more fully her idea that communication operated as an intervening variable between deafness and its developmental outcomes. In addition, Meadow discussed at length how the presence of a deaf child put tremendous pressures on a hearing family. These pressures either created stress, acted as a focus for existing stress, or provided a rallying ground for increased family cohesion. According to Meadow, how the possibilities for stress or growth emerged depended on a number of factors, including the quality of family resources.

In related work, Freeman, Malkin, and Hastings (1975) agreed with Meadow that several factors intervened between deafness and its impact on both the child and the family. Freeman et al. studied 120 deaf children and their families in Greater Vancouver, Canada, and concluded that there were several factors, including delay in diagnosis and the influence of educational controversies, that "make it difficult to sort out the inevitable primary consequences of childhood deafness from the secondary social, medical and educational factors" (p. 391).

As we approach the end of the twentieth century, professionals in the field of deafness seem to be arriving at a consensus that the relationships between a family and a deaf child are much more complex than previously realized. In a discussion of the adaptation of families with school-aged deaf children, Calderon and Greenberg (1993) note that research has not supported a stress-pathology model. In other words, it is not necessarily true that the stress involved in rearing a deaf child always results in negative outcomes for both child and family. According to the authors, a complex web of everchanging variables may interact to mitigate or exacerbate the impact of deafness on the family or, conversely, of the family on the deaf child. Thus, whether deafness in a child results in positive or negative outcomes for a family may be impossible to predict at the outset.

Families and Deafness: Research Perspectives

In review, the challenges faced by families adapting to a deaf child fit the stress-coping paradigm suggested by psychologists and family theorists. Individuals or families in stressful situations must choose strategies to regulate emotions and to solve problems. Coping strategies include intrapsychic mechanisms, information search, direct action, and inhibition of action. In addition, the use of coping strategies necessitates accessing coping resources, such as problem-solving skills, educational programs, social support, etc. Parents of deaf children must cope with the emotions associated with grief, understand information on deafness and its implications, and make critical decisions regarding communication methods and educational interventions. These aspects of parents' coping processes have been addressed in a number of recent research studies.

Research on family stress and coping in response to a deaf child can be organized into the following categories: survey studies, comparative studies, correlational studies, and qualitative studies. These studies examine various aspects of the stress and coping process. According to both psychologists and family scientists, the outcome of the coping process depends upon the family's or individual's appraisal of the situation as well as on the evaluation and use of available resources. According to Hill's ABC-X model, A (stressor) + B (resources) + C (meaning or appraisal) = X (outcome). B and C can be seen as variables intervening between A, the stressor, and X, the outcome.

The first group of investigations, survey studies, depends upon self-report rather than direct observation and thus, by design, focus on parents' appraisals of the stressor, deafness, and the available resources, educational methods, and programs. The goal of survey studies has been to examine parents' attitudes toward communication methods and educational programming. Kluwin and Gonter Gaustad (1991) sent questionnaires to the families of 364 students in a longitudinal study involving the schools of the National Research and Development Network for Public School Programs for the Hearing Impaired. The purpose of the survey was to determine which factors influenced the families' choice of communication method. The researchers found that mothers' mode of communication predicted both fathers' and siblings' mode of communication. In addition, a greater degree of hearing loss, the use of manual communication in preschool, and a higher level of maternal education were all correlated with maternal use of manual communication. The main conclusion drawn from the study was that mothers are the primary decision-makers with regard to communication mode. From a stress and coping viewpoint, mothers' appraisal and choice of coping strategies strongly influence the behavior of other family members.

A survey study undertaken by Bernstein and Martin (1992) examined another aspect of parents' coping process, that is, decision-making with regard to educational placement. The researchers surveyed 357 hearing parents of hearing-impaired children to gather information on factors that may have influenced parents to place their children in residential settings. The researchers were also interested in assessing parents' satisfaction with both the placement information they received and their child's placement. The survey responses indicated that, although a large percentage of the parents were satisfied with their child's school placement, only 36% of the parents were satisfied with information they had received. Interestingly, although the greatest number of parents stated "better education" was presented to them as a primary advantage of residential schooling, the ability to communicate turned out to be the primary advantage based on their experiences. Thus, parents' appraisals of available resources indicated satisfaction with educational programming, but dissatisfaction with information on programming.

In another survey study, Bernstein and Barta (1988) compared and contrasted parents' and professionals' views on educational programming for parents. Questionnaires were sent to parents and professionals in Texas. Results indicated that parents and professionals agreed that communication and education were the most important topics in programming for parents of hearing-impaired children. However, there were differences of opinion with regard to the importance of topics across the child's age span. Parents rated almost all topics as important across the child's age span, whereas professionals viewed audiology and speech as important in the early years and discussion of the child's future as important only in the later years. In other words, parents and professionals differed in their evaluation of the importance of various coping resources.

In summary, although survey studies permit general conclusions regarding the knowledge and attitudes of the parents who participate, they reveal little detail about how families adapt to a deaf child. A second type of study is the comparative study in which families with hearing-impaired children are compared to families without hearing impaired children. According to a stress and coping paradigm, the goal of comparative studies is to find a connection between stressor (hearing loss) and outcome (family distress or well-being). Some comparative studies address mediating variables, such as family perceptions and family resources, while others do not. In a study evaluating the emotional and marital adjustment of hearing parents of hearing-impaired youths, the investigators found that the parents of hearing-impaired youths reported fewer symptoms of distress than did parents of hearing youths, and that there were no differences in the marital satisfaction of parents in intact families (Henggeler, Watson, Whelan, & Malone, 1990). Interestingly, family cohesion was the most consistent predictor of parental adaptation and was associated with less distress in mothers and greater marital satisfaction for both spouses. As the authors point out, this result meshes with the research in the field of family studies indicating that family cohesion is related to positive outcomes in reaction to stress.

Attempts to find the correlates of successful family adjustment to deafness represent a third category of studies. In general, the goal of these investigations is to determine which factors (resources or perceptions) mediate the impact of the stressor (hearing loss) on the outcome (family functioning). Calderon (1988) assessed 36 hearing families with school-aged profoundly deaf children who were being educated in self-contained, total communication classrooms in public school programs. She evaluated the general personal adjustment of both parents as well as their specific adjustment to the deaf child. The child's adjustment was also measured. Calderon's analysis was based on the Folkman et al. model of stress and coping. Thus, she reasoned that parental adjustment was a function of the use of coping resources, specifically, social support, problem-solving skills, utilitarian resources, beliefs, and health/energy/morale. Calderon found that mothers who experienced fewer life stressors in the past or reported greater satisfaction with social support had better personal adjustment. In addition, mothers' specific adjustment to the deaf child was most related to satisfaction with social support. Interestingly, the amount of utilitarian resources available was not related to parental adjustment.

In examining paternal adjustment, Calderon found no relationship between coping resources and adjustment. In fact, fathers' adjustment was found to be dependent on maternal adjustment and maternal use of coping resources. The impact of maternal adjustment on paternal adjustment meshes with Kluwin and Gonter Gaustad's (1991) finding that mothers play a key role in determining communication mode not only for themselves but for the family as well. When Calderon examined child adjustment, she found that it was highly associated with maternal and paternal personal adjustment.

In a related study, Calderon, Greenberg, and Kusche (1989) examined the influence of family coping on the cognitive and social skills of deaf children. Again, the Folkman et al. model of stress and coping was used. According to the authors, the purpose of the study was to examine how five factors of coping resources (health/energy/morale, beliefs, social support, problem-solving skills, utilitarian resources) affect the family's adaptation and influence the child's development. Study participants included the 36 families of Calderon's (1988) earlier study. Numerous instruments were used to assess parental use of coping resources and child outcomes. Results indicated the following relationships: maternal problem-solving skills were positively related to the child's emotional understanding, reading achievement, and cognitive problem-solving skills; maternal belief in chance was negatively related to the child's social problem-solving skill; utilitarian resources were correlated with reading achievement; and, finally, positive maternal adjustment to the child was related to lower child impulsivity, greater cognitive flexibility, and higher social understanding. Conversely, the investigators found no relationship between child outcomes and maternal life stress, social support, and religiosity. There was also no relationship between maternal assessment of her own personal adjustment and child outcomes.

The failure to find a relationship between the two maternal factors, personal adjustment and experience of social support, and the child outcomes, cognitive and social skills, contrasts with Calderon's (1988) prior finding that child adjustment was most related to parental personal adjustment and maternal experience of social support. Also, in her earlier analysis, Calderon found no relationship between child adjustment and utilitarian resources, whereas a significant relationship was found between reading achievement and utilitarian resources in the Calderon et al. analysis. It seems child adjustment and achievement are differentially related to parental coping factors, with child adjustment being related to parental adjustment and social support, and child achievement being related to parental problem-solving ability and utilitarian resources.

In addition to Calderon, a number of other researchers have suggested that access to social support moderates or buffers the stress involved in rearing a child with a hearing loss (Koester & Meadow-Orlans, 1990; MacTurk, Meadow-Orlans, Koester, & Spencer, 1993). In fact, MacTurk et al. (1993) found that the families of deaf infants had social support networks equivalent to those of the families of hearing infants, and for both groups "the amount of support mothers received from family, friends, and professionals contributed significantly to the quality of later mother-child interaction" (p. 22).

Nonetheless, Quittner, Glueckauf, and Jackson (1990) have advised caution in the face of "widely held notions about the role of social support, and premature recommendations that increased support will be beneficial to those under high levels of stress" (p. 1266). Quittner et al. assessed parenting stress in 96 mothers of deaf children and 118 matched controls. The investigators also examined social support and distress symptoms, such as depression and anxiety. They found no moderating effects for social support. In contrast, parenting stress was associated with lowered perceptions of emotional support and greater symptoms of depression and anxiety. The authors concluded that social support mediated the relationship between stressors and outcomes. In other words, when mothers were experiencing stress, social support did not protect them from depression and anxiety. On the contrary, mothers experiencing stress tended to experience their relationships as less supportive and less helpful. Quittner et al. interpret their results to mean that social support may function as a buffer in situations of acute stress, but fail in chronic stress situations, such as parenting a deaf child. But Gallimore et al. (1989) demonstrate even greater caution and suggest that coping resources, such as social support and income, are not good or bad in themselves, but rather acquire their positive or negative value in the context of the family's particular circumstances and family-constructed themes or meanings. Thus, Gallimore et al. reiterate a feature of both psychologists' and family scientists' stress and coping models, that the meaning ascribed to both the stressor and various resources is critical to outcomes.

A final category of studies on family adaptation to deafness is qualitative research. The majority of qualitative research consists of personal interviews and thus focuses on family perceptions of the stressor and available resources. In other words, qualitative research examines how perception or appraisal mediates the impact of a deaf child on family functioning. Morgan-Redshaw, Wilgosh, and Bibby (1990) interviewed five hearing mothers of hearing-impaired adolescents on their experiences in rearing a hearing-impaired child. Mothers were also asked to keep journals for a period of two to three weeks. Journal entries and a second interview were used to validate the information gathered during the first interview. Transcripts of the first interview were analyzed for recurrent themes, and the following six topics emerged as significant: (1) the mothers' personal growth, (2) the mother-child relationship, (3) parent-professional relationships, (4) concerns about educational programming, (5) the importance of fluent communications, and (6) support systems available to the mothers.

Interestingly, content analysis of the interviews supported many of the conclusions drawn from quantitative research. First, the mothers often expressed dissatisfaction with professionals and with educational programming. Second, mothers stressed the importance of access to social support and of developing fluent communication with their children. And finally, the mothers assessed their child-rearing experience as challenging, but personally satisfying.

In a similar study, Israelite (1985) interviewed 14 female adolescent siblings of younger children with severe to profound hearing losses. Results indicated a mixed pattern of sibling reaction to a hearing-impaired child. In general, positive reactions were associated with positive family relationships and negative reactions with negative family relationships. Variability in sibling response seemed to be related to variability in parent attitudes and behavior. Israelite concluded that the presence of a hearing-impaired child strengthens relationships in some families and exacerbates tenuous situations in others.

As a final note on qualitative research, Gregory (1995) followed up her initial study of 122 deaf children and their families by reinterviewing the families 20 years later. According to Gregory, many of the parents remained concerned about their children, although the focus of their concerns had shifted somewhat. Many parents were concerned with their children's relationships with persons beyond the family and with the stability of their employment.

In summary, it seems that writers and researchers have made progress in their understanding of the impact of a deaf child on a normally hearing family, but that much remains to be learned. Traditionally, writers focused on the negative effects of a deaf child on a hearing family. While it is true that hearing parents experience grief in reaction to the diagnosis of their child's deafness, the pattern of family response following the initial mourning period appears to be variable. Much of the research on family adjustment to a deaf child provides only general insights into the adjustment process. For example, surveys indicate that parents are not completely satisfied with the resources available (i.e., information delivery and educational programming. In addition, surveys indicate that mothers play a key role in family adjustment. Comparative studies as well as qualitative research suggest that having a deaf child in the family may not be as detrimental as professionals once believed. In one study, measures of marital satisfaction and family cohesion showed no difference in families with a hearing-impaired member. In other studies, personal reports suggested that adjustment to a deaf child can result in personal growth and enhanced family relationships. Correlational studies indicate that the presence of coping resources, such as problem-solving skills and social support networks, contributes to successful adaptation to a deaf child. Indeed, the use of a stress and coping paradigm adapted from the field of psychology has increased our understanding of families and deafness.

Implications for Research and Practice

It is notable that, although investigators in the field of deafness have adopted the conceptual framework provided by the literature on individual stress and coping, they have neglected the significant body of research in the field of family stress management. Family researchers are interested in how stress affects family roles and relationships, in how families use coping strategies to survive and reach a new level of functioning, and in how family coping behavior changes over time. Adopting a family systems perspective suggests new questions about how families adjust to a deaf child. How do family roles and relationships change when families learn of their child's deafness and attempt to adopt new communication modes? How does the search for appropriate educational placement affect family functioning? What coping strategies do families use in response to changing demands throughout the deaf child's development? Do families vary significantly in their use of coping strategies and in their pattern of adjustment?

Wikler's (1986) analysis of research on families of children with mental retardation suggests that a stress management paradigm is useful in understanding family response to a child with a disability. According to a stress management viewpoint, family resources and family perceptions operate as intervening variables affecting the impact of the stressor on outcomes. Furthermore, as Wikler points out, the use of a stress management model reveals that, while many studies have examined the coping resources available to families, few have examined family perceptions of stressor or resources. With regard to the disability of deafness, it seems obvious that a hearing family's perception of the hearing loss itself, of its implications for the child and family, and of the resources available to the family is a critical factor affecting the family's adaptation. Indeed, qualitative studies involving in-depth interviews of family members have demonstrated the importance of family perceptions (Gregory, 1976; Israelite, 1985).

Currently, a number of debates in the field of deafness would be better informed if a family stress management view were adopted. Two issues under discussion are cochlear implants and bilingualism/biculturalism. A cochlear implant is a device that is surgically implanted to stimulate the auditory nerve of the deaf patient. Cochlear implants do not restore full hearing and are only appropriate for a small number of deaf children. Nonetheless, the issue of medical treatment for deafness presents an example of how perceptions of available resources vary. Many hearing parents of recently identified deaf infants react to information about cochlear implants positively, whereas deaf parents often react negatively. Although a complete discussion of the dynamics underlying the different evaluations of cochlear implants is beyond the scope of this article, the important point is that family (and community) dynamics should be considered in discussion of cochlear implants.

In addition, the pros and cons of a bilingual/bicultural approach to the education of deaf children have been debated without reference to the response of hearing families to such an approach (Stuckless, 1991). Again, a full discussion of this issue is beyond the scope of this article, but professionals in the field of deafness need to remind themselves that educational trends as well as medical treatments need to be examined in the context of family dynamics. Indeed, several writers point out that even larger social, economic, and political contexts need to be considered as well as the family context (Seligman, 1991; Gallimore et al., 1989).

In conclusion, psychologists' stress and coping paradigm and family researchers' stress management model have proved useful in furthering our understanding of family adjustment to deafness. Examining the reciprocal influences between deaf children and their families will not only further our understanding of the complex processes involved in family adaptation, but, ultimately, lead to more effective intervention for deaf children and their families.

References

Altshuler, K. (1974). The social and psychological development of the deaf child: Problems, their treatment and prevention. *American Annals of the Deaf, 119*, 365-376.

Bernstein, M., & Barta, L. (1988). What do parents want in parent education? *American Annals of the Deaf, 133*, 235-246.

Bernstein, M., & Martin, J. (1992). Informing parents about educational options: How well are we doing? *American Annals of the Deaf, 137*, 31-39.

Bodner Johnson, B. (1986). The family environment of deaf students: A discriminant analysis. *Exceptional Children, 52*, 443-449.

Boss, P. (1988). *Family stress management.* Newbury Park, CA: Sage.

Burr, W., & Klein, S. (1994). *Reexamining family stress.* Thousand Oaks, CA: Sage.

Calderon, R. (1988). *Stress and coping in hearing families with deaf children.* Unpublished doctoral dissertation, University of Washington.

Calderon, R., & Greenberg, M. (1993). Considerations in the adaptation of families with school-aged deaf children. In M. Marsehark & M. D. Clark (Eds.), *Psychological perspectives on deafness* (pp. 27-47). Hillsdale, NJ: Lawrence Erlbaum.

Calderon, R., Greenberg, M., & Kusche, C. (1989). The influence of family coping on the cognitive and social skills of deaf children. In D. Martin (Ed.), *The second international symposium on cognition, education, and deafness* (Vol. II, pp. 385-407).

Freeman, R., Malkin, S., & Hastings, J. (1975). Psychosocial problems of deaf children and their families: A comparative study. American Annals of the Deaf, 120, 391-405.

Folkman, S. (1992). Making the case for coping. In B. Carpenter (Ed.), *Personal coping: Theory, research, and application* (pp. 31-46). Westport, CT: Praeger.

Folkman, S., Schaefer, C., & Lazarus, R. (1979). Cognitive processes as mediators of stress and coping. In V. Hamilton & D. Warburton (Eds.), *Human stress and cognition* (pp. 265-300). New York: John Wiley.

Gallimore, R., Weisner, T., Kaufman, S., & Bernheimer, L. (1989). The social construction of ecocultural niches: Family accommodation of developmentally delayed children. *American Journal on Mental Retardation, 94*, 216-230.

Greenberg, M. (1983). Family stress and child competence: The effects of early intervention for families with deaf infants. *American Annals of the Deaf, 128*, 407-417.

Gregory, S. (1976). *The deaf child and his family*. New York: John Wiley.

Gregory, S. (1995). *Deaf children and their families*. Cambridge: Cambridge University Press.

Henggeler, S., Watson, S., Whelan, J., & Malone, C. (1990). The adaptation of hearing parents of hearing-impaired youths. *American Annals of the Deaf, 135*, 211-216.

Israelite, N. (1985). Sibling reaction to a hearing impaired child in the family. *Journal of Rehabilitation of the Deaf, 18*, 1-5.

Kluwin, T., & Gonter Gaustad, M. (1991). Predicting family communication choices. *American Annals of the Deaf, 136*, 28-34.

Koester, L., & Meadow-Orlans, K. (1990). Parenting a deaf child: Stress, strength, and support. In D. Moores & K. Meadow-Orlans (Eds.), *Educational and developmental aspects of deafness* (pp. 299-320). Washington, DC: Gallaudet University Press.

Levine, E. (1967). *The psychology of deafness*. New York: Columbia University Press.

Luterman, D. (1979). *Counseling parents of hearing impaired children*. Boston, MA: Little, Brown, & Co.

MacTurk, R., Meadow-Orlans, K., Koester, L., & Spencer, P. (1993). Social support, motivation, language, and interaction: A longitudinal study of mothers and deaf infants. *American Annals of the Deaf, 138*, 19-25.

Meadow-Orlans, K. (1980). *Deafness and child development*. Los Angeles, CA: University of California Press.

Mindel, E., & Vernon, M. (1974). *They grow in silence: The deaf child and his family*. Silver Spring, MD: National Association of the Deaf.

Moores, D. (1987). *Educating the deaf: Psychology, principles, and practices*. Boston, MA: Houghton Mifflin.

Morgan-Redshaw, M., Wilgosh, L., & Bibby, M. (1990). The parental experiences of mothers of adolescents with hearing impairments. *American Annals of the Deaf, 135*, 293-298.

Moses, K. (1985). Infant deafness and parental grief: Psychosocial early intervention. In F. Powell, T. Finitza-Hieber, S. Friel-Patti, & D. Henderson (Eds.), *Education of the hearing impaired child* (pp. 85-102). San Diego, CA: College Hill Press.

Myklebust, H. (1964). *The psychology of deafness.* New York: Grune & Stratton.

Quitmer, A., Glueckauf, R., & Jackson, D. (1990). Chronic parenting stress: Moderating versus mediating effects of social support. *Journal of Personality and Social Psychology, 59,* 1266-1278.

Schlesinger, H., & Meadow, K. (1972). *Sound and sign: Childhood deafness and mental health.* Los Angeles, CA: University of California Press.

Seligman, M. (1991). Family systems and beyond: Conceptual issues. In M. Seligman (Ed.), *The family with a handicapped child* (pp. 27-53). Boston, MA: Allyn & Bacon.

Stuckless, E. (1991). Reflections on bilingual, bicultural education for deaf children. *American Annals of the Deaf, 136,* 270-272.

Wikler, L. (1986). Family stress theory and research on families of children with mental retardation. In J. Gallagher & P. Vietze (Eds.), *Families of handicapped persons: Research, programs, and policy issues* (pp. 167-195). Baltimore, MD: Paul H. Brooks.

Parental Reaction to a Child's Hearing Impairment

Charlene M. Kampfe

Abstract: *Traditionally, parental reactions to a child's hearing loss have been discussed in terms of stages of the mourning process. Although this framework has been helpful in describing parent adjustment, it appears too simple. Parents react in complex ways to their children's disabilities; these complexities must be considered when working with families. A model of transition that accounts for individual differences is used to discuss the potential interaction among variables associated with the mourning process.*

Learning that one's child is deaf can be an intensely stressful event. It has been described as the loss or death of a parent's dreams for a normal child (Luterman, 1979; Mitchell, 1981). Because of the monumental nature of this loss, parents are thought to react by actively mourning or grieving (Schlesinger & Meadow, 1972; Luterman, 1979; Moses, 1985).

The mourning process is considered a catalyst for growth, a period that facilitates the transition from disbelief to reality, a process that helps parents shed broken dreams and generate realistic new hopes for their child (Solnit & Stark, 1961; Moses, 1985; Mindel & Feldman, 1987). Although the literature is inconsistent regarding terminology and the epigenetic nature of the process, most writers agree that parents experience emotional states or stages in response to their child's deafness. Luterman (1979) labels these stages as shock, recognition, denial, acknowledgment and constructive action.

Shock is characterized by numbness or a sense of having no feeling. Some consider it the initial affective state upon diagnosis (Shontz, 1965; Schlesinger & Meadow, 1972; Luterman, 1979; Mitchell, 1981). Shock may last a few hours or several days (Luterman, 1979). During this time, parents are typically unable to understand or remember information about the disability (Luterman, 1979).

Recognition. When parents finally realize the severity and permanence of the situation, they react with a multitude of feelings. Guilt, anger and/or depression are reported most often. Parents may experience these feelings separately or simultaneously and reexperience them again and again (Moses, 1985; Seligman, 1985; Mindel & Feldman, 1987).

Guilt is thought to be one of the most disconcerting states and manifests in a variety of ways. Parents may blame themselves, logically or illogically, for their child's deafness. Some blame poor prenatal care or family history. Others perceive the deafness as punishment (Moses, 1985; Mindel & Feldman, 1987). Guilt may show itself as preoccupation with discovering the cause, blaming the other parent, overdedication to and overprotection of the child, and/or rejection of the child (Solnit & Stark, 1961; Stream & Stream, 1978; Luterman, 1979, 1984).

Anger also is common, because the event seems unfair and communication with the child is difficult, because deafness can be disruptive, because it consumes time, energy and money and because deafness in a child can cause feelings of impotence, frustration, disappointment and confusion (Mindel & Vernon, 1971; Luterman, 1979, 1984; Moses, 1985; Mindel & Feldman, 1987). Much of this anger is directed toward the child, but may be displaced to other things and people. Parents may become critical of, demanding of, argumentative with and resistive to professionals who work with the child. They may argue within the family about issues completely unrelated to the disability (Stream, 1978; Luterman, 1979, 1984; Mitchell, 1981; Moses, 1985). This anger maybe more socially acceptable than child-directed hostility, but it prevents parents from dealing with their feelings. Subsequently, they may express their anger through nonverbal cues, overprotection or punitive actions (Mindel & Vernon, 1971).

When anger is not expressed, it may be manifested as depression (Luterman, 1979; Moses, 1985). Depressed parents lack the energy to deal with daily life, much less the energy to make decisions, seek intervention or offer emotional support to the child and family (Luterman, 1979; Mindel & Feldman, 1987).

Denial is thought to be a normal defense mechanism used to maintain homeostasis. Although it allows parents to retreat from painful feelings (Shontz, 1965; Luterman, 1979; Mindel & Feldman, 1987), it is believed to be an active process during which parents gather strength and prepare to deal with the reality of their child's disability (Mitchell, 1981). Denial can occur at many points in time. Prior to diagnosis, parents can assume their child's symptoms are the result of other variables such as stubbornness or familial tendency to speak late (Mindel & Feldman, 1987). Later, they may reject the diagnosis itself, the permanence or implications of the condition or their feelings about the deafness (Mitchell, 1981). Denial also may occur after parents recognize the reality of the situation. A period of intense feelings of impotence, frustration, guilt, anger, panic, anxiety or depression may trigger denial. At this time, parents may be attempting to retreat from a situation they cannot control (Shontz, 1965; Luterman, 1979).

Parents may express denial with repeated requests for new diagnoses, anger with the physician, wishful thinking, unwillingness to think about, seek or follow through with intervention, over-involvement in advocacy projects or collection of facts regarding deafness, over-dedication to business outside of the home, or unwillingness or inability to recognize or talk about feelings (Shontz, 1965; Luterman 1979, 1984; Mitchell, 1981).

Acknowledgment and Constructive Action are considered by some to be the final outcomes of the grieving process. Parents display a willingness to confront reality, discuss the deafness openly, assimilate information regarding the disability, and take action toward intervention. They enter the community more often with their children and encourage the maintenance of assistive devices. Because parents reexperience the reality of their child's deafness at this time, they might also reexperience many of their earlier feelings. These, however, are not felt as severely as before, and gradually subside (Shontz, 1965; Stream & Stream, 1978; Luterman, 1979).

If parents are able to work through the affective states associated with grieving, it is assumed that they eventually develop a renewed sense of well-being. They will have reevaluated and restructured their lives and values to accommodate the disability, and will emerge with new, realistic dreams for their child. If parents are not able to work through the mourning process, however, they may never reach a state of constructive action (Shontz, 1965; Luterman, 1979; Mitchell, 1981; Moses, 1985; Mindel & Feldman, 1987). Professionals disagree about whether the affective states/stages are sequential. Most, however, concur that the states are reexperienced repeatedly at significant milestones of the child's life (Moores, 1973; Luterman, 1979; Mitchell, 1981. Moses, 1985; Seligman, 1985). Professionals also agree that parents experience different affective states, for different lengths of time and at different intensities. Furthermore, parents may differ in their expressions of these states, the degree to which their reactions are adaptive or maladaptive, and the probability of their achieving constructive action (Mindel & Vernon, 1971; Gregory, 1976; Stream & Stream, 1978; Luterman,1979; Mitchell, 1981; Seligman,1985). It has been suggested that these differences owe to a variety of factors influencing the family, and that to understand the mourning process, one must consider the entire system (Buboly & Whiren, 1984; Seligman, 1985). A model that incorporates multiple variables can facilitate this understanding.

Model of Transition

Assuming that discovery of a child's deafness represents a significant event and transition for parents, a model of transition might offer some insight. One model that lends itself to the potentially complex interaction among variables associated with parental mourning is the House Model of Social Stress (House, 1974), described and modified by George (1980, 1982). Integral to this model is the concept that individuals respond to life transitions in a variety of ways. People have broad ranges of social status factors, experiences and personal resources that can interact in complex ways to moderate the perception of, reaction to and outcome of a stressful event (George, 1982). The model seems closely related to the cognitive phenomenological theory of psychological stress, that theorizes an interaction between the person and the environment and an influence of perception on the reaction to an event (Lazarus, 1966; Folkman & Lazarus, 1980; Lazarus, Kanner & Folkman, 1980).

The model, as modified for the present discussion, comprises five types of variables: conditions conducive to stress, perception of event, responses, outcomes and conditioning variables. Figure 1 illustrates the potential interaction among these. The solid lines represent hypothesized causal relationships while the broken lines represent possible mediators.

Figure 1

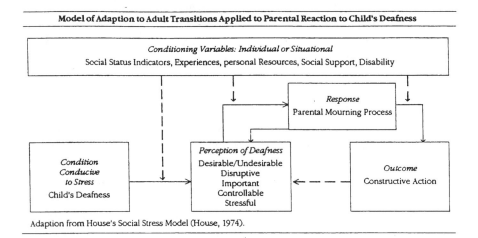

Model of Adaption to Adult Transitions Applied to Parental Reaction to Child's Deafness

Conditioning Variables: Individual or Situational
Social Status Indicators, Experiences, personal Resources, Social Support, Disability

Response
Parental Mourning Process

Condition Conducive to Stress
Child's Deafness

Perception of Deafness
Desirable/Undesirable
Disruptive
Important
Controllable
Stressful

Outcome
Constructive Action

Adaption from House's Social Stress Model (House, 1974).

Conditions conducive to stress are events that have the potential for causing stress (George, 1982). For this discussion, the condition will be a child's deafness. Perceptions refer specifically to the meanings attached to the event, in this case, the parent's appraisal of the deafness. Aspects of perception include degree of importance, desirability, disruption, control and stress associated with the event. Conditioning variables and responses may influence perceptions (Folkman & Lazarus, 1980; George, 1982). Responses are short-term reactions to events that facilitate adjustment. For this discussion, responses refer to the early stages of the mourning process. Responses can be influenced by both perceptions of the event and conditioning variables. Outcomes are long-term consequences of transitions that both responses to the event and conditioning variables can affect. The outcome of interest here is the degree to which parents achieve constructive action (e.g., generation of new realistic hopes). Conditioning variables are individual or situational variables that are potential moderators of the perception of, the response to or the outcome of a transition. For this discussion, conditioning variables include social status indicators, experiences, personal resources, social support and aspects of the disability that might facilitate or impede the mourning process.

The model demonstrates a complex interaction among conditioning variables, perceptions of, responses to and outcomes of a transition. These are discussed below as they apply to parental reactions to a child's hearing loss.

Perception of the Event. Parental perceptions of their child's hearing impairment vary depending upon a variety of conditioning variables. Social status indicators such as parental age, gender and ethnic background might all have impact on the degree to which the event appears undesirable, disruptive, important, controllable or stressful.

Experience with deafness is also likely to affect parents' perceptions. Those who are deaf or have deaf family members may have very different perceptions of the event than those who have never known anyone with a severe hearing loss (Mindel & Vernon, 1971; Schlesinger & Meadow, 1972). Likewise, those who have experienced other disabling conditions might attach different meanings to the deafness than those who have never had such experiences. The nature of these past experiences (positive or negative) might also have an impact.

Personal resources such as personality, coping strategies and attitudes might act as moderators (Mindel & Vernon, 1971; Mindel & Feldman, 1987). Persons who tend to overemphasize events will have different perceptions than those who typically deemphasize them or those who attempt to characterize them nominally. Persons who prefer to be independent of their families, who expect perfection/achievement in themselves and others, or who are extremely sensitive to public opinion may find the child's behavior, slow progress, passivity and extra need for help to be extremely stressful (Mindel & Vernon, 1971; Luterman, 1984; Mindel & Feldman, 1987). Mothers who prefer to work, but who forfeit professional plans, might be more likely to feel that the disability has been disruptive than those who prefer to remain at home (Mitchell, 1981; Luterman, 1984). Parents who over-identify with their child may perceive the deafness as extremely stressful and disruptive (Mindel & Feldman, 1987).

Education and finances are expected to have an impact, also. Parents who attach importance to education might find the child's language and reading limitations more stressful and disruptive than those who deemphasize it. Resource limitations such as reduced income because of reduced opportunities to work (Mitchell, 1981; Luterman, 1984; Mindel & Feldman, 1987), disability-related expenses (Luterman, 1984) and lack of time for working parents (Mitchell, 1981) are likely to influence their perceptions.

Support from family, society and service agencies might also moderate parental perceptions of the hearing loss. Feelings regarding the current marital relationship and degree of support given by the spouse and other family members may have an impact (Mindel & Vernon, 1971; Buboly & Whiren, 1984; Luterman, 1984). Changes in the marital relationship have been found to occur as the result of the child's disability (Gregory, 1976). The magnitude and direction of these changes may affect the degree to which the disability is viewed as negative, disruptive or stressful. Siblings have also been found to react in various ways (Gregory, 1976) that might affect parental sense of family disruption.

Availability of services may condition parents' views of the loss. When no appropriate programs are available locally, relocation of the child or the family can prove particularly disruptive (Mitchell, 1981; Luterman, 1984). Even where services are available, their quality varies. Parents may receive too much, too little, inaccurate or biased information (Gregory, 1976; Luterman, 1979; Mitchell, 1981). Counselors may not be empathetic (Mitchell, 1981) and the range of services may seem confusing and disjointed if not centrally coordinated. All of these might contribute to a decreased sense of control and/or increased sense of disruption and stress.

Variables associated with the disability also influence parental perceptions of the diagnosis. Type, degree, cause of and age at loss all create their own set of problems (Mindel & Vernon, 1971). The length of time between the first suspicion of deafness and the actual diagnosis may also make a difference. Although most parents feel the event is devastating (Mitchell, 1981), those who have suspected the deafness for quite some time may feel relief when their child is finally diagnosed (Gregory, 1976; Luterman, 1979; Mitchell, 1981).

Social standards regarding disability might also affect parental perception. Cultures that accept anomalies, for example, might result in very different parental views of the child's deafness than those which are less accepting (Mitchell, 1981; Moses, 1985).

The number and variety of these and other conditioning variables are expected to have a complicated impact on parental perception of the child's hearing loss, but the interaction among variables is even more complex.

Response (Mourning Process). Conditioning variables are thought to have an impact on the affective states of the mourning process. Social status factors such as age, gender and ethnic background might influence the type and degree of feelings parents have. Previous experience with the disability might also moderate parental affective responses (Stream & Stream, 1978; Luterman, 1979; Mitchell, 1981). Parents who are deaf or who have deaf family members typically adjust to the child's disability with greater ease (Mindel & Vernon, 1971; Schlesinger & Meadow, 1972; Meadow, 1980). Parents never exposed to deafness might have less information and less realistic expectations about the disability. They are, therefore, more likely to experience the affective states, and then to reexperience them as they discover unexpected limitations (Luterman, 1979; Mitchell, 1981).

Personal resources are expected to have an impact on the affective states (Mindel & Vernon, 1971; Stream & Stream, 1978; Mindel & Feldman, 1987). Parents have different abilities to face new challenges, delay gratification and persevere (Mindel & Feldman, 1987). Those who believe that displaying feelings is inappropriate may repress them, ultimately failing to achieve renewed, realistic dreams about their child. Parents who regularly deny and rationalize may be more inclined to prolong these states (Mindel & Vernon,1971; Mindel & Feldman,1987). Those who have rigid high expectations of themselves and their families may be more inclined to reexperience the states of frustration, anger and denial as expectations are not met. Parents' abilities to work through the initial adjustment are also expected to affect their subsequent responses to milestones in their child's life (Mitchell, 1981; Mindel & Feldman, 1987).

Parental education and financial status might also influence their emotional states. Parents who value education may be more likely to reexperience anxiety as they realize the educational limitations of their child. On the other hand, these parents might be more inclined to learn about the disability, and thus have fewer surprises and more resources. Parents' financial status might influence their abilities to obtain services, and ultimately, their affective responses (Mindel & Feldman, 1987).

Social support might also have a mediating effect (Mindel & Vernon, 1971; Buboly & Whiren, 1984). In the early stages, physicians and health care providers might encourage denial by failing to consider parents' suspicions about the child's hearing loss or by using relatively ineffective informal methods of testing for deafness (Gregory, 1976; Stream & Stream, 1978; Luterman, 1979; Mindel & Feldman, 1987).

Parents who have access to support programs after the diagnosis may experience very different feelings than those who do not. Parents forced to act in isolation are likely to harbor less realistic understandings and expectations regarding their child's disability and may, therefore, be more likely to reexperience the affective states as the child reaches important stages in life (Luterman, 1979; Mitchell, 1981). Quality of services also influences parental reactions. Professionals might provide too much information at inappropriate times or biased, unrealistic information leading to parental anxiety, panic, confusion or guilt (Lutherman,1979; Mindel & Vernon, 1987).

The type of social support one receives will likely depend upon society's attitudes toward grieving. Persons who live in cultures that suppress grieving may have greater difficulty because those around them may discourage feelings of guilt, anger, anxiety and depression (Mitchell, 1981; Moses, 1985). Conversely, parents who are given the opportunity to express their feelings in a nonjudgmental, empathetic and accepting atmosphere will be more likely to work through these, and eventually achieve constructive action (Schlesinger &Meadow, 1972; Luterman, 1979; Mitchell, 1981; Moses, 1985; Mindel & Feldman, 1987).

Family support may affect parents' responses to the loss. A warm, open spousal or intergenerational relationship may offer a great deal of comfort, ultimately affecting their emotional reactions (Mindel & Vernon, 1971; Mindel & Feldman, 1987). Family members may, however, be at varying stages of loss. Parents who avail themselves of services or who spend more time with the child may have more realistic understandings of the deafness and respond likewise (Mindel & Vernon,1971; Luterman,1984). When parents are at different stages, it is difficult for them to understand and support each other. Grandparents may also influence the parents' reaction. Their ideals, abilities to care for the deaf child, relationships with their children, coping strategies and personalities may all have an effect. Grandparents are thought to remain in denial for an extended time. In this stage, they are unable to give support, and may even encourage denial (Mindel & Vernon, 1971; Luterman, 1984; Mindel & Feldman, 1987).

Other parents of deaf children can provide valuable support. Having access to these individuals seems to help parents accept their own child's deafness (Mindel & Feldman, 1987).

Variables associated with the disability might affect emotional reactions. For example, if the child is able to hear environmental noises, denial may be prolonged, or the states of shock and anger maybe reexperienced as parents discover the unexpected limitations of the disability (Luterman, 1979;

Mitchell, 1981; Mindel & Feldman, 1987). The length of time parents have suspected the deafness before diagnosis might also have an impact. Mothers who did not suspect deafness may respond with a greater degree of shock and disbelief than those who believed the child was deaf before the diagnosis (Mindel & Vernon, 1971; Gregory, 1976; Luterman, 1979 Mitchell, 1981).

Just as conditioning variables influence the mourning process, so do perceptions of the loss. Parents who see the deafness as extremely undesirable, disruptive, important, uncontrollable and stressful are likely to respond differently than those who see it as less so. For example, parents who perceive the disability as less disruptive, less important or less stressful may experience fewer of the affective states of the mourning process, or may experience them, but with less intensity. Those who feel they have little control over the situation may use different coping strategies than those who feel they have some control. Those who perceive that they caused the deafness might experience severe feelings of guilt for extended periods of time (Moses, 1985; Mindel Feldman, 1987).

Outcome. Certainly, the variables discussed here do not include all potential moderators. These, however, should be sufficient to demonstrate the potential influences on parents' responses to their child's disability and, ultimately, on their abilities to achieve constructive action.

Summary

The highly individual, multivariate and extremely complex set of perceptions, social status indicators, experiences, personal resources, social supports and disability factors presented in the model can account for some differences in parental responses to their child's deafness. Since most literature regarding parental response is based on theory rather than research findings, no definitive statements can be made. The model, as modified here, or as others may modify it, can provide a framework by which these hypothesized interactions can be understood and studied further, ultimately leading to the identification of variables associated with successful parental adaptation to a child's deafness.

References

Buboly, M.M., & Whiren, A.P. (1984). The family of the handicapped: An ecological model for policy and practice. *Family Relations, 33*, 5-12.

Folkman, S., & Lazarus, R. (1980). An analysis of coping in a middle-aged community sample. *Journal of Health & Social Behavior, 21*, 219-239.

George, L. K. (1980). *Role transitions in later life.* Monterey, CA: Brooks/Cole.

George, L. K. (1982). Models of transition in middle and later life. *The Annals of the American Academy, 464,* 22-37.

Gregory, S. (1976). *The deaf child and his family.* New York: Wiley Press.

House, J. S. (1974). Occupational stress and coronary heart disease: A review and theoretical integration. *Journal of Health and Social Behavior, 15,* 12-27.

Lazarus, R. S. (1966). *Psychological stress and the coping process.*

Lazarus, R.S., Kanner, A., & Folkman, S. (1980). Emotions: A cognitive-phenomenological analysis. In R. Plutchik and H. Kellerman (Eds.), *Theories of emotion* (pp. 189-217). New York: Academic Press.

Luterman, D. (1979). *Counseling parents of hearing-impaired children.* Boston: Little, Brown & Co.

Luterman, D. (1984). *Counseling the communicatively disordered and their families.* Boston: Little, Brown & Co.

Meadow, K. P. (1980). *Deafness and child development.* Berkeley: University of California Press.

Mindel, E. D., & Feldman, V. (1987). The impact of deaf children on their families. In E.D. Mindel & M. Vernon (Eds.), *They grow in silence: Understanding deaf children and adults* (2nd Edition). Boston: Little, Brown & Co.

Mindel, E. D., & Vernon, M. (1971). *They grow in silence. The deaf child and his family.* Silver Spring, MD: National Association of the Deaf.

Mitchell, C. J. (1981). Counseling for the parent. In R. J. Rosser & M.P. Downs (Eds.), *Auditory disorders in school children.* New York: Thieme-Stratton, Inc.

Moses, K. L. (1985). Infant deafness and parental grief: Psychosocial early intervention. In F. Powell, T. Finitzo-Hieber, S. Friel-Patti, & D. Henderson (Eds.), *Education of the hearing impaired child.* San Diego: College Hill Press.

Schlesinger, H. S., & Meadow, K. P. (1972). *Sound and sign: Childhood deafness and mental health.* Berkeley: University of California Press.

Seligman, M. (1985). Current trends: Handicapped children and their families. *Journal of Counseling and Development, 64,* 274-277.

Shontz, F. C. (1965). Reactions to crisis. *The Volta Review, 67,* 364-370.

Solnit, A. J., & Stark, M. H. (1961). Mourning and the birth of a defective child. *Psychoanalytic Study of the Child, 16,* 532-537.

Stream, R.W., & Stream, K. S. (1978). Counseling the parents of the hearing-impaired child. In F. Martin (Ed.), *Pediatric audiology.* Englewood Cliffs, NJ: Prentice-Hall.

Stress and Coping among Black and Hispanic Parents of Deaf and Hearing-Impaired Children: A Review of the Literature

Idalia Mapp

Abstract: *An analysis of the research literature on stress and coping among African American and Hispanic parents in the U.S. with deaf or hearing-impaired children, as well as other disabilities, shows that little attention has been paid to this topic, even though these groups compose 25 percent of the U.S. population, and about 33 percent of all deaf or hearing-impaired children are African American or Hispanic. Findings show that, collectively, the parents use a wide variety of coping mechanisms, which often are effective in alleviating stress, especially those that involve personal, neighborhood, and familial factors, such as beliefs, religious faith, and informal support networks. Because both groups, however, occupy relatively low positions in the social hierarchy, especially as regards socioeconomic status and formal educational attainment, they are often deprived of using coping resources such as psychotherapy, private counseling, and medical technologies. In addition, Hispanics in America are often challenged to overcome linguistic barriers, as well as barriers that derive from traditional values and attitudes, which can impede coping efficacy. More studies are needed to discern differences between both African American and Hispanic parents and parents in the different Hispanic groups. Several suggestions are offered to improve the coping ability of minority parents with deaf or hearing-impaired children, including improved stress and coping paradigms or models, use of psychotherapy, counseling and support groups, and new social policies.*

Special Challenges Faced by African American And Hispanic Parents

Over the past several decades, many studies have documented that when parents learn they have a hearing impaired child, or a child with another disability, they often experience grief, depression, anxiety, panic, and other negative states, with which they are forced to cope (Feher-Prout, 1996; Kashyap, 1986; Mapp, 1995; Mapp & Hudson, 1997; Moores, Jatho & Dunn, 1996; Tavormina et al., 1981; Tavormina et al., 1981; Vernon, 1972; Wallrabenstein, 1984). In this process, social and professional supports are often crucial for parents to surmount psychological and emotional impairments and resume normal functioning. Overcoming challenges associated with having a hearing impaired or otherwise disabled child is especially difficult for many members of ethnic and racial minority groups in America, because research suggests coping efficacy is inversely related to economic and educational status (Fujiura, Yamaki & Czechowicz, 1998; Moores, Jatho & Dunn, 1996).

In addition, Latinos, among other ethnic groups with disabled children in America , commonly face barriers related both to communication difficulties (Steinberg, 2003) and cultural traditions that impede contacting and dealing effectively with service professionals, such as beliefs about the benefits of "folk" cures, reliance on family members as opposed to professionals to cope with problems, and *machismo* attitudes, among others. In this context, it should be mentioned that, although some individuals refer to the concept of *machismo* to describe an Hispanic male as "tough," "chauvinistic," "sexist," or "insensitive", the correct and true meaning of the word refers to a man who takes responsibility for the well-being of his family, sacrifices his own needs, works hard to provide for his loved ones, treats women with respect, and prides himself on being a good husband, father, and son.

The Demographics of Childhood Deafness and Hearing-Impairment in America

African American and Hispanic parents have a disproportionate number of children with severe hearing disabilities, as well as other developmental disabilities, compared to non-Hispanic Caucasian Americans. As regards hearing disabilities, nearly one-third of hearing-impaired children in America are either Black or Hispanic (Cohen & Clarkson, 1987; Deaf and African American Children, 2003), whereas these two groups compose about 25 percent of the U.S. population, with each group numbering around 12.5 percent of the total (U.S. Bureau of the Census, 2003). These data suggest that the changing demographics of deafness require special skills, sensitivities, and sociocultural information on the part of professionals, such as social workers, physicians, and nurses, working with African American and Hispanic parents of deaf or hearing-impaired children.

As regards childhood disabilities in general, Fujiura, Yamaki, and Czechowicz (1998) described the relationship of disability prevalence, low socio-economic status, and family structure among ethnic and racial minorities in the United States. Across all ethnic/racial and age cohorts, rates of disability were higher among low-income households; above the low-income threshold, group differences were greatly attenuated. Black and Hispanic children with a disability lived disproportionately in low-income, single-parent homes. Based on their findings, the researchers argued that the analysis of ethnic/racial differences in disability represent much more than a concern for "minority affairs." The data suggest the importance of risk embedded in the social and economic context of the nation and the need for disability policy to be directly engaged in the broader domestic discussions on poverty, social risk, and income inequality.

The Literature on African American and Hispanic Parents of Deaf and Hearing-Impaired Children

Despite these facts, the writer has discovered through a review of the research literature over the past two decades, that researchers have devoted little attention to studies on African American and Hispanic parents of deaf or hearing-impaired children, and barely any attention at all to comparative studies of the two groups, regarding the stress they experience, coping styles they exhibit, or supports they receive related to having a deaf or hard of hearing child. In addition to these studies, the review of the literature shows that some other studies have been done on Black and Hispanic parents of children with a variety of developmental disabilities, which have value for understanding the complex nature of parental dynamics related to coping with a deaf or hearing-impaired child.

In considering these studies, the researcher was interested in answering three basic questions: (a) What does the literature say about African American and Hispanic parents with deaf or hearing-impaired children, as well as other disabilities, especially as regards their coping behavior? (b) Can cognitive, emotional, or behavioral modalities be discerned either within or between the two groups of parents? (c) Do the two groups of parents have special needs compared to non-Hispanic Caucasian Americans that should be addressed more vigorously and knowledgeably by the helping professions?

The purpose of the article is to answer these and related questions, in two sections. First, studies are discussed that include African American parents, Hispanic parents, or both types of parents whose children are either deaf or hearing-impaired, or who have other types of developmental disabilities, including multiple disabilities that may include hearing deficits.

In the second section, the writer summarizes and synthesizes the main points of the literature review and presents recommendations for social workers and other professionals who are concerned about African American and Hispanic parents of deaf or hearing-impaired children.

Research Studies

Only a few research studies have included both African American and Hispanic parents of deaf or hearing-impaired children (Mapp, 1995; Mapp & Hudson, 1997; Mary, 1990; Wu, 2002). Based on an initial study by Mapp (1995) — who found unexpectedly low levels of stress among African American and Hispanic parents deaf or hearing-impaired children but more effective coping among the Hispanic parents—Mapp and Hudson (1997) conducted a correlational study of 98 parents of children with hearing loss to determine the relationships among the parents' stress levels, their reported coping strategies, and the demographic characteristics of themselves and their hearing-impaired children. The study revealed that racial and ethnic group membership was significantly related to the degree of use of several coping strategies. Hispanics differed significantly from African Americans in that they made greater use of coping strategies, including confrontive, distancing, self-control, social support, planful problem solving, and positive reappraisal coping strategies. They also differed from other groups in the sample in their use of confrontive and planful problem-solving coping strategies. In addition, the researchers found, as predicted, that the communicative ability through signing of the child was significantly related to levels of parental stress. The predicted relationships between a parent's marital status, a parent's educational level, the child's sex, and the age at onset of the hearing loss were not confirmed.

Wu (2002) examined the critical community resources and social supports of 10 inner city, African American and Latino families with deaf or hard of hearing children, aged 6 years and below. In identifying and evaluating these families' past and current resource supports, Wu's primary objective was to gain participants' input to inform program development. The children in the study attended their local public school program for deaf and hard of hearing students, and were enrolled in a community-based multi-service agency for deaf and hard of hearing youth and their families. The research design combined a naturalistic-ethnographic orientation and collective case-study approach. The process involved a semi-structured interview format that included community resource and temporal mapping measures, to both identify and evaluate the coping resources that these families used in the past and present. It also addressed what they considered was still then missing from their community support system. By analyzing the responses thematically and by a cross-case analysis, the researcher was able to determine the larger and more global themes shared across cases, which became the basis of recommendations to be incorporated into the community-based agency's program development planning. Findings from the study indicated that the most helpful resources and supports to the families were those that (a) provided "service with heart"; (b) were both child and family-centered in approach and content of services; and

(c) satisfied the most basic needs of the family first, in order to allow the family the time and energy to follow through on prescribed early intervention plans. Once family needs were met, resource emphasis was on inclusion of the family in child development activities and programming. Raising awareness, acceptance, and accommodation to deafness and hearing loss in the family's cultural and geographical community were also areas of critical need that parents felt strongly about, which were not yet met by resources or supports around them. The findings from the study clearly reinforced the current trend of family-centered support in early intervention practice of recognizing the child as a member of the family unit. Recognizing family strengths and assets upon which to expand, coupled with addressing the family needs, as the parent defined them, significantly enabled, empowered, and strengthened overall family functioning and the sense of competency a parent had, especially when they addressed the unique needs of their deaf or hearing impaired hard of hearing child.

Mary (1990) interviewed 20 Black, 20 Hispanic, and 20 White mothers of disabled children less than 6 years of age, to explore their feelings and reactions toward disabled children. The findings suggested that Hispanic subjects reported an attitude of self-sacrifice toward disabled children and greater spousal denial of disabilities more often than Black or White subjects. Stages of reaction from strong negative feelings to later periods of adjustment were most often reported by Hispanic and White subjects, and by 75 percent of subjects with disabled children with Down's syndrome. Although severity of retardation was not predictive of parental reporting of stages, subjects who received diagnoses within one month of the disabled children's births were more likely to report subsequent adjustment stages.

Several studies have been conducted of Hispanic families in the United States with a deaf or hearing-impaired child that focused on coping. Steinberg et al. (2003) examined the decision-making process among 29 Hispanic families who had a child with a hearing loss, in four geographical areas. The parents shared their experiences with the researchers, about searching for appropriate interventions and making choices regarding communication and education. The researchers explored the impact of language, culture, minority status, and access to information and services on the parents' decision-making process. The results indicated that the deliberations of Hispanic parents are often complicated by language and cultural barriers, and by limited access to information, resources, and a full range of options. The communication method chosen by the parents tended to be the one recommended by professionals, which was usually a combination of spoken English and sign language. Parents frequently expressed the hope that their child would learn Spanish as well. These subjects displayed a higher degree of assertiveness in obtaining services for their children than other studies have suggested, according to the researcher.

In another study, Steinberg (1997) examined the perceptions, attitudes, and beliefs about deafness and disability in nine Hispanic families with deaf children aged 6-13 years, using in-depth interviews that focused on the families' experiences in adjusting to the child's hearing loss. The interviews emphasized, in particular, concepts of causation of deafness; communication with the deaf child; and perceptions of the accessibility of services. The findings showed that most parents expressed either positive or neutral feelings about deafness, and that their concepts of causation varied, with some parents attributing deafness to divine will, others to heredity or physical insult. In addition, many parents reported that their extended families and communities stigmatized the deaf child.   Most families were satisfied with the services available.   Parents' appraisals of the children's receptive and expressive abilities for oral language were profoundly contradictory.

Jones and Kretschmer (1988) surveyed the parents of 46 Black hearing-impaired students aged 3-19 years regarding their attitudes, feelings, and knowledge about their children's hearing handicaps. The findings revealed that these parents were highly satisfied with their children's educational programs but involved themselves only minimally in the formal educational process. These parents were also unfamiliar with many of the methods and procedures commonly used by teachers when working with hearing-impaired students. The findings could suggest the parents used distancing or denial as ways to cope with their deaf or hearing-impaired child.

Several researchers have studied either African American or Hispanic parents of children with different types of disabilities, including hearing impairment combined with other disabilities, which have focused on parental coping and utilization of social supports.   Dothitt (2002) investigated the relationships between stress, multiple role involvement, and coping resources among African-American women who were wives, paid employees, and mothers of a child with a developmental disability. The sample of 55 African American women, who resided in the Washington, D.C. metropolitan area, were administered four questionnaires: a demographic questionnaire, a qualitative questionnaire, the Women's Role Strain Inventory, and the Coping Resources Inventory. Based on analysis of the data using chi-square, Fisher's exact test, ANOVA, the Pearson correlation coefficient, and multiple regression, Dothitt claimed a major finding of the study was that "spiritual/philosophical" was the highest coping resource domain espoused by the subjects, and that the "physical" coping resource domain was the lowest. Other significant findings were that the dependent variable, multiple role stress, was related to, respectively, the independent variables of husband support, gender of the child, and coping resources; and that the mean stress within the mother role was significantly different from the mean stress within the paid employee and wife roles.

Pickett, Vraniak, Cook and Cohler (1993) claimed that family studies in the area of severe mental illness have focused primarily on the problems of white parents caring for a psychiatrically disabled child. In response to such neglect of the unique experiences of Black families, this study compared the coping mastery ability and self-esteem scores of 24 Black and 185 White parents of severely mentally ill offspring to determine the different effects of caregiving on these two groups of parents. T-test analyses revealed that Black parents had higher feelings of self-worth and lower levels of depression than the white parents.

According to Blue-Banning, Turnbull and Pereira (2002), the rapid increase of culturally and linguistically diverse populations in the U.S. has important implications for service delivery. Addressing the needs of individuals transitioning from adolescence to adulthood and their families requires that outcomes of service recognize the cultural differences of people with disabilities. Because the Hispanic population is one of the fastest growing of the culturally and linguistically diverse populations in the United States, a clearer understanding is needed of the perspectives of Hispanic parents of youth and young adults with disabilities, concerning their hopes and expectations for their child's future, in order to provide them with effective support services. To address this issue, the researchers conducted focus group interviews with 38 Hispanic parents of youth and young adults with developmental disabilities. The findings showed a diversity of viewpoints among the parents, rather than a monolithic or narrow set of cognitions, regarding the parents' hopes and expectations for their children's future living, employment, and free-time options.

Lian and Fantanez-Phelan (2001) utilized a bilingual questionnaire to investigate perceptions relating to cultural and linguistic issues and advocacy among 100 Latino parents whose children participated in school programs for limited English proficient students with disabilities in a large urban district. The questionnaire included 56 Likert scale items in 3 categories: cultural and linguistic issues, parental rights, and home-school partnership. The results of the study supported the concern that Latino families need the tools to guide them through the special education process and encourage their involvement. The researchers concluded that there needs to be an enhancement of the provision of culturally and linguistically appropriate collaborative services that are individualized and interactive between parents and the school system.

Several researchers compared Mexican and Puerto Rican parents of disabled children. In an interview study, Skinner, Correa, Skinner and Bailey (2001) investigated 250 parents of Mexican and Puerto Rican origin living in the U. S. who had young children with developmental delays. The purpose of the study was to determine the role of religion in their lives. The mean age of the parents was 29.7 years and the mean age of the children was 3 years.

According to the researchers, the interviews indicated that parents in both groups largely viewed themselves as religious, were affiliated with a formal religion, and participated in religious activities. Most parents viewed both church and faith as supportive, but faith was shown to provide more support.

Bailey et al. (1999) interviewed 200 Latino parents (50 Mexican couples and 50 Puerto Rican couples, with an overall mean age 30.3 years) living in the U. S. to determine their needs and supports related to raising a child, under age 6 years of age, with a disability; and to identify variables related to reported needs and supports. The researchers reported that the pattern of needs expressed was similar to that found in previous studies, but that the number was substantially higher. More support was reported from family and formal sources than from friends or informal sources. Using repeated measures of analysis of covariance involving 6 family variables and 3 child variables, the researchers found that English language proficiency was the only variable to account for significant variance in needs and supports.

To examine the nature of "blame" Hispanic mothers attribute for having a disabled child, and how that might affect their coping and stress, Chavira, Lopez, Blacher, and Shapiro (2000) examined the applicability of attribution theory to mothers' perceptions and reactions to their child's problem behavior. The participants were 149 Latina mothers (with an average age of 40.6 years) and their children (between 3 and 19 years of age) with developmental disabilities or mental retardation. The mothers were interviewed regarding specific incidents in which their child exhibited a behavior problem, and the researchers also assessed the severity of the child's disability and mother's attributions of responsibility and behavioral and emotional reactions to the child's behavior problems. The findings indicated that most mothers viewed their child as not being responsible for the behavior problem. Furthermore, as predicted by attribution theory, mothers who ascribed relatively high responsibility to the child were significantly more likely to report negative emotions (anger and frustration) and aggressive/harsh behavioral reactions than mothers who ascribed low responsibility. Also, mothers were more likely to ascribe high responsibility to the child when the problem was characterized as a behavioral excess than as a behavioral deficit. According to the researchers, the results provide support for the applicability of an attributional framework, and may have important implications for helping parents in addressing the problem behaviors of their children with developmental disabilities.

Skinner, Bailey, Correa, and Rodrigues (1999) examined how 150 Latino mothers (with a mean age of 28.5 years) of children (with a mean age 3 years) with developmental disabilities used narratives to express and create self-understandings *vis-à-vis* their child. The purpose of the study was twofold: (1) to introduce narrative as a tool that people use to make sense of disability, and (2) to demonstrate how these mothers draw on cultural belief and the narrative form to construct meanings of self in relationship to disability. From an analysis of the participants' spontaneous narratives of self and disability, the research found that the majority of mothers portrayed themselves as good mothers in line with larger cultural notions, and viewed their child as bringing about positive transformations in their lives.

Reyes-Blanes, Correa, and Bailey (1999) compared the family needs and sources of support as perceived by (a) 55 Puerto Rican mothers 21-49 years old with young children 3 months to 5 years old with disabilities, residing in Puerto Rico, and (b) 39 of their counterparts living in Florida. The researchers also explored the relationship between the mothers' perceived family needs and sources of support and both mother and child background characteristics. In the interview process, the ABILITIES Index, the Family Needs Survey, and the Family Support Scale were used to measure, respectively, mothers' perception of (a) child's extent of delay, (b) family needs, and (c) sources of support. The results indicated that family needs did not differ in the Puerto Rican and Florida samples. Mothers from the Puerto Rican sample did, however, perceive significantly more sources of support than mothers in the Florida sample.

Sontag and Schlacht (1994) investigated ethnic differences in parent perceptions of their information needs and their sources of information, and the nature of parent participation in early intervention and participation preferences. They conducted interviews with Hispanic, White, and American Indian families (N = 536) with infants and toddlers who had developmental problems. A major finding from the study was that medical doctors were the only source a majority of the participants identified as providing them with useful information about their child. The parents also reported a high degree of involvement in meeting their child's service needs. Less than half of the parents, however, had attended program-planning meetings, while few parents identified this activity as a useful way to become more involved in meeting their child's needs. Hispanic and American Indians reported more difficulty than Caucasians in obtaining information about their child's problem, according to the researchers.

Harry (1992) examined the views of 12 low-income Puerto Rican families whose children were classified as learning disabled or mildly mentally retarded. In nine of the families, only mothers and one grandmother participated. Different cultural meanings of disability and normalcy led parents to reject the notion of disability and focus on the impact of family identity, language confusion, and detrimental educational practices on children's school performance. Parents' views were in line with current arguments against labeling and English-only instruction, according to Harry.

Prieto-Bayard and Baker (1986) described a group parent-training program for 20 lower socioeconomic status Spanish-speaking families with a developmentally disabled child, aged 3.5-16 years. Nine families received group training, and 11 control families received delayed training. The researchers took measures of mothers' teaching ability, children's self-help skills, children's behavior problems, mothers' knowledge of teaching principles, and families' home teaching. The findings showed that the trained parents gained significantly more than the control parents on the latter three measures, and that trained families gained significantly on all of the measures.

Summary and Conclusions

African Americans and Latinos compose about 25 percent of the total U.S. population, but about 33 percent of all deaf and hard of hearing children are born to such parents, as well as a disproportionate percentage of children with other disabilities. The literature shows that these parents often experience stresses with which they must cope; and that individual mothers and fathers use one or several coping mechanisms, but not nearly all the coping options available to such parents. As this study has shown, collectively the parents use avoidance, religious devotion, denial, faith, optimism, social support groups, economic assistance, medical technologies, psychotherapy, narratives, mainstreaming, subcultural isolation, individual distancing, attribution of blame, fatalism, training courses, and rationalization, among various other coping mechanisms.

Despite the size of the African American and Latino population in the United States, and the stresses of coping with disabled children, especially among sociocultural groups with relatively low amounts of economic, educational, and linguistic resources in American society, it is surprising to see that almost no studies have been conducted that have compared the two groups of parents on their ability to cope with having a deaf or hearing-impaired child, or other type of disabled child. Most significantly in this area, the work of Mapp (Mapp, 1995; Mapp and Hudson, 1997) has shown that Hispanics differ significantly from African Americans in making greater use of coping strategies, including confrontive, distancing, self-control, social support, planful problem solving, and positive reappraisal coping strategies.

Studies that have solely involved either African American or Hispanic parents with hearing impaired or otherwise disabled children have not focused on exactly the same phenomena or used the same methodology. As a result, reliable comparisons of the two groups of parents from the disparate studies cannot be made. The need for more well-designed studies of coping among African American and Hispanic parents of deaf or hearing-impaired children, especially comparative studies, is highly important, for a variety of reasons. While these parents' attempts to achieve a positive attitude and overcome the negative potentials of having to raise a deaf or hearing-impaired, or otherwise disabled, child represents a valiant effort on their part, there are many reasons to believe their task is more difficult than may at first seem apparent; and this, in turn, suggests these parents may need additional supports, including supports they have rarely or never utilized. Some reasons for this suggestion are attributable to the relatively low socioeconomic status that African American and Hispanic individuals, on the whole, occupy in American society, while other reasons are related to barriers associated with their social and cultural backgrounds, such as language, customs, and educational barriers.

These suppositions are supported by Moores, Jatho and Dunn (1996), in their review of literature published in the periodical _American Annals of the Deaf_ during the period 1996-2000 concerning families with deaf members. They found that the examined literature primarily discussed four themes: (a) support services, (b) interaction and involvement, (c) stress and coping, and (d) decision making. Most important for this study, according to the researchers, the literature shows that services were more effective for families with higher education levels and higher socioeconomic status, thereby indicating the need for more comprehensive services for families from less affluent backgrounds and with lower levels of education. Interestingly, the heterogeneity of the families reported on in the studies was a striking factor, and the literature showed an expanding awareness and concern with fathers, siblings, extended family members, and members of the deaf community, as opposed to the traditional mother-child dyad.

Even several decades earlier, Vernon (1972) reported findings based on a literature review that went back to 1952, that the key variables affecting parents' coping procedures are the character of the parents, the counseling they receive, their attitude toward having a child, the degree toward which denial is used, and the stress resulting from communication problems. As can be seen, several of these variables are linked to either economic, educational, or cultural factors, which can either impede or enhance coping ability and stress. According to Farrugia (1991-92), when a deaf child is born to parents who do not cope well with the demands of any parent-child relationship, the additional demands associated with deafness and early development can only lead to greater pressures on an already strained parent-child relationship. These conditions can lead to the kind of abusive or unavailable parenting that may result in borderline personality disorder. Given the high rate of single-parents and unemployed or underemployed households in which African American and Hispanic children are raised, one can logically assume that the negative impact on single or unemployed parents with low incomes is expected to be profound, in many instances. As suggested by Klein (1977), these problems can be expected to be even worse for parents of deaf-blind children. The dual handicaps have greater pervading ramifications for their families than most professionals are likely to perceive.

This claim related to deaf or hearing-impaired children with at least one other handicap was supported by Tavormina et al. (1981), who assessed the personality styles, attitudes, perspectives, and coping strategies of 133 mothers and 93 fathers of hearing-impaired children who also were diabetic, asthmatic, and cystic fibrotic, aged 5-19 years. The instruments used included the Eysenck Personality Inventory, Missouri Behavior Problem Checklist, and Hereford Parent Attitude Survey. Across measures, both the essential positive adjustment levels and special problems of the sample were demonstrated, such that they formed a distinct group whose functioning fell between that reported for either "normal" or poorly adjusted parents. Furthermore, the presence of the ill child served as the primary contributor to these patterns, with types of illness providing a secondary but significant thrust to its extent. Mothers consistently reported both more problems and involvement than fathers, which the researchers claimed illustrated their differential roles within these families as well as their typical modes of response to the stress of the ill child. Without a doubt, the stress was taking its toll on the parents, according to the researchers, who suggested that a focus on parental needs is necessary in the total management program for the physically ill child.

Practice Implications

Given the findings from this study and their implications for parents, especially mothers and fathers of African American or Hispanic descent in America, the researcher recommends the following for social workers and other concerned professionals.

Develop a Family Stress and Coping Paradigm. Workers and other professionals should develop a paradigm or model that can address the issues of stress and coping among parents of deaf or hearing-impaired children, especially a paradigm that includes cultural criteria consistent with the backgrounds and experiences of hearing African American and Hispanic parents (Feher-Prout, 1996; Greenberg, Lengua & Calderon, 1997; Kampfe, 1989). Feher-Prout (1996) found, in a literature review study, that 90% of deaf children are born to hearing parents who experience stress, not only in response to the initial diagnosis, but also in adapting to the unique needs of their deaf child. Feher-Prout pointed out that professionals have increasingly had to develop their understanding of the reciprocal influences between deaf children and their families, and concluded that adoption of a family stress and coping paradigm would inform discussion of current issues in deafness, such as cochlear implants and bilingualism/biculturalism.

Greenberg, Lengua and Calderon (1997) also proposed the development of a conceptual model of coping for parents of deaf or hearing-impaired children, especially as the model fits within a larger process model for understanding factors that influence the psychosocial development of deaf children and youth. They most stressed variables related to contextual and cultural issues, social-cognition, and personality factors that impact the deaf child and his or her family. In addition, Kampfe (1989) presented a model of transition that accounts for individual differences in parental reactions to a child's hearing loss. Supporting the findings of the current study, Kampfe pointed out that there are highly individual, multivariate, and extremely complex sets of perceptions, social status indicators, experiences, personal resources, social supports, and disability factors that affect one's ability to perceive the event and respond with effective coping behaviors.

Help Parents Overcome Disappointment Based on Failed Expectations. New parents naturally expect to have a healthy child in every respect, and are often severely disappointed when they learn their infant has a developmental disability. This disappointment, in turn, can lead to depression or hostility against the child, among other negative reactions, which can further harm the integrity of the family unit and all relationships within it. To the extent this situation exists, effective coping becomes difficult or impossible. For these reasons, parents should be helped to work through negative emotions based on disappointment by trained professionals. In this regard, a study by Kashyap (1986) is instructive. Kashyap discussed problems of communication between a deaf child and parents and siblings and related coping mechanisms in a sample of 100 deaf Indian children, aged 5-14 years, and their families. Parents' expectations for their deaf children were violated by the hearing impairment. For many parents, the child's deafness threatened their sense of invulnerability and triggered mourning and anxiety. Many felt they could have no expectations for the child's future. Most parents viewed the presence of the deaf child as a negative influence on the family, although they simultaneously felt the overall impact on their daily life was neutral. According to Kashyap, social work intervention should focus on helping parents resolve their feelings about the deafness in terms of their expectations and their perceptions of its impact on the family.

Provide Extended Psychosocial Intervention, Including Support Groups. The more severe the hearing impairment, or other disability, of the child, the more difficult it is for parents to cope. This is especially true when the child has a hearing impairment and at least one other disability. In such cases, extended psychotherapy and the use of support groups can be crucial for parents to overcome their stresses and cope effectively. Hintermair (2000) examined the stress experiences and social networks of parents of children aged 1-12 years with hearing impairments. A total of 317 parents of hearing-impaired children provided demographic information and completed the Parenting Stress Index. From the study, Hintermair found that parents who frequently met with other parents both shared practical help and showed evidence of warm, accepting, and trusting relationships with their children; and that parents with children having severe hearing impairments exhibited more problems in establishing mutual child relationships than did parents of children with less severe hearing loss. According to the researcher, the findings from the study suggested that social support is important for reducing stress in parents with hearing-impaired children, especially when the disability exists in conjunction with another disability, and that these parents also should be provided with extended psychosocial intervention.

Teach New Parents to Use Bonding Behaviors. When parents first discover that their child has a hearing impairment, they should use the natural parent-infant bond as a basis for overcoming the stresses placed on the relationship. Leigh (1987) discussed the natural attachment (bonding) process between mother and child, and the strains placed on it when the child has a hearing impairment. The author thus suggested that pressures can be alleviated by using and enhancing this natural bonding force to improve relationships with children while helping them to grow. In this process, coping strategies should take into account the parents' emotions, allowing them to begin to actively foster communicative and behavioral development in their children. Coping strategies also should include the effects of parental responsivity on a child's later emotional health, the experience of letting go as a part of allowing a child to develop, the expanding role of fathers, and special considerations when the parents are themselves hearing-impaired.

Encourage "Total Communication" Along with Therapy and Counseling. Many parents of deaf or hearing-impaired children fail to communicate effectively with their children, due to lack of education and training; and this failure can impact negatively on coping efficacy. Vernon and Wallrabenstein (1984) examined events and parental reactions to the diagnosis of deafness in their children with regard to the parents' final coping dynamics. They found that common parental reactions included denial, isolation of affect, feelings of impotence, blaming the doctor, guilt, and depression. Constructive coping by parents can only begin after the irreversibility of the condition is acknowledged and the implications understood and accepted. Habilitation and education, if not properly planned, often represent a greater liability to deaf children and their families than the deafness itself. According to the researchers, this liability is due largely to a pervasive adherence to oralism and mainstreaming at the expense of more appropriate total communication and a specialized approach. Thus, parent counseling and the use of total communication together offer the best promise for the success of deaf children in reaching their potential.

Create a New National Policy for Low-Income Parents. Ultimately, the ability of parents to cope with the stresses placed upon them by having a disabled child rests largely on the resources they can draw upon, including but not limited to economic, educational, therapeutic, and medical resources. Because access to many of these resources are unequally distributed in society, those groups with relatively less resources will have a more difficult time coping effectively. They must compensate, in fact, by drawing upon strong familial, neighborhood, and personal attributes, such as belief, faith, conviction, determination, will, and religion, among many others. Oftentimes, however, these factors are not enough to overcome the structural inequities embedded in society, including the unequal distribution of children with disabilities, which is more prevalent among minority and poor people. Fujiura, Yamaki, and Czechowicz (1998) described the relationship of disability prevalence, low-income status, and family structure among ethnic and racial minorities in the U. S. Across all ethnic/racial and age cohorts, rates of disability were higher among low-income households; above the low-income threshold, group differences were greatly attenuated. Black and Hispanic children with a disability lived disproportionately in low-income, single-parent homes. Based on their findings, the researchers argued that the analysis of ethnic/racial differences in disability represents far more than a concern for "minority affairs." The data suggest both the importance of risk embedded in the social and economic context of the nation, and the need for disability policy to be directly engaged in the broader domestic discussions on poverty, social risk, and income inequality.

References

Bailey, D., Skinner, D., Correa, V., Arcia, E., Reyes-Blanes, M., Rodriguez, P., Vazquez-Montilla, E., & Skinner, M. (1999). Needs and supports reported by Latino families of young children with developmental disabilities. *American Journal on Mental Retardation, 104*(5), 437-451.

Blue-Banning, M.,Turnbull, A., & Pereira, L. (2002). Hispanic youth/young adults with disabilities: Parents' visions for the future. *Research & Practice for Persons with Severe Disabilities,27* (3), 204-219.

Chavira, V., Lopez, S., Blacher, J. & Shapiro, J. (2000). Latina mothers' attributions, emotions, and reactions to the problem behaviors of their children with developmental disabilities. *Journal of Child Psychology & Psychiatry & Allied Disciplines, 1* (2), 245-252.

Deaf and African American Children Website (2003), http://deafness.about.com

Douthitt, C. (2002). An investigation of stress and coping resources among African-American women who are married, working, and mother of a child with a developmental disability. *Dissertation Abstracts International: Section B: The Sciences & Engineering, 62*(10-B), 4780.

Farrugia, D. (1991-1992). Borderline personality disorder and deafness. *Journal of the American Deafness & Rehabilitation Association, 25* (3), 8-15.

Feher-Prout, T. (1996). Stress and coping in families with deaf children. *Journal of Deaf studies & Deaf Education, 1* (3), 155-166.

Fischgrund, J., Cohen, O. & Clarkson, R. (1987). Hearing-impaired children in Black and Hispanic families. *Volta Review, 89* (5), 59-67.

Fujiura, G., Yamaki, K. & Czechowicz, S. (1998). Disability among ethnic and racial minorities in the United States: A summary of economic status and family structure. *Journal of Disability Policy Studies, 9* (2), 111-130.

Greenberg, M., Lengua, L., & Calderon, R. (1997). The nexus of culture and sensory loss: Coping with deafness. In Wolchik, S. & Sandler, I. (Eds), *Handbook of children's coping: Linking theory and intervention. Issues in clinical child psychology* (pp. 301-331).

Harry, B. (1992). Making sense of disability: Low-income, Puerto Rican parents' theories of the problem. *Exceptional Children, 59* (1), 27-40.

Hintermair, M. (2000). Hearing impairment, social networks, and coping: The need for families with hearing-impaired children to relate to other parents and to hearing-impaired adults. *American Annals of the Deaf, 145* (1), 41-53.

Hintermair, M. (2000). Children who are hearing impaired with additional disabilities and related aspects of parental stress. *Exceptional Children, 66* (3), 327-332.

Jones, R. & Kretschmer, L. (1988). The attitudes of parents of Black hearing-impaired students. *Language, Speech, & Hearing Services in Schools, 19* (1), 41-50.

Kampfe, C. (1989). Parental reaction to a child's hearing impairment. *American Annals of the Deaf, 134* (4), 255-259.

Kashyap, L. (1986). The family's adjustment to their hearing impaired child. *Indian Journal of Social Work, 47* (1), Special Issue: *The Family,* 31-37.

Klein, C. (1977). Coping patterns of parents of deaf-blind children. *American Annals of the Deaf, 122* (3), 310-312.

Leigh, I. (1987). Parenting and the hearing impaired: Attachment and coping. *Volta Review 89* (5), 11-21.

Lian, M. & Fantanez-Phelan, S. (2001). Perceptions of Latino parents regarding cultural and linguistic issues and advocacy for children with disabilities. *Journal of the Association for Persons with Severe Handicaps, 26* (3), 189-194.

Mapp, I. (1995). *Coping and stress among parents of children with hearing impairment.* Doctoral Dissertation. New York: New York University, School of Social Work.

Mapp, I. & Hudson, R. (1997). Stress and coping among African American and Hispanic parents of deaf children. *American Annals of the Deaf, 142*(1), 48-56.

Mary, N. (1990). Reactions of Black, Hispanic, and White mothers to having a child with handicaps. *Mental Retardation, 28*(1), 1-5.

Moores, D., Jatho, J., & Dunn, C. (2001). Families with deaf members: *American Annals of the Deaf,* 1996 to 2000. *American Annals of the Deaf, 146*(3), 245-250.

O'Hare, E. (1999). The effects of stress and affect on parenting behavior: A study of mothers of deaf and hearing children. *Dissertation Abstracts International: Section B: The Sciences & Engineering, 59*(9-B), 5102.

Pickett, S., Vraniak, D., Cook, J., & Cohler, B. (1993). Strength in adversity: Blacks bear burden better than Whites. *Professional Psychology: Research & Practice, 24* (4) 460-467.

Prieto-Bayard, M. & Baker, B. (1986). Parent training for Spanish-speaking families with a retarded child. *Journal of Community Psychology, 14*(2), 134-143.

Pruchno, R., Patrick, J. & Burant, C. (1997). African American and White mothers of adults with chronic disabilities: Caregiving burden and satisfaction. *Family Relations: Interdisciplinary Journal of Applied Family Studies, 4*(4), *Special Issue: Family Caregiving for Persons with Disabilities,* 335-346.

Reyes-Blanes, M., Correa, V., & Bailey, D. (1999). Perceived needs of and support for Puerto Rican mothers of young children with disabilities. *Topics in Early Childhood Special Education, 19*(1), *Special Issue: 62,* 54-62.

Skinner, D., Bailey, D., Correa, V. & Rodriguez, P. (1999).Narrating self and disability: Latino mothers' construction of identities vis-a-vis their child with special needs. *Exceptional Children, 65* (4), 481-495.

Skinner, D., Correa, V., Skinner, M., & Bailey, D. (2001). Role of religion in the lives of Latino families of young children with developmental delays. *American Journal on Mental Retardation, 106*(4), 297-313.

Sontag, J. & Schacht, R. (1994).An ethnic comparison of parent participation and information needs in early intervention. *Exceptional Children, 60*(5), 422-433.

Steinberg, A. et al. (2003). Decisions Hispanic families make after the identification of deafness. *Journal of Deaf Studies & Deaf Education, 8*(3), 291-314.

Steinberg, A. (1997). "A little sign and a lot of love. . . .": Attitudes, perceptions, and beliefs of Hispanic families with deaf children. *Qualitative Health Research, 7*(2), 202-222.

Tavormina, J., et al. (1981). Psychosocial effects on parents of raising a physically handicapped child. *Journal of Abnormal Child Psychology, 9*(1), 121-131.

U. S. Bureau of the Census (2003). http://www.census.gov.

Vernon, M. (1972). Psychodynamics surrounding the diagnosis of a child's deafness. *Rehabilitation Psychology, 19*(3), 127-134.

Vernon, M. & Wallrabenstein, J. (1984). The diagnosis of deafness in a child. *Journal of Communication Disorders, 17*(1), 1-8.

Vernon, M. (1972). Psychodynamics surrounding the diagnosis of a child's deafness. *Rehabilitation Psychology, 19*(3), 127-134.

Wu, C. (2002). Resource-based early intervention with multicultural deaf/hard of hearing infants, toddlers and their families. *Dissertation Abstracts International: Section B: The Sciences & Engineering, 62*(9-B), 4245.

The Diagnosis of Deafness in a Child

McCay Vernon
James M. Wallrabenstein

Abstract: *Communicating to parents the diagnosis of an irreversible disease or disability in their child is a difficult task for medical practitioners. In order for the parents, as well as the physician, to cope constructively with the severe psychological consequences, disappointment, and grief, it is critical that there be a clear understanding of common reactions to such trauma. Beginning with mixed feelings about the pregnancy common to most parents, through birth, and up to the actual diagnosis, important events take place that are examined with regard to the parents' final coping dynamics. Common reactions include denial, isolation of affect, feelings of impotence, questioning the reasons for deafness, turning to religion, blaming the doctor, guilt, "doctor shopping," depression, and others. Constructive coping by parents can only begin after the irreversibility of the condition is acknowledged and the implications understood and accepted. Beyond this, an understanding of what lies ahead for their child is important. In this regard, habilitation and education, if not properly planned, often represent a greater liability to deaf children and their families than the deafness itself. This is due largely to a pervasive adherence to oralism and mainstreaming at the expense of a more appropriate total communication specialized approach. Thus, parent counseling and use of total communication together offer the best promise for the success of deaf children in reaching their potential.*

Introduction

Among the more difficult responsibilities faced by otolaryngologists and other physicians is communicating the diagnosis in a child of an irreversible disease or disability and then coping, in a constructive manner, with the psychological effects of this severe trauma on the family and the child (Freeman, Malkin, and Hastings, 1975; Mindel and Vernon, 1972). There are very few professionals whose training prepared them to assist parents in their need to discuss, ventilate, and understand their feelings about such a diagnosis (Vernon, 1976).

    The reactions of parents to the discovery that their child has a permanent disability need to be clearly acknowledged and understood if positive approaches are to occur. What follows is a discussion of the diagnosis of sensorineural deafness, with the realization that the psychodynamics operative in deafness have generality to other irreversible disabilities as well. The best perspective on how parents cope is gained by a chronological look at events beginning with pregnancy and continuing through early habilitation and education efforts.

Pregnancy

Few pregnancies occur when planned (Vernon, 1976). Confirmation of the pregnancy is often greeted with mixed feelings. On one hand, there are the joyous hopes and expectations associated with becoming parents. These good feelings, however, may be mixed with feelings of anxiety or even hostility related to the additional responsibilities, loss of individual freedom, and increased financial burdens incurred with raising a child (Show and Nerbonne, 1981). In some cases, the expectant mother, as well as the spouse, may fantasize that the pregnancy will terminate, or even attempt to induce abortion either through mild attempts, such as lifting heavy laundry, or more direct efforts, such as taking quinine or probing the uterus (Vernon, 1979). The point is that later, when the child is discovered to be deaf, the parents often feel directly responsible, thus guilty.

Birth to Diagnosis

Surprisingly, most cases of childhood deafness are not diagnosed until between 18 months and 3-years-of-age (Mindel and Vernon, 1972). This is true for a number of reasons, one of which is that deafness is invisible. Secondly, some residual hearing is usually present and the child may react to some loud noises in the environment. Thirdly, the major complaints of parents of deaf children are also common among those with normal hearing children, e.g., "Why doesn't my child talk?" (Vernon, Griffin, and Yoken, 1981). In addition, most medical practitioners are unaware of the various etiologies of congenital deafness that may serve as warning signs of its presence (Vernon, Griffin, and Yoken, 1981). As a result of this lack of awareness, early auditory screening of infants has not been common, even in high risk cases.

The final identification of deafness often represents the culmination of a long emotionally draining series of events for the parents (Liben, 1978). As suspicion mounts that something is wrong, based on the family's observations that the child doesn't seem to pay attention, is hard to manage, or does not seem to begin talking when expected, the anxious parents may find relief in the advice from extended family members and well meaning friends, as well as frequent assurances from the pediatricians, that there is "nothing to worry about," that the child is just "developing more slowly, but will soon catch up" (Freeman, Malkin, and Hasting, 1975).

In short, early diagnosis of deafness is rendered difficult by its infrequency, invisibility, and uniqueness, and by the sharing of symptomatology with other childhood ailments. As a result, one-third of all deaf children, in the past, have been misdiagnosed as retarded, aphasic, autistic, brain damaged, or schizophrenic (Vernon, Griffin, and Yoken, 1981). This situation is illustrated by the documented report of a psychologist who, in his own private practice, found 50 deaf persons in institutions for the mentally retarded who were not retarded (Vernon and Kilcallen, 1972). Thus, when the parents, deaf child in hand, finally appear in the office of the audiologist or otolaryngologist, frequently they bring with them much frustration, fear, and anxiety (Mindel and Vernon, 1972).

Diagnosis

When the diagnosis of deafness is finally made, it may come as a relief. Finally, the parents know what is wrong. However, this temporary feeling of relief is followed quickly by overwhelming complications. The diagnosis of deafness is, in fact, a traumatic blow, the full depth of which is rarely felt by the professional making the diagnosis (Vernon, 1976). Many a parent in such a situation has later commented, "After being told Jimmy was deaf, I can't remember a thing the doctor said."

Accepting and Coping

In their desire for the child to be an extension of themselves, parents ask, "Will our child be normal?" (Crowley, Keane, and Needham, 1982). It is at this point that the professional making the diagnosis, as gently but firmly as possible, must ensure that the parents begin to acknowledge the irreversibility of the condition. Even more, parents need to be helped to understand and accept its full implications. The fact is that, for sensorineurally deaf children, there are no cures and none are projected for the foreseeable future (Vernon, Griffin, and Yoken, 1981). Further, unlike a visual defect, which can be corrected through wearing of corrective lenses, no hearing aid or any amount of auditory training and speech therapy will ever totally erase the problem of profound sensorineural deafness.

The role of the professional in helping parents cope constructively with their reactions to the diagnosis of deafness cannot be overemphasized. In many respects, the professional's reaction tends to be the same as the parents, but at a less intense emotional and transparent level (Crowley, Keane, and Needham, 1982).

Why is this so? Just as parents have a great investment in their child, the professional who chooses otolaryngology or a related medical field, has a deep commitment to the maintenance and restoration of hearing. The professional views hearing as very important and has both a personal investment and professional life devoted to its study. Thus, it is not just the parent who senses the diagnosis of deafness as traumatic (Mindel and Vernon, 1972).

A basic principle to be recognized, following diagnosis, is that the supportive habilitation of the deaf child can begin only after both parents and professionals have acknowledged the irreversibility of the condition and the full implications of it are understood (Freeman, Carbin, and Boese, 1981).

Reactions to the Diagnosis

During the process of suspecting, recognizing, and identifying the handicap, it is common for parents to experience feelings of shock, bewilderment, frustration, sorrow, anger, and guilt. To cope with these intense feelings, a number of defense mechanisms come into play (Mindel and Vernon, 1972).

Denial, as a defensive reaction to deafness, is universal. If chronic, it is devastating because it precludes more constructive coping. Denial is a normal first reaction to trauma. This is clearly evidenced in our reactions to death, cancer, a serious accident, or other emotional shock (Vernon, 1979).

Isolation of affect occurs when the parent accepts the diagnosis intellectually, but expresses no feeling about it. Such a reaction is unhealthy because the diagnosis of deafness represents a major human loss. This loss requires a degree of mourning and grief, just as that experienced with the death of a loved one. If a child's deafness does not result in a period of parental grief, something is seriously wrong (Vernon, 1979).

Feelings of impotence represent another reaction. Both the parent and the diagnostician want more than anything to help, to find a cure. This desire often leads to unrealistic endeavors, the most common of which is a move towards oralism as the only approach, i.e., insisting that the child learn to speak and otherwise appear as a normal hearing person at the expense of other more appropriate means of communication, such as finger-spelling and sign language along with speech (Pahz, Pahz, and Lloyd, 1978).

"Why me?" and "What did I do?" are examples of a third reaction, that of questioning the reason for the deafness. Parents often have ambivalence about knowing the reasons for their child's deafness. Feeling it cannot be chance, many worry that they were somehow directly responsible.

Some parents turn to religion. Such a response can be constructive if it leads to true acceptance of the situation. Unfortunately, in some cases, this type of religion represents a frantic denial and an effort to transform the loss of hearing into a "heaven sent blessing in disguise." This sort of reaction formation denies the real implications of irreversible deafness.

Another coping mechanism and, perhaps, the "in thing" with respect to the mushrooming number of cases involving alleged malpractice, is to blame the doctor. Many people, especially parents, tend to attribute to the physician powers beyond medicine. Then when things go wrong, the doctor is blamed for negligence. While such charges are usually unfounded, the large number of cases of misdiagnosis involving deaf children, give substance to some of the cases (Schlesinger and Meadow, 1972).

Guilt feelings about having a deaf child are almost universal. They may arise from early fantasies that the pregnancy would terminate, actual efforts to induce abortion, or general feelings of ambivalence. Some interpret the child's deafness as God's punishment for their earlier sins. Regardless, unresolved guilt is destructive. It must be resolved if parents are to play a supportive role in the growth and development of the deaf child (Denmark, 1969).

Another common reaction to the diagnosis of deafness is for parents to seek a multitude of opinions or cures. "Doctor shopping" is typical in many cases, as parents search for an alternate less painful "solution" for the situation. Anyone professing a "cure" for the child, including a variety of greedy quacks with offers such as healing clothes, or finger surgery, are sought out in vain hope. Another variation of this reaction is the reading of medical literature in a "do-it-yourself" search for a cure. Such reactions serve to exemplify the extreme vulnerability of parents of deaf children.

Grief and depression, unless chronic, are normal reactions of parents to their sense of loss. Parents who never work through their grief to achieve a mature acceptance of the deafness are forced to assume a double burden of unacknowledged (and, thus, unexpiated) grief and pretense (Moores, 1978).

Additional reactions of parents may include a fear for the future, epitomized by such concerns as whether the child will be self-sufficient and assume a productive role, or become a life-long burden. In some cases there may be an increase in physical activity as a way of avoiding thought about the situation or repressing emotional responses. In some severe cases, anger, a natural consequence of the parents' frustration and disappointment, may be directed at the child and result in complete overt rejection.

Finally, in discussing parental reactions to the diagnosis of deafness, it is important to note that women cope with deafness, and handicaps in general, better than men. Thus, attention must be given to both parents with fathers also being encouraged to express their feelings and concerns (Crowley, Keane, and Needham, 1982).

Education and Habilitation

It is sad but true that education and habilitation often represent a greater liability to deaf children and their families than the deafness itself (Meadow, 1980). Let us examine briefly why this is so.

In contrast to the fact that deaf individuals in over 60 studies have shown intelligence equal to that of those who hear (Vernon, 1968), the educational achievement of most deaf persons constitutes what has been termed a national disgrace. Recent statistics indicate that 50% of deaf students at age 20 read at less than a mid-fourth grade level, that is, below or barely at a newspaper literacy level (Koelle and Convey, 1982). At best, only 10% of hearing impaired students can read at or above an eighth grade level (Trybus and Karchmer, 1977).

While it is not expected that medical or audiologic practitioners become experts in the education of deaf people, a clear understanding of the status of educational efforts and, more importantly, some of the reasons for their failure, can be invaluable to professionals in assisting parents to cope constructively and develop realistic expectations for their child.

Perhaps the greatest contribution to our society's failure in the education of deaf children has been the stubborn adherence to an oralism only philosophy, i.e., the exclusive reliance on residual hearing, speech, and lipreading, for communication (Moores, 1978; Bornstein, 1973). Such a limited approach to education of deaf children symbolizes normally hearing persons' denial of the implications of deafness (Mindel and Vernon, 1972). While educational institutions serving deaf persons are gradually moving away from this narrow approach to the use of total communication, the transition has been slow (Jordan, Gustason, and Rosen, 1979). Total communication involves the combined use of traditional oral methods complemented by the use of natural gestures, finger-spelling, and sign language. The sole reliance on lipreading, hearing aids, and speech therapy, in an effort to make a deaf child appear normal, is not only extremely harmful to the child's mental well-being and damaging to the child's educational potential, it is a pathologic denial of the implications of a permanent disability (Mindel and Vernon, 1971).

Conclusion

It is critical for the otolaryngologist, audiologists, and physicians, in general, to provide parents with more than a medical diagnosis of deafness or other irreversible disability. Initial counseling of the parents in coping with and understanding the implications of their child's condition is essential at the time of diagnosis. Certainly, referral to further mental health counseling is appropriate, but parents must be offered initial support, encouragement, and basic factual information if they are to avoid faltering at the first step of the long journey before them.

References

Bornstein, H. (1973). A description of some current sign systems designed to represent English. *Am. Ann. Deaf 118*: 454-463.

Crowley, M., Keane, K., and Needham, C. (1982). Fathers: The forgotten parents. *Am. Ann. Deaf 127*: 38-40.

Denmark, J. C. and Eldridge, R. W. (1969). Psychiatric services for the deaf. *Lancet ii*: 259-262.

Freeman, R. D., Carbin, C. F., and Boese, R. J. (1981). *Can't Your Child Hear?* Baltimore: University Park Press.

Freeman, R. D., Malkin, S. F., and Hastings, J. O. (1975). Psychosocial problems of deaf children and their families: A comparative study. *Am. Ann. Deaf 120*: 391-405.

Jordon, I. K., Gustason, G., and Rosen, R. (1979). An update on communication trends at programs for the deaf. *Am. Ann. Deaf 124*:350-357.

Koelle, W. H. and Convey, J. J. (1982). The prediction of achievement of deaf adolescents from self concept and locus of control measures. *Am. Ann. Deaf 127*:769-779.

Liben, L. S. (1978). *Deaf Children: Developmental Perspectives*. New York: Academic Press.

Meadow, K. P. (1980). *Deafness and Child Development*. Berkeley: University of California Press.

Mindel, E. D. and Vernon, M. (1972). *They Grow in Silence*. Silver Spring: National Association of the Deaf, pp. 98-102.

Moores, D. F. (1978). *Educating the Deaf: Psychology, Principles and Practices*. Boston: Houghton Mifflin.

Pahz, J. A., Pahz, C. S., and Lloyd, G. T. (1978). *Total Communication*. Springfield, IL: Charles C. Thomas.

Schlesinger, H. S. and Meadow, K. P. (1972). *Sound and Sign: Childhood Deafness and Mental Health*. Berkeley: California University Press.

Show, R. L. and Nerbonne, M. A. (1981). *Introduction to Aural Rehabilitation*. Baltimore: University Park Press.

Trybus R. and Karchmer, M. (1977). School achievement scores of hearing impaired children: National data on achievement status and growth patterns. *Am. Ann. Deaf 122*:62-69.

Vernon, M. (1979). Parental reactions to birth defective children. *Postgraduate Medicine 65*:183-189.

Vernon, M. (1976). The importance of early diagnosis. *Medical Opinion 5*:34-41.

Vernon, M. and Kilcallen, E. (1972). *The Rehabilitation Record 13*:24-27.

Vernon, M. (1968). Fifty years of research on the intelligence of deaf and hard of hearing children: A review of literature and discussion of implications. *J. Rehab. Deaf 1*:1-12.

Vernon, M., Griffin, D. H., and Yoken, C. (1981). Hearing loss: Problems in family practice. *J. Family Pract. 12*:1053-1058.

Families with Deaf Members:
American Annals of the Deaf 1996 to 2000

Donald F. Moores
Jerry Jatho
Cynthia Dunn

Abstract: *The authors provide an overview of 21 articles from several countries focusing on families with deaf members published in the literary issues of the* American Annals of the Deaf *from 1996 to 2000. Four categories were identified: Interaction and Involvement, Support Services, Stress and Coping, and Decision Making. The articles represent a commendable expansion of focus from the mother-child dyad to increased attention to fathers, siblings, extended family members, and significant nonfamily members such as deaf adults. The heterogeneity of families was a striking factor, even within those studies dealing with relatively homogeneous populations. Services appeared to be most effective within middle-class, educated family units, illustrating the need for more comprehensive services sensitive to the needs of families from less affluent backgrounds and with lower levels of education. In general, services to families with deaf children may be characterized as better than in the past but still in need of significant sensitivity and improvement. The presence of a deaf child in a family with hearing parents may cause stress, but parents have the flexibility to respond in a positive and beneficial way, especially when provided adequate information and support. The idea that hearing parents go through a grieving process involving the identification of deafness in their child seems to be an overstatement.*

Continuing the series begun in the April 2001 issue investigating trends in *Annals* articles during the 1996-2000 period ("Issues and Trends in Instruction and Deafness: *American Annals of the Deaf* 1996-2000" and "Literacy Publications: *American Annals of the Deaf* 1996-2000") this article reports on articles published in the literary issues of the *American Annals of the Deaf* from 1996 to 2000 that address topics concerning families with deaf members. Our goal was to identify areas of importance within this category, as indicated by publication on the topics during a 5-year period. Several people read the articles, and discussions followed their preliminary recommendations. Because some of the articles dealt with federal mandates to identify deaf infants as early as possible and to provide services to the children and their families from time of identification, there was some question whether these articles might be categorized more appropriately as "Instruction" (Moores, Jatho, & Creech, 2001) rather than the present "Family." The authors concluded, however, that although some of the articles treated here may have some educational or service component, all have a family orientation.

Twenty-one articles, or approximately 15 percent of all articles published in the *Annals* during the 5-year period, met our criteria. The topics were quite diverse. Most dealt with deaf children, but others concentrated on deaf parents, hearing parents, and extended families. We divided the articles into four categories:

Interaction and Involvement,

Support Services,

Stress and Coping,

Decision Making: Cochlear Implants and Communication Modes.

We were especially interested in the extent to which federal mandates, technical developments such as cochlear implants, and trends in research with families in the general population influenced the work reported. One very obvious area is work addressing the pluralistic nature of our society and the growing attention to multiculturalism. Another is the question of whether the federal mandate to move from individual educational plans (IEPs) to individualized family service plans (IFSPs) is reflected by a change of focus from the traditional mother-child dyad to include fathers, siblings, and extended family members. Finally, we were interested in ascertaining the extent to which research on families in general influenced work in our field.

Categories

Interaction and Involvement

As anticipated, there has been a clear movement away from concentrating solely on the mother child dyad to include fathers, siblings, grandparents, and members of the deaf community. Although not explicitly stated, this represents tacit awareness that the deaf child does not live in a vacuum or interact only with the mother, but rather participates in an intricate social network. Calderon and Low (1998) reported that children whose fathers or other male figures were present in the home had significantly better academic achievement than children who had no significant adult male presence. Nybo, Scherman, & Freeman (1998) found that hearing grandparents provided diverse kinds of positive support to their hearing children and deaf grandchildren and that the quality of preexisting relationships was related to the influence of grandparents.

Morton (2000) also addressed the importance of extended family dynamics, with emphasis on the potential contribution of grandparents. Hintermair (2000) reported on data from 317 parents of deaf children in Germany and found that parents who frequently met with other parents of deaf children and with deaf adults showed a strong sense of competence and warm, accepting, trusting relationships with their deaf children.

Through participant observation, interviews, and videotapes in natural settings, Evans (1998) conducted a qualitative study over 6 months to investigate the ways in which being the only deaf child in a large family affects the child's experiences and the ways in which her deafness affects the hearing members of the family. Kristin (not her real name) was a 7-year-old profoundly deaf child, the fifth of eight children from 2 to 14 years of age. Her parents and siblings were all hearing. Both parents were teachers, and the family lived on a farm. Observations and videotapes were made in various settings, including the home, cheerleading, basketball games, ice-skating, and Kristin's First Holy Communion. The parents reported a struggle to prioritize time for jobs, child care, and home maintenance, as would any family with eight children under 15 years of age. The mother reported that there was the need to balance Kristin's special needs as a deaf child and the parents' own need not to have deafness be the primary focus of the family. Within this context, Evans concluded that there may be a fundamental difference between beliefs held about deafness by teachers and by parents who interact with children in a greater variety of environments. Kristin had access to a fluent signing communication partner approximately two-thirds of the time, mostly in one-to-one or small group situations. At other times, such as at a basketball game with siblings, she was more of an observer. Although she occasionally had problems understanding others who did not sign, she had little difficulty in communicating her intentions and exhibited sensitivity to the communication skills of others.

Kluwin & Corbett (1998) conducted interviews with 105 mothers of deaf and hard of hearing children in five large cities. Approximately 80 percent of the sample were classified as minority, more than half received public assistance, and in general, family income was low. The authors identified five subgroups: younger mothers who were high school dropouts, older mothers who were high school dropouts, older mothers who were high school graduates, mothers with some college experience, and older caregivers.

Kluwin & Corbett reported that the younger dropouts, barely out of childhood themselves, typically left school while pregnant, did not identify with school values or understand school culture, lived near the poverty line, and lacked the resources to respond to their children's needs. The situation for the older dropouts was similar, with the authors concluding that both groups will require social system support to overcome their educational and financial limits.

High school graduates report high levels of interest in visiting class and participating in IEPs, but often lack sufficient time or resources to devote to the activities. College educated mothers reported that they participated in all forms of contact. Senior caregivers showed a preference for reading material, disliked the IEP process and did not want to visit classrooms. Kluwin & Corbett concluded that parents of deaf children in America do not represent a monolithic group: They are quite diverse.

In a different orientation, Powers & Saskiewicz (1998) investigated the involvement in their children's education of hearing parents of deaf children and hearing parents of hearing children from five to twelve years of age. They reported high levels of involvement in both groups, and in general, there were no significant differences between the two groups, except that the parents of deaf children observed more in the classroom and parents of hearing children volunteered more in the classroom. Powers & Saskiewicz speculated that perhaps the parents of deaf children did not feel competent in interacting with deaf children other than their own.

Jones & Dumas (1996) gathered data on communication interactions with hearing children from 7 to 11 years of age with deaf parents and with hearing parents. There were no differences between children in deaf-parented families and in hearing-parented families on measures of self-assertion, separateness, permeability, and mutuality. For the parents there were no statistically significant differences, with the exception that hearing mothers evidenced a significantly higher percentage of self-assertive communications than did deaf mothers; that is, they had a higher number of direct suggestions for their children.

Prendergast & McCollum (1996) studied the interactions of deaf mothers and hearing mothers with deaf toddlers. The deaf mother/deaf child dyads experienced significantly more episodes of mutual attention. Not only were the deaf mothers more active, but their deaf toddlers were more responsive. Prendergast & McCollum concluded that hearing mothers are less knowledgeable about the needs of visual learners and need guidance specific to visual communication to develop skills to interact easily with their toddlers.

Koester, Karkowski, & Traci (1998) reached the same conclusion in their research on how deaf and hearing mothers regain eye contact when 9 month old deaf and hearing infants break contact. While hearing mothers compensate for a deaf child's inability to perceive auditory cues, Koester et al. found that deaf parents may offer important insights into the use of other modalities to elicit and maintain a deaf infant's attention.

Support Services

Meadow-Orlans, Mertens, Sass-Lehrer & Scott-Olson (1997) reported the responses of 407 parents of 6 and 7 year old deaf and hard of hearing children enrolled in 137 different programs in 39 states to a questionnaire concerning support services. Of the responses 46 percent were from parents of deaf children and 54 percent were from parents of hard of hearing children. Almost 40 percent of the mothers had some education beyond high school; approximately 30 percent of the children were classified as minority or mixed-race, and one or both parents were deaf in 13 percent of responding families, a somewhat larger percentage than is found in the general deaf American school age population. Hearing loss was confirmed at an average age of 14.3 months for the deaf children and 28.6 months for the hard of hearing children. In regard to original communication approaches, 66 percent used sign + speech, 24 percent used speech alone, 5 percent used sign alone, 3 percent used cues, and 3 percent used some combination of cues and signs. Because only 46 percent of children were classified as deaf, the fact that 66 percent used sign + speech seems a little surprising. In fact, signs + speech were used with 78 percent of the deaf children and 54 percent of hard of hearing children. Apparently professionals and parents in this study no longer believe the old myth that the use of signs will inhibit speech development. Respondents were very positive about support services that they received, with teachers receiving the highest ratings, followed by spouses, therapists, other parents, and deaf adults. Hearing mothers tended to evaluate their programs more positively than deaf or hard of hearing mothers. White mothers evaluated the programs more positively than mothers with minority racial/ethnic identification. MeadowOrlans et al. concluded that, apparently, programs are doing a good job of providing relevant information and services to families.

Calderon, Bargones, & Sidman (1998) conducted a follow-up of the families of 28 deaf children from 42 to 87 months who had participated in an early intervention program, with emphasis on child, family and ecological factors. All of the parents were hearing and predominantly middle class. One hundred percent of fathers and 89 percent of mothers had graduated from high school. Two-thirds of the families had experienced stress during the period of intervention, identified as major life events such as divorce, birth of an additional child, unemployment, serious illness, etc. Seventy eight percent of the children had one or more siblings. The early intervention program employed a total communication philosophy. From 9 to 42 months after completing the early intervention program, 26 were enrolled in total communication classes, one in an ASL class, and one in an oral only class. Parents reported that 75 percent of the children wore hearing aids and most received benefit from them.

Calderon et al. reported that intervention began on the average around 21 months, far too late. The apparently homogeneous population studied really was quite heterogeneous. There was great diversity. Calderon et al. concluded that any attempt to create a "typical profile" of a child with hearing loss and his or her family or the services received is quickly defeated.

Watkins, Pittman, & Walden (1998) reported on the Deaf Mentor Experimental Project in which parents received home visits from a hearing parent advisor who concentrated on English, listening, and literacy skills and a deaf parent advisor who shared ASL, culture, and personal knowledge of deafness with the families. They reported greater gains in vocabulary, communication, language and syntax compared to children in another state who received parent advisor services, but without the input of a deaf mentor.

Stress and Coping

Fisiloglu and Fisiloglu (1996) used a Turkish version of the Family Assessment Device (FAD) to compare responses of parents of 40 children attending a program for deaf and hard of hearing children in Ankara to parents of 20 matched hearing students. The FAD assesses seven areas; Problem Solving, Communication, Roles, Affective Responses, Affective Involvement, Behavior Control, and General Functioning. There were no statistically significant differences, except in Problem Solving, where families of hearing children tended more toward dysfunctionality than families of deaf children. Fisiloglu and Fisiloglu concluded that families of deaf and hard of hearing children adjusted quite well to the stressor of raising a child with a hearing loss and that such families may be special but they are not necessarily dysfunctional. Stress on families is not necessarily a negative force. Stress can be an occasion for growth.

Mapp & Hudson (1997) investigated stress levels and coping strategies of 98 parents of children attending a school for the deaf. Sixty-seven percent classified themselves as Hispanic, 20 percent as African American, and 9 percent as other. Three of the parents identified themselves as white and one as Asian American. Parents reported low levels of stress and this was especially true for parents who reported frequent church attendance. The authors hypothesized that there would be higher levels of stress reported by parents of males. This was not borne out. There were no significant differences related to the gender of the child. Also, the presence or absence of a spouse or other partner was not related to stress. Stress was lower for parents of children who signed fluently. It should be noted that although the school the children attended used signs, the parents rated 31 percent of the children as either not signing well or signing "adequately." Independent evaluation was not conducted. In terms of coping, Hispanic parents reported a higher degree of confrontive coping, distancing, self control, social support, planful problem solving, and positive appraisal than African Americans. They also showed higher degrees of planful problem solving and confrontive coping than white, Asian American and "other" parents in the sample.

Lampropoulou and Konstantareas (1998) studied child involvement and stress in 42 Greek mothers of deaf children enrolled in three schools for the deaf. Seventy one percent of the children had older siblings. Mothers of younger children and of boys in general reported greater stress and had longer and more frequent involvement with their children. Mothers with greater stress were more likely to view their involvement as more like a chore. The mothers reported few areas of support, except for neighbors.

Calderon and Greenberg (1999) used a competency-based model of stress and coping in 36 hearing mothers of deaf and hard of hearing children. Social support emerged as an important predictor of maternal adjustment as well as a buffer between current life stress and maternal adjustment. Four elements of support were identified: community, friends, intimate relations, and extended family. Maternal problem solving skill was a predictor of child adjustment and as a mediating factor between child's age and teacher rating of child adjustment. Problem solving was assessed by responses to four hypothetical situations: finding someone knowledgeable about deafness to talk with, identifying resources, arranging the provision of more speech therapy, and arranging for remediation of academic delays. The authors concluded that a competency-based rather than a pathological model should be employed. They specifically recommended services to teach, expand, and encourage parents knowledge and use of problem-solving skills; facilitation of strong social networks; and implementation of a developmental approach that recognizes parents' and children's varying needs at different ages.

Koester & Meadow-Orlans (1999) studied the interactions of 19 deaf infants and 19 hearing infants with their hearing mothers. The samples consisted of relatively homogeneous, middle class, educated families. Fathers were present in all but one family. All of the fathers were Caucasian, as were 34 of the mothers. One was Asian American and one was "mixed race." Children were videotaped with their mothers in normal play and a "still-face" episode. Deaf children assessed by their mothers as "difficult" displayed significantly more repetitive behavior in the play situation and more gaze aversion in the still face situation compared to "easy" deaf babies and both "easy" and "difficult" hearing babies. The authors reported that mothers classified deaf babies who were physically active and frequently avert their gaze as "difficult." They argue that intervention specialists should perceive these behaviors as positive efforts of their infants to influence their environment and communicate their feelings. This would enhance mothers' ability to "read" their infants nonverbal cues and enhance development of the child's self regulating capacities regardless of temperamental style.

Decision Making: Cochlear Implants and Communication Modes

Kluwin & Stewart (2000) conducted phone interviews with 35 parents of children who had received cochlear implants through a large scale university implant program. The primary sources of information for 80 percent of the parents were either other parents (N = 15) or medical personnel (N = 13), which included pediatricians, audiologists, or members of the implant team.

Motivation was usually a desire for "normal" or improved speech skills. Parental reaction was positive, with 29 stating they would do it again and that communication skills had improved. Two parents would not do it again, three had some reservation, and one was uncertain. Kluwin & Stewart noted that the sample consisted of parents who had already made the decision and had an implant for their children. Also, they tried to contact 75 families and succeeded with only 35, so the sample was biased in favor of families that had maintained contact with the implant program. The authors concluded that until researchers have access to large populations of implant recipients, and the resources to look at the missing as well as the present, we will not have the information to respond to the issue of implants for young children.

Peters (2000) described the decision process of one family as they considered an implant for their deaf daughter. He discusses-and rejects-the extreme arguments for and against implants and argues that the majority of parents fall between the extreme poles. Their primary concern is doing the right thing for a child in the face of conflicting advice. Peters presents the rationale for his family's decision not to have a cochlear implant for their daughter.

Eleweke & Rodda (2000) conducted in-depth research on factors influencing communication mode with two families of children attending a preschool audiology clinic in England. All parents were hearing. One family used British Sign Language (BSL) with their daughter and the other used aural/oral communication with their two children. The first family reported that they had not been adequately informed of options until they met a deaf signing social worker. The second family felt that they had been adequately informed about choices, but that teachers seemed hesitant about providing as much information as possible. Both sets of parents initially had high hopes for the benefit of hearing aids, believing their children would hear normally and experiencing disappointment when benefits were quite limited. Both sets also felt that hearing loss had been diagnosed late and that counseling and support services were inadequate. The parents using signs believed that professionals who worked with them did not understand their feelings. Similarly the aural/oral parents said about the professionals, "They just don't care. To them it is just a job." Regardless of the communication mode selected, neither set of parents expressed satisfaction with the process of identification, counseling, or services provided. The authors, acknowledging that the data come from only two families, nevertheless conclude that the findings underline the need for core support services for parents of deaf children.

Discussion

The family-related articles that appeared in the literary issues of the *American Annals of the Deaf* from 1996 to 2000 are quite impressive in their range and quality. One area of interest to us was the extent, if any, to which authors of various articles reflected the mandates of federal legislation and the influence of work in general child development to expand the focus from the child or mother-child dyads to include fathers, siblings, extended family members, and significant nonfamily members. It is clear that in most families the mother is the primary care giver and has the greatest influence on the developing child, but the impact of other family and nonfamily members usually is significant.

The family related articles reviewed here show an important expansion of focus. Calderon & Low (1998) reported that the presence of fathers or other significant adult male figures was correlated with improved academic achievement of young deaf children. Morton (2000) and Nybo, Sherman & Freeman (1998) addressed the importance of the extended family unit, especially grandparents, in facilitating the development of deaf children. Hintermair (2000) and Watkins, Pittman & Walden (1998) documented the importance of parental contact with deaf adults, either as mentors coming into the home or on a less formal basis.

Calderon, Bargones, & Sidman (1998) in the United States and Lampropoulou & Konstantareas (1998) in Greece both reported that in more than 70 percent of the families studied, the deaf child had one or more siblings, illustrating the complexity of the family dynamics. Evans's (1998) qualitative study of a deaf girl in a family with eight children under fifteen years of age highlighted the decisions and trade-offs parents have to make in meeting obligations to all family members.

Research on parental interactions with children produced some intriguing findings. Powers & Saskiewicz (1998) reported that hearing parents of elementary school age deaf children and hearing parents of elementary school age hearing children were quite similar in their participation in their children's education, with the exception that parents of hearing children volunteered more and parents of deaf children observed more. The implication is that programs for the deaf should find ways to facilitate hearing parents' participation in class activities. On a different note, Jones & Dumas (1996) found deaf and hearing parents to be similar in their interactions with their oldest hearing children, with the exception that hearing mothers tended to be more assertive with their children. The results suggest there are more commonalities than differences in families with deaf parents and families with hearing parents. The major exception seems to be that in communication with deaf infants deaf mothers, as might be predicted, make better use of the visual modality than hearing mothers in sustaining communicating with young deaf children (Koester, Karkowski, & Traci, 1998; Prendergast & McCollum, 1996).

Research on services to families produced varying results, sometimes related to family stress and coping and sometimes not. To some extent this may be due to the heterogeneity—cultural, racial, ethnic, socioeconomic, nationality, etc.—of the samples studied and to some extent it may be a function of the different assessment instruments. Meadow-Orlans et al. (1997), in the largest study reported, found parents of young deaf children in general to be quite positive about the services they received, but deaf parents and parents with minority racial/ethnic identification expressed lower levels of satisfaction. Kluwin & Corbett (1998) identified 5 types of families in a sample drawn from 5 large cities, ranging from young single mother school dropouts to college educated parents. Services simply were not reaching those mothers most in need of help, young girls with few family, financial, or academic resources. Calderon et al. reported similar findings with what on the surface was a more homogeneous group of parents. Lampropoulou & Konstanareas (1998) reported a neutral affect and stress among Greek mothers of deaf children, especially when the children were males. Mothers had few sources of support from schools, family or professional service providers. On the other hand, Mapp & Hudson, (1997) found little reported stress among African-American and Hispanic American parents of deaf children, but problems in coping behavior of the African American parents. Fisiloglu & Fisiloglu (1996) reported that Turkish families with hearing parents and deaf children adjusted quite well to the presence of a deaf child. They concluded that families with deaf children clearly are not dysfunctional and that stress can be an occasion for growth. In contrast, Eleweke & Rhoda (2000) reported the deep dissatisfaction of two families in England with deaf children with the advice and services they received.

These "mixed" results are intriguing. As previously noted, they may be due to factors such as heterogeneity of subjects and of assessment instruments. It should be noted that samples were drawn from England, Germany, Greece, Turkey, and the United States. This fact itself illustrates the importance educators of deaf children across the world attribute to families. In general, it appears that most parents are resilient. The presence of a deaf child in a family with hearing parents may cause stress, but stress is a fact of life. It is clear that there is a great need for more comprehensive services for families with deaf children starting from the time of identification, which ideally should be at birth. The types of services must be individually designed to meet the unique needs of each family. How this can be accomplished will be one of the most important research questions in our field for generations to come.

References

Calderon, R., Bargones, J., & Sidman, S. (1998). *Characteristics of hearing families and their young deaf and hard of hearing children: Early intervention follow-up, 143*(4), 347-362.

Calderon, R., & Greenberg, M. T. (1999). *Stress and coping in beating mothers of children with hearing loss: Factors affecting mother and child adjustment. 144*(1), 7-18.

Calderon, R., & Low, S. (1998). *Early social-emotional, language, and academic development in children with hearing loss: Families with and without fathers. 143*(3), 225-234.

Eleweke, C. J., & Rodda, M. (2000). *Factors contributing to parents' selection of a communication mode to use with their deaf children, 145*(4), 375-383.

Evans, J. F. (1998). *Changing the lens: A position paper on the value of qualitative research methodology as a mode of inquiry in the education of the deaf, 143*(3), 246-254.

Fisiloglu, A. G., & Fisiloglu, H. (1996). *Turkish families with deaf and hard of hearing children: A systems approach in assessing family functioning. 141*(3), 231-235.

Hintermair, M. (2000). *Hearing impairment, social networks, and coping: The need for families with hearing-impaired children to relate to other parents and to hearing-impaired adults, 145*(1), 41-51.

Jones, E. G., & Damas, R. E. (1996). *Deaf and hearing parents' interactions with eldest hearing children, 141*(4), 278-283.

Kluwin, T. N., & Corbett, C. A. (1998). *Parent characteristics and educational program involvement, 143*(5), 425-432.

Kluwin, T. N., & Stewart, D. A. (2000). *Cochlear implants for younger children: A preliminary description of the parental decision process and outcomes, 145*(1), 26-32.

Koester, L. S., Karkowski, A. M., & Traci, M. A. (1998). *How do deaf and hearing mothers regain eye contact when their infants look away? 143*(1), 5-13.

Koester, L. S., & Meadow-Orlans, K. P. (1999). *Responses to interactive stress: Infants who are deaf or hearing, 144*(5), 395-403.

Lampropoulou, V., & Konstantareas, M. M. (1998). *Child involvement and stress in Greek mothers of deaf children, 143*(4), 296-304.

Mapp, I., & Hudson, R. (1997). *Stress and coping among African American and Hispanic parents of deaf children, 142*(1), 48-56.

Meadow-Orlans, K. P., Mertens, D. M., Sass-Lehrer, M. A., & Scott-Olson, K. (1997). *Support services for parents and their children who are deaf or hard of hearing: A national survey, 142*(4),278-288.

Moores, D. F., Jatho, J., & Creech, B. (2001). *Issues and trends in instruction and deafness: American Annals of the Deaf 1996 to 2000, 146*(2), 72-76.

Moores, D. F., & Miller, M. S. (2001). *Literacy publications: American Annals of the Deaf 1996 to 2000, 146*(2). 77-80.

Morton, D. D. (2000). *Beyond parent education: The impact of extended family dynamics in deaf education, 145*(4), 359-305.

Nybo, W. L., Scherman, A., & Freeman, P. L. (1998). *Grandparents' role in family systems with a deaf child: An exploratory study, 143*(3), 260-267.

Peters, E. (2000). *Our decision on a cochlear implant, 145*(3), 263-267.

Powers, G. W., & Saskiewicz, J. A. (1998). *A comparison study of educational involvement of hearing parents of deaf and hearing children of elementary school age, 143*(1), 35-38.

Prendergast, S. G., & McCollum, J. A. (1996). *Let's talk: The effect of maternal hearing status on interactions with toddlers who are deaf, 141*(1), 11-18.

Watkins, S., Pittman, P., & Walden, B. (1998). *The deaf mentor experimental project for young children who are deaf and their families, 143*(1), 29-34.

"A Little Sign and a Lot of Love . . .":
Attitudes, Perceptions, and Beliefs of
Hispanic Families With Deaf Children

Annie G. Steinberg, Jose R. Davila, Jorge Collazo, Sr.
Ruth C. Loew, Joseph E. Fischgrund

Abstract: *The authors studied the perceptions, attitudes, and beliefs about deafness and disability in 9 Hispanic families with deaf children. In-depth interviews were conducted, focusing on the families' experiences in adjusting to the child's hearing loss and emphasizing, in particular, concepts of causation of deafness; communication with the deaf child; and perceptions of the accessibility of services. Most parents expressed positive or neutral feelings about deafness. Concepts of causation varied, with some parents attributing deafness to divine will, others to heredity or physical insult. Many parents reported that their extended families and communities stigmatized the deaf child. Most families were satisfied with the services available. Parents' appraisals of the children's receptive and expressive abilities for oral language were profoundly contradictory. These interviews provide valuable insight into the belief systems and needs of this minority group. Increased awareness of these needs and concerns is necessary to improve services for Hispanic deaf children and their families.*

Introduction

The Hispanic Population and Disability

One factor influencing the response by a family to a child's disability is that family's cultural background. The manner in which individuals from different ethnic groups view and treat disabilities varies considerably, with cultural elements such as language, family structure, gender roles, beliefs about health and healing, and acculturative stress all playing significant roles in the symptom manifestation, rehabilitation, and treatment of disabilities (Arnold, 1987).

The United States is a pluralistic society composed of many ethnic minorities, each with its own beliefs, values, attitudes, and norms (Seligman & Darling, 1989). Because these minorities also share some aspects of the culture of the larger society, they constitute subcultures within that society. Individuals from other parts of the world bring into this country their own sets of values, but they also, to varying extents, adopt those of the more encompassing society.

Individuals of Hispanic background have a distinct heritage with roots in Spain, Africa, the Caribbean, and Central and South America. Americans of Hispanic origin are the second largest ethnic minority in the United States, constituting [by 1990] approximately 8% of the total U.S. population (U.S. Bureau of the Census, 1990, Series P-20, No. 444). This group is characterized by a language and a lifestyle distinct from those of mainstream Americans as well as by a high incidence of poverty. As an immigrant group, the Hispanic population is prone to the vicissitudes and stresses of acculturation, including poor working conditions, inadequate housing, and lack of access to health and human services. The Hispanic population of the United States is itself diverse, with Mexican Americans, Puerto Ricans, Cuban Americans, and Salvadorans, among others, sharing certain cultural traits but differing in others (Becerra & Zambrana, 1985; Seligman & Darling, 1989). Sabogal, Marin, Otero-Sabogal, Marin, and Perez-Stable (1987) found a strong common pattern of attitudes toward family among individuals of Hispanic origin, although there were specific identifiable differences among the various Hispanic subgroups (Sabogal et al. 1987). In the present study, generalizations about "Hispanic culture" should be viewed accordingly.

A family's beliefs about what constitutes normality and about the causes and management of illness have significant implications for its adaptation to disability (Rolland, 1994). Researchers have identified several influential factors in the Hispanic individual's perceptions and beliefs about disabilities (Triandis, Marin, Betancourt, Lisansky, & Chang, 1982) and described persons of Hispanic origin as sharing strong feelings of solidarity and loyalty to both nuclear and extended families (Triandis et al., 1982). The family has been described as the most important institution for Mexican Americans, Puerto Ricans, Cuban Americans, and Central and South Americans (Alvirez & Bean, 1976; Cohen, 1979; Glazer & Moynihan, 1963; Szapocznick & Kurtines, 1980). As a whole, the Hispanic community is a tightly knit group whose members have typically responded to disability by offering increased support and comfort in both home and community (Cruz, 1979). Some have noted that this support can be excessive, with protection of the disabled individual being of primary concern. Thus, according to Cruz (1979), "Hispanic families tend to overprotect and paternalize their disabled. Even if a disabled individual wants to learn to be independent and self-sufficient, he is seldom allowed to do so" (p. 33).

Others have studied the Hispanic individual's beliefs about the nature of disease and disability. Spector (1985) pointed out that Chicanos may regard illness as a punishment for wrongdoing (Spector, 1985). Lafitte noted that individuals of Hispanic origin may interpret a disability as a divine punishment for sin, the sin typically believed to be that of the parents of the individual with the disability (Lafitte, 1983, pp. 51-58). In addition to, or instead of, the services of a health care professional, individuals who believe in folk medicine may seek the help and services of a *curandero* (folk healer) who derives his or her ability to cure from the supernatural (Seligman & Darling, 1989).

The well-defined gender roles of the Hispanic culture may also influence the individual's beliefs about disabilities. Rodriguez and Santiviago (1991) argued that in traditional Hispanic families, "the father is considered the main source of authority and final arbitrator, and the mother is the emotional and service broker, conducting the daily business of running the family" (Rodriguez & Santiviago,1991, pp. 89-97). Thus, according to Rivera (1983), it may be difficult for the father, as the authority figure, to accept a disability within the family. On the other hand, it is the mother who generally conducts interactions with institutions, including the school.

Linguistic and cultural barriers may render health care and education services inaccessible to families of Hispanic origin. Educators and health care providers have reported minimal involvement with educational support services (Cohen, Fischgrund, & Redding,1990, pp. 67-73). The institutional and professional structure of the school may be so intimidating to parents of Hispanic heritage that these individuals seldom participate in the development of their children's Individual Educational Plans (Bennett,1989; Stein, 1983). The prevalence of academic failure among Hispanic families renders the underutilization of educational services a particular concern.

Deafness: Background Information

For people who have not experienced hearing loss, it may seem natural and obvious to regard deafness as a disease or a disability. As such, it may be seen as something to be cured or ameliorated. However, particularly among deaf people themselves, a cultural definition of deafness has evolved in the United States during the past decade. These individuals emphasize the role of common linguistic, educational, social, and political experiences and attitudes in uniting deaf people into a unique community (Noshpitz, 1997; Steinberg, 1997). They regard deafness primarily as a cultural phenomenon rather than a disability. It has become common to use the capitalized word *Deaf* to refer to the culture and the lowercase form to designate the audiological condition (Battison,1980, pp. 58-68; Padden,1980).

Deaf culture is unusual, however, in that the culture is typically not transmitted from parent to child, because most deaf children are born to hearing parents who may have no prior knowledge of deafness or of any sign language. Because deafness limits the child's access to the language spoken by hearing family members, without educational intervention, communication in a nonsigning home may remain limited to simple gestures and "home signs" (nonstandard coined signs) for basic necessities.

Cohen et al. (1990) demonstrated that the problems in communication and academic achievement experienced by deaf children from Hispanic families are more severe than those of their non-Hispanic peers (Carlisle, 1984, pp. 58-68; Cohen et al., 1990). They suggested that the child's problems may result from an insensitive educational system that fails to integrate the language spoken at home (mostly Spanish) with the English taught in school. A deaf child from a hearing Hispanic family may be receiving Spanish cues (via speech reading, use of residual hearing, and print) in the home but English cues at school (via audition, speech reading, print, and often a structured sign system). Although a hearing child can assimilate bilingual input and master two languages, the flow of inconsistent linguistic signals described above may be an impediment to the development of communication skills for a deaf child who is having difficulty in mastering even one spoken language (Carlisle, 1984, pp. 58-68).

The quality of the parent-child relationship is seen as important to the later functioning of deaf adults. Although only a small minority of deaf individuals have deaf parents, Corson (1973) suggested that parental acceptance of deafness, in addition to the presence of a signed language model, may be a factor in the superior achievement of deaf children of deaf parents as compared with those of hearing parents.

The importance of Hispanic families' cultural perceptions, attitudes, and beliefs about deafness in particular, and about disability in general, have not been extensively examined, especially through qualitative research methodologies. The purpose of this study is to gain insight into the Hispanic population's perceptions and beliefs about deafness by exploring the experiences and responses of Hispanic families (particularly families of primarily Puerto Rican origin) in discovering and adjusting to a child's hearing loss. We interviewed the families of deaf children of Puerto Rican background, emphasizing five major topics: demographics, concepts of the causation of deafness, reactions to deafness, communication with the deaf child, and perceptions of the accessibility of services.

Participants

Ten of the 16 families of Hispanic origin with a child attending the Pennsylvania School for the Deaf, a day school in Philadelphia, were interviewed about their perceptions of, and experiences with, deafness. One family was excluded from the analysis because their child was profoundly developmentally delayed and not officially enrolled at the school; this left 9 participating families. A school staff member contacted the participating families by telephone to request their involvement in the study. All families contacted agreed to be interviewed. Two fathers, two grandmothers, and one aunt participated, in addition to the nine mothers. However, the mother was the principal informant in all nine interviews.

Method

Unlike the hypothesis-testing model of research, the ethnographic approach used for this study emphasizes the qualitative description of individuals' experiences and the development of theories that may be testable in subsequent research (Kirk & Miller, 1986). In analyzing the interviews, we attempted to reconstruct the evolution of beliefs and behaviors as participants, who for the most part had no experience with deafness prior to the discovery that their child was deaf, encountered information about deafness and about the available health care and educational services. Careful analysis of the interview protocols yielded information about how Hispanic cultural beliefs and perceptions about disability pertain to deafness.

The study used a semistructured interview to gather data about, and to gain an understanding of, the families' demographics, status as immigrants, beliefs about deafness, attitudes toward school and health care professionals, expectations for their children, and communication with the deaf child.

Interviews were conducted orally, in either English or Spanish, depending on the respondent's preference. The investigators (Annie Steinberg and Jose R. Davila) were accompanied by a staff member at the Pennsylvania School for the Deaf. This staff member, who is of Hispanic origin, is employed as a support person and communication facilitator with students and families of Hispanic background at the school.

Each interview lasted about 1 hour and was completed in one session. All 10 interviews were conducted in the families' homes—all of which are in the largely Hispanic section of North Philadelphia—and were audiotaped for subsequent analysis.

Although most of the interviews were conducted in Spanish, they were translated into English. In the process of translation, we found expressions, metaphors, and idioms that could not be translated successfully. Many of these Spanish expressions captured the "music" of this study, containing within them beliefs and perceptions. To preserve the richness of this study, some of the expressions will be presented verbatim.

Results

Demographics

The age range for the deaf children in these families was from 6 to 13 years, the average age being 8.1 years. All of the mothers were married at the time of the interview. The average number of children for the families interviewed was three. All families had more than one child. One of the deaf children had been adopted at the time of birth; deafness had not been diagnosed prior to adoption. The diagnosis of deafness occurred at 2 years of age in seven families. The other two reported diagnosis at 1 year and at 3 years, respectively. Although medical histories for the children were not reviewed, one student was noted to have an additional disability (absence of a lower extremity).

Length of residence in the United States was less than 5 years for five of the nine families interviewed. Two families had been in the United States for more than 30 years, and the remaining two had lived in the United States for 8 and 10 years, respectively. All families, except for one father who was born in El Salvador, identified themselves as Puerto Rican.

Six of the nine families reported Spanish as the language spoken in the home and also preferred to be interviewed in Spanish. Two families specified both English and Spanish as the languages spoken in the home; the remaining family reported communicating only in English. These three interviews were conducted primarily in English, although there was some switching between English and Spanish throughout the interviews.

Concepts of Causality

Kleinman (1980) defined explanatory models as "the notions about an episode of sickness and its treatment that are employed by all those engaged in the clinical process" (p. 104). They are tightly related to general beliefs about sickness but are gathered in response to a particular illness. Even though deafness is not generally defined as a disease, it is often considered to be a disability. This study examined the explanatory models of different family members in response to a family member's deafness.

The Hispanic population has been described as having deep religious beliefs about disability (Lafitte,1983, pp. 51-58; Spector, 1985). Six of the nine families interviewed spontaneously made reference to God in explaining why their own child was deaf or why other children were deaf. They believed that God caused the child's deafness. Although the interviewers did not pursue a more complete understanding of the complex notions about both the world and the deaf child that would lead to this belief, some family members spontaneously offered additional related information. Most viewed deafness positively or neutrally rather than as a punishment, although the latter was expressed also by a few individuals. One father felt that his daughter was a gift from God and that he had to "take care of it [the gift]." Another mother responded, "There was a reason for God to bring him down like that. So I'm happy; I can't complain." Two of the families not only referred to God as the causal agent but also believed that God would restore the child's hearing: "And when God gives him back his hearing, let it be God that gives him his hearing back."

Others reported different explanations for their children's deafness, which we did not attempt to verify. For example, one of the mothers had flown to Puerto Rico 25 days after her daughter was born and reported that the etiology was the noise from the plane. Some were skeptical about the medical explanation of the etiology of the child's deafness. One mother said that even though doctors claim that her son's deafness was caused by meningitis, she believes that it may be hereditary because "there are many people who are deaf on my mom's side of the family." In fact, four of the nine families interviewed reported family histories of deafness.

Family and Community Responses to Deafness

Family Responses

Extensive research has been conducted in the area of the family's reaction to, and acceptance of, a child's deafness (Fischgrund, Cohen, & Clarkson, 1988; Luterman, 1979; Moses, 1985). However, the specific reactions of Hispanic individuals have not been studied. This study explored the reaction of the Hispanic family to having a deaf family member. Each of the mothers interviewed reported her thoughts and feelings at the time of diagnosis.

Most (7 of 9) mothers reported feeling sad, hurt, shocked, and/or frustrated at the time of diagnosis. Some explained that these feelings described their initial reactions but that they had "learned to deal with" their children's deafness. Other parents expressed feeling hurt because they wanted their children to speak to them. Three of the mothers in the study said that they felt upset because they will never be able to hear their children tell them, "I love you." One mother expressed her feelings as follows: "It hurt me a lot and still hurts me, that I have never heard her tell me that she loves me."

The father's powerful shock and grief at the deafness diagnosis was spontaneously reported by four mothers. One mother explained that her husband's reaction differed from hers: "I didn't have that shock that my husband had of sadness and crying. . . . The first day [when he found out], he forgot about everything he had to do and locked himself up in the room." One mother reported that her husband "*no está lleno*" (is still not full/satisfied) with having a deaf daughter. She also said that her daughter is not close to her father. Only one of the fathers interviewed expressed his opinion about having a deaf son: "It's very hard for a father to have a kid like that [*un nene así*]. Because how much would a father give so that his son could hear?"Studies of the Hispanic population indicate that the mother is generally the one who conducts the family business (Cohen et al,1990, pp. 67-73; Rivera,1983). She is the one who deals with the children on a day-to-day basis. Our results are consistent with this claim: Mothers reported being responsible for attending to the needs of the deaf child. One mother said that she moved to the United States without having a job, home, or command of the language for her son's benefit because she "was meant to do it" ["*me toca hacerlo*"]. To acknowledge this mother's courage in addressing her son's needs, her own mother sent her a plaque that hangs above the home's mantelpiece. The grandmother said, "I say that my daughter is a heroine because she moved to the States for her son's sake."

Seven of the nine families reported making no distinctions between the deaf child and the other children in the family. They explained that they want their child to grow up feeling that he or she is normal, just like his or her siblings. All of the mothers reported assigning comparable responsibilities to hearing children and to the deaf child. One mother with five children responded by stating: "They are all the same. I see it that because he has a problem, you shouldn't treat him differently from the other kids."

The Hispanic population has been characterized as depending on the extended family for support (Alvirez & Bean, 1976, pp. 271-291; Rodriguez & Santiviago,1991, pp. 89-97). Most of the parents interviewed came from large families (of more than 5 children). However, none of them reported receiving help from the extended family with their deaf children. Two said their families are not close, that "they really don't care." Others (2 of 9) were surprised that their families accepted their deaf children. One mother said, "I would understand if they [the extended family] didn't care, but they all love him."

Community Stigma

A recurring theme was the stigma associated with having a deaf child. Parents described situations in which the child seemed to have lost his or her individual identity in the community. For example, a common experience was to hear people referring to the child without using his or her name. Four of the nine families explained that members of the Hispanic community, and even family members, referred to their son or daughter as "*sordo*," "*sorda*" (the deaf one), or "*mudo*," "*muda*" (the mute one). Parents felt the child's own identity became subsidiary to the disability. This situation was emotionally charged and upsetting to parents, many of whom told neighbors to call the child by his or her own name. One mother moved from her neighborhood in Puerto Rico because the neighbors used to call her daughter "*la sordita*" (diminutive, little deaf one) and throw rocks at her; even "in her father's side [of the family] nobody calls her by her name. They call her '*la sordita de B*' [B's little deaf one]."

Similar experiences were reported in the Hispanic community of Philadelphia as well. One mother, who has resided in the mainland United States most of her life, said that her Hispanic neighbors in North Philadelphia would not allow their children to play with her son because he was deaf. They thought that her son had an infectious disease and were afraid that their own children might "catch it." Another mother reported having approached neighborhood children, who had been harassing her daughter, to tell them that "the fact that she doesn't hear doesn't mean that she's stupid."

Also, mothers reported that deaf Hispanic children were viewed with pity by the Hispanic individuals they encounter. Direct evidence was obtained from one mother's description of how family members treat her deaf child: "I get mad with my mother-in-law because she '*la quiere pero con una pena*' [loves her (her deaf daughter) with pity]. The language used by the family members interviewed also conveyed sentiments of pity. Six of the nine families interviewed attached the diminutive "-*ito*" (masculine) or "-*ita*" (feminine) when referring to the deaf child: "*sordito*," "*pobrecito*" (little deaf one, poor little one). In comparison with other disabilities such as mental retardation, blindness, and orthopedic handicaps, deafness was viewed positively by those interviewed. Even though deafness was still viewed as a handicap or disability, it was not seen as negatively as other conditions: "There are others worse off than she is. There are those who can't see; others can't use their legs." Therefore, they expected their child to do better in life than individuals with "other" disabilities. One mother commented on a man with Down's syndrome who worked as an auto mechanic: "If a man who is a *mongolito* [little mongoloid] can do that, why can't N [do this type of work] if all he's lacking is his hearing?"

Some family members note that other people tend to assume that their son or daughter is mentally retarded. These situations are upsetting for them, and they attempt to explain that their child is deaf, not retarded: "There are people who think that he is retarded because they don't know him. That's because they don't know what is happening, and they think that it's a huge fight dealing with him. But it's not."

Communication with the Deaf Child

Eight of the nine families reported that communication with their deaf children did not present a problem. Subjects provided varied examples to demonstrate the child's level of comprehension: "Oh, yes . . . sometimes when I stamp my foot she looks at me, and I tell her to get me water from the kitchen [makes a gesture, not the ASL (American Sign Language) sign for water], and she does." Furthermore, four respondents reported that their deaf children are able to understand spoken language, both English and Spanish. These family members did not think that deaf children become confused by variation in language input: "I don't understand why his teacher says that M is going to get confused if I speak to him in Spanish and she speaks to him in English. I don't think that's confusing." Another mother suggested that God helps her son to comprehend speech: "I don't know if it's God who wants him to understand only me, but he understands me."

Not only did many respondents feel that their deaf child could fully understand their speech, but four of the nine families reported that the child could speak without difficulty. This seemed to prove to the family members that no communication problem existed. One mother reported, "He talks plenty to me, even though you may not believe it. I can communicate with that child with no trouble." A father explained that his son, almost 9 years old, can speak in both languages: "He talks in English and Spanish. In English he says, 'stop' and 'give me'; in Spanish he says, '*papi*' [daddy] and '*abuela*' [grandmother]." In other contexts, however, some parents did acknowledge communication difficulties. Each of three mothers spontaneously reported that her deaf child experienced behavioral difficulties, which she attributed to the fact that the child could not successfully communicate with the family.

Regardless of the primary language used in the home, all families mentioned the use of sign language as an additional means of communication. Five of the mothers reported participation in a sign language course offered by the school for Hispanic families, and five of the nine families mentioned a sign language book as an aid in communicating with the deaf child, although most admitted to have little knowledge of signs. Three of the nine mothers said they learned signs from their children. However, some parents reported that they saw no reason to constantly use sign language because, in their opinion, the child was able to understand speech. One mother replied, "With him it's different because you talk to him and he understands what you are saying, so I hardly sign to him." The only aunt interviewed in the study emphasized the importance of sign language saying, "I don't think he gets confused because he doesn't hear the language; he only watches the signs."

One of the mothers interviewed saw no use for spoken language in order to communicate with her deaf son. She reported that she communicates with him "with a little sign and a lot of love," that "when you live in the same environment, when you are family, words are not necessary, one communicates with looks and love."

Perceived Accessibility of Services: United States versus Puerto Rico

Many of the families interviewed have either remained (3 of 9) in the mainland United States (instead of going back to Puerto Rico) or moved (2 of 9) to the mainland because of the services available for their deaf son or daughter. These services include education, hearing aids, doctors, hospitals, and school transportation. One mother moved to the mainland 28 days after she found out her son was deaf and planned to stay here for 20 years, the amount of time she considered necessary to enable her deaf son to be "independent and happy." Other families remained on the mainland, despite a wish to return to Puerto Rico, because of the benefits available to the deaf child.

Education was a priority for most parents, who expressed the opinion that in Puerto Rico the schools are either not as good in quality, are too far away, or do not provide an adequate education. One mother said, "Here they fight so the [deaf] child can develop . . . so that he can be a normal person like you and me." Another interviewed mother observed that in Puerto Rico, parents must pay for their child's specialized school, but "here they have this school [Pennsylvania School for the Deaf (PSD)], and the government helps you. In Puerto Rico, if your dad can't pay for the school, then . . ." She explained that her mother's deaf cousins who live in Puerto Rico did not attend school because of the cost of specialized education.

The health-related services provided at no cost for the deaf child were also determining factors in keeping the families from moving back to Puerto Rico. Three of the families interviewed stressed the importance of being able to obtain free hearing aids in the mainland United States. One of the mothers, who moved to the mainland in search of less costly health care services for her deaf daughter and herself, explained that she was not able to afford a hearing aid for her daughter in Puerto Rico. Here on the mainland, she has received them at no personal expense. When another mother found, on a return visit to Puerto Rico, that she could not even purchase hearing aid batteries there, she observed, "What importance did they give my child there? . . . What other surprises would have awaited me in other areas?"

Although others have described the difficulties in obtaining health care services for individuals of Hispanic origin (Seligman & Darling, 1989), none of the people interviewed reported difficulty in accessing medical services on the mainland for a deaf son or daughter. In fact, even those individuals who did not feel confident with their English reported no problems. They were able to find an interpreter at the hospital or brought someone proficient in English to accompany them and act as an interpreter.

The free health-related services, hearing aids, and education available on the mainland for deaf children, which are either not available or very costly in Puerto Rico, seem to affect the family's belief that their deaf child has better opportunities and more hope in the mainland United States. One mother's response captured these beliefs: "I think that in Puerto Rico they [deaf individuals] are seen as more handicapped. Here, they see them with more possibilities." Another mother was counseled to move to the mainland by the pediatrician who made the diagnosis of deafness in her son. The physician, by her report, told her that her son "would not be able to do this and that" "*el nene no va a ser nada*" [that her son would be nothing]. Upon arrival in the mainland United States, it was "as if they opened the doors to me . . . in Puerto Rico a person who is deaf is not as valued as he is here. There are no schools; not as many benefits." One mother summed up her appreciation of the professional attention she and her child receive on the mainland as follows: "Maybe since you are used to Puerto Rico . . . I felt that those [professionals on the mainland] were people who descended from heaven;" ("*con calidad humana*") [people with human quality].

Discussion

As befits an exploratory ethnography, this discussion focuses on that which can be learned from the experiences of the individual. The small sample size (nine families) and the unique characteristics of the PSD, among other factors, limit generalizability.

Subjects were recruited at the PSD, a unique educational environment that may not be representative of many other educational facilities serving deaf children. For example, this school has hired a half-time cultural translator, offers sign language classes in the Hispanic community, and celebrates Hispanic Awareness Week, demonstrating their commitment to increasing the cultural sensitivity of both the school staff and the family. The school's cultural translator held an essential role in the recruitment of participants for this study and facilitated communication and sharing of information between the interviewers and the families. This study involved no corroboration of family members' perceptions and experiences. No record review was conducted to assess the language skills or the academic performance of the students whose families participated. Because all but one of the individuals interviewed identified him- or herself as Puerto Rican, the study would need to be replicated in other Hispanic populations to assess the degree to which cultural differences within the Hispanic community at large are reflected in attitudes toward deafness.

Thus, although predictions about a larger population cannot be made from these data with any confidence, such was not our intent. It is precisely in the richness of these reports of personal experiences that the value of this study can be found.

Concepts of Causality

The subject matter of this study included attitudes, perceptions, and beliefs about deafness and disability among families of Hispanic origin. These belief systems are often overlooked by individuals who serve this population. Professionals must begin to examine the explanatory models held by these families when offering counseling and educational or medical services. These models of causality provide not only an understanding of how parents perceive the etiology of the child's deafness but also may indicate beliefs about appropriate treatment and successful outcome.

Some families spontaneously made reference to God as the causal agent, reporting the expectation that God would restore the child's hearing. Unfortunately, we did not have the opportunity to determine if this event was anticipated in this world or an afterlife; if the former, this belief may interfere with the family's acquisition of sign language skills and other vital information.

All parents, including the mother who reported that her child's deafness was caused by airplane noise as well as the families who maintained that the deafness was hereditary, need to have their concepts of causality taken seriously and addressed by the professionals who deal with them and their children. The former explanation is extremely unlikely, the latter quite plausible; however, both enter into the belief systems that these families bring to bear on their children's deafness.

Family and Community Responses to Deafness

Although in recent years mainstream American society has embraced deafness as a diversity worth celebrating, the families interviewed experienced powerful stigma and distancing from both their extended families and the Hispanic community at large. These negative attitudes in the child's home community may significantly contribute to poor academic and vocational outcomes. Positive self-image programs may be of benefit not only to the individual child but also to the family and to the community. Community education and sensitivity training should be components of programs that serve the Hispanic deaf community.

Parental experiences and perceptions of support have been correlated with positive maternal-child interaction in dyads with deaf children (Meadow-Orlans & Steinberg,1993, pp. 407-426). Although the literature describes family support as a key characteristic of the Hispanic population, many of the mothers (6 of 9) did not feel that they could rely on their families for assistance or comfort. This is of particular interest and concern because many of these families were uprooted because of the child's deafness. One possible explanation for this surprising finding is that families with deaf children must choose between remaining in Puerto Rico and benefiting from a larger support system or coming to the mainland where they can obtain better services but lack the extended family support.

It is significant, however, that the nuclear family members who were interviewed often expressed positive, supportive attitudes toward their deaf children. The willingness to relocate for the benefit of one child, the effort to assign comparable responsibilities to deaf and hearing siblings, and the pain the parents report at their child's stigmatization in the Hispanic community all attest to strong bonds with the deaf child within the nuclear family.

Communication With the Deaf Child

An interesting, albeit confusing, finding was the inconsistency of comments made about communication within the family of a deaf child. Although we did not attempt to corroborate the information provided, the responses were often inherently contradictory. Families reported knowledge of sign language, despite the fact that most had attended only a few classes. In the course of the interviews, the same family members who claimed to know sign language also admitted to have little knowledge of signs. Accounting for these discrepancies goes beyond the scope of this study, although it would be a fruitful area for further research. It is possible, for example, that the parents lacked information about the complexity of a signed language and thus did not know how to evaluate their own skills. Family members alternated between acknowledging and denying the consequences for communication of their child's deafness: "I know he's deaf, but he can hear and understand what I say to him in both English and Spanish." Some of the parents seemed to be interpreting any evidence of comprehension or production of speech as evidence of a far broader mastery of these skills. For instance, a school-age child whose expressive communication consists of "stop," "give me," "daddy," and "grandmother," in Spanish and/or English as mentioned above, may have a very limited vocabulary and virtually no command of syntax in either oral language. Similarly, if the strongest evidence of language comprehension is that a child can bring water in response to the stamp of a foot and a manual gesture, that child probably has limited comprehension of syntactic structure or of more abstract vocabulary. The examples of language behavior that the parents cited often did not support the claims they made for their child's communicative skills.

Hearing parents of a deaf child commonly wish intensely for their child to function as much as possible as if he or she were hearing. Any evidence of communicative success can be interpreted as evidence of progress toward what is seen as normality. It is sometimes possible for families to deny the pervasive consequences of deafness by focusing on these small accomplishments (Mindel & Vernon, 1971; Moores, 1978; Schlesinger & Meadow, 1972). From these interview responses alone, we cannot determine the reasons for the contradictions inherent in these families' comments on communication. Perhaps they result from rationalization or denial, or perhaps from lack of information about deafness, its consequences for communication, and the development of language in both deaf and hearing children.

Perceived Accessibility of Services: Mainland United States versus Puerto Rico

All of the families interviewed felt that there was a significant difference between the services available to deaf children in Puerto Rico and in the mainland United States. More than half of the individuals in this study are now residing on the mainland because of this profound disparity.

As a U.S. territory, Puerto Rico is mandated by federal regulations and congressional acts to provide free, appropriate, individualized public education for all students who are deaf (Downey, 1989, pp. 158-161). The parents have the right to due process, that is, to review and challenge educational recommendations for their children. The enactment of the Americans With

Disabilities Act of 1990 additionally legislates accessibility of facilities and equipment in all public entities, including schools, hospitals, physicians' offices, day care centers, vocational training centers, and so on (Chaikind,1992). Other relevant mandates include the Federal Individuals With Disabilities Education Act (IDEA) and a recent judicial decision in Pennsylvania (Cordero vs. the Commonwealth of Pennsylvania), which set the stage for parent/school collaboration in the education of disabled children; and the Child and Adolescent Service System Program (CASSP), which emphasizes community-based care, culturally competent services, and parent/professional collaboration (Cross & Benjamin, 1989). Even mandates that refer to other disabled groups nonetheless set precedents that are potentially generalizable to deafness. The parents interviewed for this study clearly do not feel that the mandated services and opportunities for parental involvement were available to them in Puerto Rico.

In marked contrast with the popular perception that many medical and educational services are difficult for lower income and minority groups to obtain, these families were quite satisfied with service accessibility on the mainland. Although perhaps this contentment is merely the result of the disparity between resources on the mainland and in Puerto Rico, it is nonetheless striking that these families consistently expressed positive reactions to the ease with which they could obtain hearing aids, medical care, and special education for their deaf children.

Conclusions

This study examined the attitudes, perceptions, and beliefs about deafness among Hispanic families with a deaf child. From this exploratory study, several hypotheses may be constructed for future investigation, including the following:

1. If given accessible and culturally sensitive information about deafness and made full participants in the decision-making process with respect to the education of their deaf children, Hispanic parents would have a better understanding of the difficulties inherent in oral communication for a deaf child.

2. Study of a larger sample of Hispanic families with deaf children would demonstrate the generalizability of the findings of the present study, for example, that (a) deafness carries a powerful stigma in the Hispanic community, which is manifested in the interactions between the nuclear and the extended family of the deaf child; and that (b) Hispanic families with deaf children are generally satisfied with the services available to themselves and to their children in the mainland United States.

Although the Hispanic deaf community is a small and often silent minority, an increased awareness of the needs and concerns of this cultural group is necessary to make services accessible and to prevent continued societal marginalization of these children and of their families.

References

Alvirez, D., & Bean, F. D. (1976). The Mexican-American family. In C. H. Mindel & R. N. Haberstein (Eds.), *Ethnic families in America* (pp. 271-291). New York: Elsevier.

Americans With Disabilities Act of 1990. PL101-336, 42 U.S.C.A. § 12101 *et seq.*

Arnold, B. R. (Ed.). (1987). *Disability, rehabilitation, and the Mexican-American.* Edinburg, TX: Pan American University.

Becerra, R. M., & Zambrana, R. E. (1985). Methodological approaches to research on Hispanics. *Social Work Research and Abstracts, 21*(2), 42-49.

Bennety, A. T. (1989). *Hispanic families and children in the special education intake process.* New York: The Lexington Center.

Carlisle, D. C. (1984). The hearing-impaired Hispanic child: Sociolinguistic considerations. In G. Delgado (Ed.), *The Hispanic deaf. Issues and challenges for bilingual special education* (pp. 58-68). Washington, DC: Gallaudet College Press.

Chaikind, S. (1992). Children and the ADA: The promise of tomorrow. *Exceptional Parent (AM Guide)*, M8-M10.

Cohen, L. (1979). *Culture, disease and stress among Latino immigrants.* Washington, DC: Smithsonian Institution.

Cohen, O., Fischgrund, J., & Redding, R. (1990). Deaf children from ethnic, linguistic and racial minority backgrounds: An overview. *American Annals of the Deaf,135*(2), 67-73.

Cordero v. Pennsylvania Department of Education and the Commonwealth of Pennsylvania, 795 P Supp.1352 (M.D. Pa. 1992).

Corson, H. (1973). *Comparing deaf children of oral deaf parents and deaf parents using manual communication with deaf children of hearing parents on academic, social and communicative functioning.* Unpublished doctoral dissertation, University of Cincinnati, OH.

Cross, T. L., & Benjamin, M. P. (1989). *Toward a culturally competent system of care* (CASSP monograph). Washington, DC: National Institute of Mental Health.

Cruz, D. (1979). Outreach problems in Puerto Rico. In G. Dixon & C. Bridges (Eds.), *On being Hispanic and disabled: The special challenges of an underserved population, conference report* (pp. 33-34). Washington, DC: Partners of the Americas.

Downey, W. S. (1989). Public Law 99-457 and the clinical pediatrician. *Clinical Pediatrics, 29*(3),158-161.

Federal Individuals With Disabilities Education Act, 20 U.S.C. §§ 1400 *et seq.*

Fischgrund, J. E., Cohen, O. P., & Clarkson, R. L. (1988). Hearing impaired children in Black and Hispanic families, *Volta Review, 89*(5),59-67.

Glazer, N., & Moynihan, D. P. (1963). *Beyond the melting pot.* Cambridge, MA: MIT Press.

Kirk, J., & Miller, M. L. (1986). *Reliability and validity in qualitative research.* Newbury Park, CA: Sage.

Kleinman, A. (1980). *Patients and healers in the context of culture.* Berkeley: University of California Press.

Lafitte, J. (1983). Counseling and rehabilitation in process. In *The special rehabilitation and research needs of disabled Hispanic persons* (pp. 51-58). Edinburg, TX: National Institute of Handicapped Research and President's Committee on Employment of the Handicapped.

Luterman, D. (1979). *Counseling parents of hearing impaired children.* Boston: Little, Brown.

Meadow-Orlans, K., & Steinberg, A. (1993). Effects of infant hearing loss and maternal support on mother-infant interactions at 18 months, *Journal of Applied Developmental Psychology, 14*, 407-426.

Mindel, E. D., & Vernon, M. (1971). *They grow in silence.* Silver Spring, MD: National Association of the Deaf.

Moores, D. F. (1978). *Educating the deaf. Psychology, principles, and practices.* Boston: Houghton Mifflin.

Moses, K. L. (1985). Infant deafness and parental grief: Psychosocial early intervention. In F. Powell, J. Finitzo-Hieber, S. Friel-Patti, & D. Henderson (Eds.), *Education of the hearing impaired child* (pp. 85-102). San Diego, CA: College-Hill.

Noshpitz, J. D. (Ed.). (1997). *The handbook of child and adolescent psychiatry* (Vol. 4). New York: John Wiley.

Padden, C. (1980). The deaf community and the culture of deaf people. In C. Baker & R. Battison (Eds.), *Sign language and the deaf community* (pp. 89-103). Silver Spring, MD: National Association of the Deaf.

Rivera, O. A. (1983). Vocational rehabilitation process and Hispanic culture. In *The special rehabilitation and research needs of disabled Hispanic persons.* Washington, DC: National Institute of Handicapped Research and the President's Committee on Employment of the Handicapped.

Rodriguez, O., & Santiviago, M. (1991). Hispanic deaf adolescents: A multicultural minority. *The Volta Review, 93*(5), 89-97.

Rolland, J. S. (1994). *Families, illness, and disability.* New York: Basic Books.

Sabogal, F., Marin, G., Otero-Sabogal, R., Marin, B. V., & Perez-Stable, E. J. (1987). Hispanic familism and acculturation: What changes and what doesn't? *Hispanic Journal of Behavioral Sciences, 9*(4), 397-412.

Schlesinger, H. S., & Meadow, K. P. (1972). *Sound and sign: Childhood deafness and mental health.* Berkeley: University of California Press.

Seligman, M., & Darling, R. (1989). *Ordinary families: Special children.* New York: Guilford.

Spector, R. E. (1985). *Cultural diversity in health and illness.* New York: Appleton-Century Crofts.

Stein, R. C. (1983). Hispanic parents' perspectives and participation in their children's special education program: Comparisons by program and race. *Learning Disability Quarterly, 6,* 432-439.

Steinberg, A. (1997). Deafness. In J. D. Noshpitz (Ed.), *The handbook of child and adolescent psychiatry* (Vol. 4). New York: John Wiley

Szapocznick, J., & Kurtines, W. (1980). *Acculturation.* Boulder, CO: Westview.

Triandis, H. C., Marin, G., Betancourt, H., Lisansky, J., & Chang, B. (1982). *Dimensions of familism among Hispanic and mainstream Navy recruits* (Tech. Rep. No. 14). Champaign: University of Illinois, Department of Psychology.

U.S. Bureau of the Census. (1990). *The Hispanic population in the United States* (Series P-20, No. 444). Washington, DC: U.S. Government Printing Office.

Social Support, Motivation, Language, and Interaction: A Longitudinal Study of Mothers and Deaf Infants

Robert H. MacTurk, Kathryn P. Meadow-Orlans, Lynn S. Koester, Patricia E. Spencer

Abstract: *This project examined the effect of early cognitive, social, and communicative experiences on later social and language development in deaf infants with hearing mothers. Interactions between mothers and deaf infants were found to be positively influenced by social support provided to mothers in the early months of the infants' lives, mothers' visual and tactile responsiveness when their infants were 9 months of age, infants' ability to cope with interactive stress at 9 months of age, and fewer attempts by infants to engage with the social environment during the mastery motivation assessment at 9 months. Neither mother-infant affective matching nor maternal visual-tactile responsiveness correlated with the deaf infants' language level.* *

A large body of research spanning more than 30 years documents the developmental impact of early deafness. In particular, deaf children with hearing parents have been found to lag behind hearing peers in language acquisition, exhibit social and behavioral problems, and have academic difficulties despite normal intelligence (Moores, 1987). Because of the usual delay in diagnosing deafness in children of hearing parents, little research has been conducted with deaf children younger than 2 years of age. Recent advances in diagnostic techniques and a growing awareness of the importance of early intervention are changing this picture, making possible the research reported here.

This project examined the effect of early cognitive, social, and communicative experiences on later social and language development in deaf infants with hearing mothers. The study focused on the relationships between four sets of independent variables (infants' mastery motivation and social coping skills, mothers' interactive responsiveness and communicative contingency) and two sets of dependent variables (infants' language level and

*Editor's note: A recent book by K.P. Meadow-Orlans, P.E. Spencer, and L. S. Koester entitled *The World of Deaf Infants: A Longitudinal Study* (Oxford University Press, 2004) provides more current analyses and syntheses of these same findings than were available at the time of this article.

dyadic interaction style). Infants' hearing status and family support were viewed as mediating variables. In order to identify and track age-related changes in these developmentally important and conceptually related areas of functioning, the multifactorial, longitudinal design included observations of mothers' and infants' behaviors when the infants were 9, 12, 15, and 18 months of age. Interviews were conducted as well.

A wealth of data indicate that infant's experiences with their environments provide the foundation for later competence (Bruner, Jolly, & Sylva, 1976). In the 1930s, several influential reports revealed the deleterious effects of extreme social deprivation on the mental and physical development of infants placed in foundling homes (Skodak & Skeels, 1949; Spitz, 1945). Initially these negative outcomes were attributed to a lack of maternal care giving (Bowlby, 1953). Yarrow's (1961) critique of this global approach to the effects of early experience provided the framework for subsequent investigations of specific patterns or dimensions of mothering. It also provided the basis for more focused theories of infant development, including consideration of the specific contributions of the social environment to later competencies (Lewis & Goldberg, 1969; Wachs & Gruen, 1982).

Ainsworth conducted a series of investigations into the relationship between early mother-infant interactions and the quality of the mother-infant relationship in the second year of life. Her findings revealed that infants whose needs were met in a socially responsive environment were more likely to have satisfactory relationships with their mothers at 18 months of age (Ainsworth & Wittig, 1969; Ainsworth, Blehar, Waters, & Wall, 1978). Moreover, these children were more likely to explore their environments, be socially competent, and to do well in school than their peers who experienced less responsive social environments (Ainsworth & Wittig, 1969; Lieberman, 1977; Sroufe, 1983). Additional studies have shown positive correlations between early maternal responsiveness and later intelligence (Bornstein & Sigman, 1986; Coates & Lewis, 1984).

The conceptual link between early maternal responsiveness and later infant competence has been termed the *secure base phenomenon* (Sroufe & Waters, 1977). The mother who is sensitive, responsive, and emotionally available to her infant provides a secure base that enables the infant to separate easily and to explore the wider environment (Frodi, Bridges, & Grolnick, 1985; Hron, Lefever, & Weintraub, 1990). Exploratory behavior has been linked to later competence (Jennings, Harmon, Morgan, Gaiter, & Yarrow, 1979; McCall, Eichorn, & Hogarty, 1977; Messer et al., 1986).

Several life events, such as maternal depression or the birth of an atypical infant, have been shown to interfere with the mother's ability to provide an appropriately responsive environment. For example, clinically depressed mothers lack the emotional resources to interact effectively with their infants (Cohn, Campbell, Matias & Hopkins 1990; Field et al., 1988). In addition, Redding, Harmon, and Morgan (1990) report that even mildly depressed mothers have infants who prefer less challenging tasks and are less motivated to explore their environments.

Field's (1977) analysis revealed a tendency for the mothers of premature infants to be more stimulating with their infants than the mothers of term infants. This increase in stimulation levels has also been observed in adult-infant conversational styles (Jaffe & Feldstein, 1970) and in feeding patterns (Stevenson, Roach, Ver Hoeve, & Leavitt, 1990). This style of interaction may result in a reduction of early, self-initiated experiences whereby infants learn to control important aspects of their environments. This increase in stimulation may be an adaptive response to decreased levels of infant responsiveness and signalling, or may be based upon maternal expectations. Mothers of deaf infants appear to offer more stimulation, have interaction patterns that are less rich, and focus on objects rather than on social play (Nienhuys & Tikotin, 1983; Spencer & Gutfreund, 1990). Such patterns may reduce deaf children's opportunities to experience appropriately contingent environments, possibly impeding their mastery of their environments.

Evidence suggests, however, that intervention can affect mother-infant interactions. For example, when Field (1977) instructed mothers to imitate their infants' actions, the infants responded with a significant increase in smiling. Watson (Watson, 1972; Watson & Ramey, 1972) reported similar findings in his work on social contingencies. Harmon, Pipp, and Morgan (1984) found that nonspecific psychiatric interventions with depressed mothers of premature infants were associated with significant increases in their infants' mastery motivation.

Another factor is the availability of family social support systems. Several studies have indicated that social support can mediate the deleterious consequences the birth of an atypical infant brings to the interactive system (Crockenberg, 1981; Feiring, Fox, Jaskir, & Lewis, 1985). Lack of social support networks are associated with decreases in maternal involvement, stimulation, and positive affect; conversely, availability of support is related to increases in maternal sensitivity and nurturing (Crockenberg, 1981; Weinrauh & Wolf, 1983).

The effect of social support networks is particularly important because they are potentially amenable to change. By distinguishing the unique variance associated with deafness that contributes to later language development and a mutually satisfying mother-infant relationship, it may be possible to identify specific intervention strategies appropriate for the deaf population.

Methods

Subjects

Forty hearing mothers participated in the study, 20 with deaf infants and 20 with hearing infants. Groups were matched according to mothers' education (mean = 16.3 years) and infant sex (12 boys and 8 girls in each group). Infants experienced births free of major complications and were developing normally with no (additional) sensory or physical impairments. Their families were middle income. All but one family had both parents present in the home. All fathers were Caucasian; one mother was Asian American, and another was of mixed-race parentage.

Fifteen of the deaf infants had a hearing loss in the severe-to-profound range; five had a more moderate loss. Hearing loss was confirmed by seven months of age in all cases (mean age at time of diagnosis was 2.8 months). All were receiving services by 10 months of age. The deaf infants were recruited from five metropolitan areas: Washington, DC, Atlanta, Dallas, Pittsburgh, and Amherst/Boston. The hearing infants were recruited primarily from the Washington, DC, metropolitan area.

Procedures

Nine Months. (1) Mother-Infant Face-to-Face Interaction was videotaped in a standard format with the infant sitting on a table in a seat facing the mother for 3 minutes of normal play, followed by 2 minutes of maternal "still-face" and another 2 minutes of play (Tronick, Als, & Brazelton, 1980). (2) Infant's Mastery Motivation (Yarrow et al., 1983) was assessed by presenting four age-appropriate toys in a fixed order for 3 minutes each. Infants sat on mothers' laps across a table from the examiner. (3) Mothers completed the Parenting Stress Index (Abidin, 1983), consisting of 101 items divided into seven Parent Domain subscales and six Child Domain subscales.

Twelve Months. (1) The Infants' Mastery Motivation was assessed using the same methodology as for the 9-month visit but with a different set of toys. (2) Mother and child were videotaped while they played together with a large set of age-appropriate toys for 20 minutes.

Fifteen Months. Mothers completed the Family Support Scale (Dunst, Jenkins & Trivette, 1984), which rated support from 18 possible sources.

Eighteen Months. (1) Mother and child were videotaped playing with age-appropriate toys for 20 minutes. The data were used to generate (1) Child's Language Level and (2) Global Ratings of Mother-Child Interaction.

Each author was responsible for coding and analyzing a specific data set. After completion of the initial descriptive analyses, each author selected two variables that appeared to capture important aspects of a specific domain and could be expected to serve as predictors of language or interaction in the final regression equation. Of the 10 variables selected, 5 met the F-to-enter criteria (F = 4.00) in the two preliminary step-wise regression analyses. These variables are shown in Table 1, with means, standard deviations, and significance levels for the between-groups differences.

Definitions of Variables

Support Index is the sum of Mean Total Score from the Family Support Scale and quintile rankings of two subscale scores from the Parenting Stress Index, Relationship with Spouse and Social Isolation.

Social Smile (Mastery Motivation, 9 months) was defined as the number of times the infant looked at the experimenter or mother with a positive facial expression.

Maternal Visual/Tactile Responsiveness (Face-to-Face Interaction: Play, 9 months) reflects co-occurring maternal and infant nonvocal behaviors, including infant attention and maternal visual display, infant social signals and maternal greeting, or infant distress and maternal tactile contact.

Affective Matching (Face-to-Face Interaction: Play, 9 months) provides a more specific measure of mother and infant's engagement in either the same affective displays (positive or negative expressions) or similar rhythmic activities (e.g., infant cycling arms, mother stroking infant's legs).

Gaze Avert (Face-to-Face: Still-Face, 9 months) is the frequency of the infant looking away from the mother, either by visually exploring the environment or by turning to look at parts of himself or herself.

Global Mother-Infant Interaction (Free Play, 18 months) is the mean of five maternal ratings (Sensitivity, Involvement, Flexibility, Affect, Consistency), four infant ratings (Compliance, Affect, Involvement, Gentleness), and three dyadic ratings (Enjoyment, Understanding, Turntaking).

Infant Language Level (Free Play, 18 months) is the frequency of infants' production of linguistically encoded communicative expressions. The measure includes all communicative expressions, vocal or signed, and reflects infants' use of language in an interactive context.

Reliability

The authors were responsible for establishing acceptable levels of reliability for their respective measures. All sessions were coded by trained observers who, as much as possible, were blind to the aims of the investigation and the hearing status of the infants. For each procedure, 10% to 15% of the videotapes were assessed for interrater reliability. Levels of agreement between the raters were greater than 80% for all the measures employed in this report.

Results and Discussion

Data Analysis

The data were analyzed in several stages. The first stage consisted of a series of descriptive data screening procedures to identify possible distributional problems of particular variables. Appropriate transformations were applied to variables violating assumptions of normality, and all measures were converted to z-scores to equalize the metric (Tukey, 1977). Data presented in this report are in the untransformed, original metric, but the analyses were conducted on the transformed z-scores.

The second stage examined the data for the presence of developmental status, sex, recruitment site, or hearing level differences. The third stage consisted of a series of one-way analyses of variance (ANOVAs) and correlational analyses as a preliminary step in building the predictive regression equation. The final stage was the computation of two step-wise multiple regressions using the 18-month dyadic Global Rating and the 18-month Infant Language Level as independent variables. These analyses were used to examine the predictive relationships between the summary measures and the two dependent measures for deaf and hearing infants at 18 months.

Preliminary Analyses

During interviews conducted when their infants were 9, 15, and 18 months of age, the mothers completed the Alpern-Boll Developmental Profile (Alpern, Boll, & Shearer, 1980) physical development and self-help subscales. These were converted into developmental quotients and the mean quotient computed across the three ages. The physical development mean quotients were 114 and 108 for the deaf and hearing infants respectively. The self-help mean quotients were 106 and 112 for the deaf and hearing infants respectively. None of these scores were significantly different.

The majority of both the deaf (n = 10) and hearing (n = 18) infants were seen in the laboratory on the Gallaudet University campus. To test for the differences between research sites, the subjects were divided into two groups (Gallaudet versus Other) and analyzed using the Student t-test. This analysis revealed no significant differences (above what would be expected by chance alone) on any of the measures contained in this report. Similar analyses were conducted on hearing level: The infants were divided according to sex and degree of hearing loss (severeto-profound loss [n = 151 and mild-to-moderate loss [n = 51). Again, no significant differences were detected.

Group Differences

A series of one-way ANOVAs were performed on the variables that displayed significant predictive relationships with the two dependent variables, as well as on the two dependent variables. Only three measures were significantly different: Maternal VisualTactile Responsiveness, Infant Gaze Avert, and the Global Interaction rating. In each measure, the hearing infants and their mothers scored higher than the deaf infants and their mothers.

The data contained in Table 1 are especially notable in two ways. First, all the variables that accounted for a significant proportion of the observed variance in the dependent measures were obtained from the 9-month visit. This suggests the origins of language acquisition and mutual enjoyment experienced by the mother-infant dyads are established during the second half of the first year of life, regardless of the infants' hearing status. This conclusion is consistent with findings of Ainsworth (1973), Bruner (1983), and Snow (1989).

Second, the groups do not differ significantly in family support. Contrary to previous reports (Greenberg, 1983), the families of the deaf infants appear to have social support networks equivalent to those of the comparison families. In all likelihood, this relates to uncomplicated access to professional services (suggested by early identification of infants' deafness).

Predictive Relationships

Global Interaction Ratings

The preliminary step-wise regression analysis revealed four summary measures that met the F-to-enter criteria of 4.00 or better for the two groups combined.

These measures (Family Support, Social Smile, Gaze Avert, and Maternal Responsiveness) were used in a linear regression by groups analysis (BMDPlR) to examine their predictive utility for the quality of mother-child interaction at 18 months.

For the deaf infants and their mothers, the four measures accounted for approximately 78% of the observed variance in the Global Interaction Ratings. The measures accounted for only 29% of the observed variance with the hearing infants (Table 2). The slope of the regression lines for the two groups were significantly different (F (5,29) = 3.22, p < .05).

For both groups of families, the amount of support mothers received from family, friends, and professionals contributed significantly to the quality of later mother-child interaction. These sources of support, especially important for the mothers of deaf infants, may be relatively amenable to manipulation in intervention strategies.

Also contributing to positive interactions at 18 months were maternal visual/tactile responsiveness during Face-to-Face Interaction. The effect was stronger for the mothers of deaf infants and may reflect the manner in which responsiveness was measured. In most research on mother-infant interactions, measures of maternal responsiveness assess both auditory and physical responses, including "babytalk," cooing, touching, and/or holding (Belsky, Taylor, & Rovine, 1984; Clarke-Stewart, 1980; McCarthy & McQuiston, 1983). Hence possible separate influences of auditory and physical contact are masked. We considered only nonvocal forms of maternal responsiveness. The frequency with which the mothers of the deaf infants visually or tactually stimulated their 9-month-old infants significantly increased the amount of explained variance in the dependent measure.

The same was not true for the hearing infants. Visual-tactile stimulation was a relatively minor contributor to their subsequent patterns of interaction. We would expect that the vocal contingent behavior of the mothers with hearing infants would also display significant predictive utility. We think this is an especially important finding. Not only does it confirm that maternal responsiveness is an influential dimension of an infant's early experience, but it also suggests that the response modality should be matched with the infant's sensory capacities. That is, visual and tactile responses appear to be particularly salient for deaf infants, whereas vocal responses may play a similar role for hearing infants.

Gaze aversion during face-to-face interaction generally, and during maternal still-face specifically, is a means by which infants manage aversive stimuli. The maternal still-face episode is inherently aversive to infants. The mothers' proximity, combined with lack of responsiveness, presents the infants with a highly discrepant situation that requires them to draw upon their own resources to regulate their emotional reactions (Tronick, Als, Adamson, Wise, & Brazelton, 1978). Table 2 shows that the relationship between the frequency of Gaze Avert and the quality of later mother-child interaction was equal for the two groups but opposite in effect. For the deaf infants, a higher frequency of gaze aversion at 9 months of age was associated with higher ratings on the measure of dyadic interaction at 18 months. For the hearing infants, fewer gaze averts during periods of maternal still-face were associated with more satisfactory interactions. As with the issues surrounding tactile versus vocal responsiveness discussed earlier, the various modalities of stimulation appear to play an important role.

Table 1 shows that deaf infants averted their gazes significantly less frequently than their hearing peers. This suggests that they were less stressed than the hearing infants or that their need to maintain visual contact with their mothers was stronger than their need to manage the ambiguity of the maternal still-face episode. Whatever the explanation, the deaf infants' ability to modulate these two competing domains (visual contact and stress management) resulted in more favorable patterns of mother-child interaction later in life.

MacTurk (in press) reports a similar phenomenon in his study of the development of mastery motivation in deaf and hearing infants. He found that, for deaf infants, social looking at 9 months of age was positively related to motivation levels at 12 months. For the hearing infants, early social looking did not relate to later task performance.

These reports suggest that deaf infants develop compensatory strategies to overcome their reduced contact with the environment. Hearing infants experience a social and object environment that provides sources of feedback that may be processed simultaneously.

Deaf infants, on the other hand, experience a social and object environment that requires them to process environmental signals sequentially. Though this adaptation does not always result in significant mean group differences, the consequences are apparent across both ages and situations.

Social smiling during the mastery motivation assessment at age 9 months was negatively related to later interaction for the deaf infants. As McCarthy and Messer (1984) have pointed out, infant smiling is a complex signal. They found that infant social smiling at 6 months of age was associated with insecure patterns of attachment at 15 months of age. Their explanation was that early social smiling, generally considered a mechanism to regulate proximity (Bowlby, 1982; Ainsworth, 1973), indexes disturbances in the quality of the mother-infant relationship. This explanation may also account for the results reported here. The deaf infants who smile more during the mastery motivation assessment may be signalling their need for increased social contact. To the extent that deafness interferes with a hearing mother's ability to read and respond appropriately to her infant's signals, we would expect to see an effect on the quality of later mother-infant interaction. This expectation is supported by our findings.

Table 1

Means, Standard Deviations, and Significance Levels Summary Measures for Dyads With Deaf and Hearing Infants

Variable	Deaf	Hearing	F (1, 39)
Support Index	8.70	9.38	.82
	(2.61)	(2.05)	
Independent Variables, Age 9 months			
Social Smile[a]	1.37	1.72	.53
	(1.49)	(1.52)	
Affective Matching[b]	3.65	5.70	2.69*
	(2.74)	(4.87)	
Maternal Responsiveness[b]	9.80	12.60	5.67**
	(3.09)	3.94	
Infant Gaze Avert[c]	4.70	7.50	3.90**
(4.54) (4.42)			
Dependent Variables, Age 18 months			
Infant Language Level[d]	7.28	23.63	3.17*
	(10.61)	(30.83)	
Dyadic Global Ratings[d]	3.04	3.78	5.10**
	(1.03)	(1.05)	

Note. *$p < .10$. **$p < .05$. [a] Mastery. [b] Face to face (normal interaction). [c] Face to face (still-face). [d] Free play.

Table 2

Dyadic Global Ratings: Standardized Regression Coefficients, Multiple Rs, and R^2s, for the Deaf and Hearing Infants

Variable	Deaf [a]	Hearing [b]
Support	.59	.32
Responsiveness	.42	.21
Gaze Alert	.47	-.48
Social smile (9 mos.)	-.45	-.04

Note. [a] Multiple R =.88; R^2 = .78.   [b] Multiple R = .53; R^2 =.29.

Table 3

Infant Language Level: Standardized Regression Coefficients, Multiple Rs, and R^2s, for the Deaf and Hearing Infants

Variable	Deaf [a]	Hearing [b]
Affective Matching	.03	.52
Responsiveness	.05	-.54

Note. [a] Multiple R =.06; R^2 = .03.   [b] Multiple R = .61; R^2 =.37.

Language at 18 Months

The preliminary multiple regression analyses conducted for the global interaction ratings were repeated for the measure of infant Language Level at 18 months of age. The step-wise multiple regression yielded two summary measures, both of which were obtained from the Face-to-Face situation at 9 months of age (frequency of Affective Matches and Maternal Responsiveness). The linear regression by groups revealed no significant differences between the slopes of the two regression lines. The two measures accounted for none of the observed variance in the language measure for the deaf infants at 18 months of age, and for 37% of the variance for the hearing infants.

More important than the degree of significance for the language regression is the direction of the effect of the two interaction measures for the hearing infants at 9 months of age: Affective Matching contributes positively to later Language Level, whereas Maternal Responsiveness contributes negatively. This implies that the predominantly physical forms of responsiveness tapped by these measures may overwhelm the infant's ability to process these experiences. The affective matching between the mother and her infant may represent a more distal form of responsiveness, and one which the infant may readily control by turning away.

We see that the mother's early social behavior makes an important contribution to the hearing infant's later language development, but not to the deaf infant's. Mothers of deaf infants, as a group, displayed somewhat less affective matching and significantly less responsiveness than the mothers of hearing infants (Table 1), indicating an absence of dyadic synchrony. Given the lower frequency of gaze aversion among the deaf infants, affective matching should be higher. This suggests that mothers of deaf infants may be less adept at reading and responding to their infants' emotional states.

Wood (1982) claims that deafness places an increased strain on the infants' developing attention, memory, and integrative capacities, possibly diminishing their early social interactions. This may help explain our findings regarding the deaf infants' language development. That is, the deaf infant must work harder to process maternal input since it is accessible only through nonvocal channels. In addition, attention to the object world and to social narratives about that world must be sequential rather than simultaneous, since both must be perceived primarily through vision. Therefore, the deaf child may have fewer opportunities to develop "output" skills such as the eliciting behaviors that appear more frequently among the hearing infants and are thought to be useful social tools for maintaining appropriate levels of stimulation.

The results presented here support the conclusion that deafness per se has little explanatory value for the developmental trajectory of deaf infants. Rather, we conclude that the major influences on the early development of these infants consist of a delicate interplay of both exogenous factors, as represented by the family support measures, and endogenous factors, as represented by the measures of mother and infant behavior. We see that the presence of family support networks, combined with the emotional resources available to the participants, has important consequences for the later mother-child relationship. The relationship between early experience and later language development is not clear, however. None of the measures employed in this report accounted for any of the observed variance in the deaf infants' language level at 18 months of age, at least when the deaf infants were compared to their hearing peers.

Our approach to the design of this investigation was driven primarily by research findings on hearing parents and infants. We are currently collecting comparable data on deaf and hearing infants of deaf parents, and expect these data to provide additional insight into the results reported here.

References

Abidin, R. R. (1983). *Parenting stress index manual.* Charlottesville, VA: Pediatric Psychology.

Ainsworth, M. D. S. (1973). The development of mother-infant attachment. In B. M. Caldwell & H. N. Riccuti, (Eds.), *Review of child development research* (Vol. 3, pp. 1-94). Chicago: University of Chicago Press.

Ainsworth, M. D. S., & Wittig, B. A. (1969) Attachment and exploratory behavior of one-year-olds in a strange situation. In B. M. Foss (Ed.), *Determinants of infant behaviour IV* (pp. 185-220). London: Methuen.

Ainsworth, M. D. S., Blehar, M. C., Waters, E., & Wall, S. (1978). *Patterns of attachment: A psychological study of the strange situation.* Hillsdale, NJ: Erlbaum.

Alpern, G. D., Boll, T. J., & Shearer, M. S. (1980). *Manual, Developmental Profile II* (rev. ed.). Aspen, CO: Psychological Development Publications.

Belsky, J., Taylor, D. G., & Rovine, M. (1984). The Pennsylvania Infant and Family Development Project II: The development of reciprocal interaction in the mother infant dyad. *Child Development, 55*, 706-717.

Bornstein, M. H., & Sigman, M. D. (1986). Continuity in mental development from infancy. *Child Development, 57*, 251-274.

Bowlby, J. (1953). *Child care and the growth of love.* London: Penguin.

Bowlby, J. (1982). *Attachment and loss: Vol. 1. Attachment.* New York: Basic.

Bruner, J. (1983). *Child's talk: Learning to use language.* New York: Norton.

Bruner, J., Jolly, A., & Sylva, K. (Eds.) (1976). *Play: Its role in development and evolution.* Harmondsworth, UK: Penguin.

Clarke-Stewart, K. A. (1980). The father's contribution to children's cognitive and social development in early childhood. In F. A. Pedersen (Ed.), *The father-infant relationship: Observational studies in a family context* (pp. 111-146). New York: Praeger.

Coates, D. L., & Lewis. M. (1984). Early mother-infant interaction and infant cognitive status as predictors of school performance and cognitive behavior in six-year-olds. *Child Development, 55*, 1219-1230.

Cohn, J. F., Campbell, S. B., Matias, R., & Hopkins, J. (1990). Face-to-face interactions of postpartum depressed and nondepressed mother-infant pairs at two months. *Developmental Psychology, 26*, 15-23.

Crockenberg, S. B. (1981). Infant irritability, mother responsiveness, and social support influences on the security of mother-infant attachment. *Child Development, 52*, 857-865.

Dunst, C. J., Jenkins, V., & Trivette, C. M. (1984). Family Support Scale: Reliability and validity. *Journal of Individual, Family, and Community Wellness, 1*, 45-52.

Feiring, C., Fox, N., Jaskir, J., & Lewis, M. (1985, April). *The relationship between social support, infant risk status and mother-infant interaction.* Paper presented at the biennial meeting of the Society for Research in Child Development, Toronto, Canada.

Field, T. M. (1977). Effects of early separation, interactive deficits, and experimental manipulations on infant-mother face-to-face interaction. *Child Development, 48*, 763-771.

Field, T. M., Healy, B., Goldstein, S., Perry, S., Bendell, D., Schanberg, S., Zimmerman, E. A., & Kuhn, C. (1988). Infants of depressed mothers show "depressed" behavior even with nondepressed adults. *Child Development, 59*, 1569-1579.

Frodi, A., Bridges, L., & Grolnick, W. (1985). Correlates of mastery-related behavior: A short-term longitudinal study of infants in their second year. *Child Development, 56*, 1291-1298.

Greenberg, M. T. (1983). Family stress and child competence: The effects of early intervention for families with deaf infants. *American Annals of the Deaf, 128*, 407-417.

Harmon, R. J., Pipp, S., & Morgan, G. A. (1984, May). *Mastery motivation in perinatal risk infants.* Invited presentation at an NICHHD conference on mastery motivation in infancy and early childhood. Bethesda, MD.

Hron, K., Lefever, G., & Weintraub, D. (1990, April). *Correlates and predictors of mastery motivation: Relations to mother-child problem-solving, temperament, attachment and home environment.* Poster presented at the International Conference on Infant Studies, Montreal, Canada.

Jaffe, J., & Feldstein, S. (1970). *Rhythms of dialogue.* New York: Academic.

Jennings, K. D., Harmon, R. J., Morgan, G. A., Gaiter, J. L., & Yarrow. L. J. (1979). Exploratory play as an index of mastery motivation: Relationships to persistence, cognitive functioning and environmental measures. *Developmental Psychology, 15*, 386-394.

Lewis, M., & Goldberg, S. (1969). Perceptual-cognitive development in infancy: A generalized expectancy model as a function of the mother-infant interaction. *Merrill-Palmer Quarterly, 15*, 81-100.

Lieberman., A. (1977). Preschoolers' competence with a peer: Influence of attachment and social experience. *Child Development, 48*, 1277-1287.

MacTurk, R. H. (in press). Social and motivational development in deaf and hearing infants. In D. J. Messer (Ed.) *Mastery motivation: Children's investigation, persistence and development.* London: Routledge.

McCall, R. B., Eichorn, D. H., & Hogarty, P. S. (1977). Transitions in early mental development. *Monograph of the Society for Research in Child Development, 42* (3, Serial No. 171).

McCarthy, M. E., & McQuiston, S. (1983, April). *The relationship of contingent parental behaviors to infant motivation and competence.* Paper presented at the Biennial Meeting of the Society for Research and Child Development, Detroit, MI.

McCarthy, M. E., & Messer, D. J. (1984, August). *Infant affect in the home and its relation to later cognitive abilities.* Paper presented at the annual meeting of the American Psychological Association, Toronto, Canada.

Messer, D., McCarthy, M., McQuiston. S., MacTurk, R., Yarrow, L. & Vietze, P. (1986). Relation between mastery behavior in infancy and comp-etence in early childhood. *Developmental Psychology, 22*, 336-372.

Moores. D. F. (1987). *Educating the deaf. Principles and practices.* Boston: Houghton Mifflin.

Nienhuys, T. G., & Tikotin, J. A. (1983). Prespeech communication in hearing and hearing-impaired children. *Journal of the British Association of Teachers of the Deaf, 7*, 182-194.

Redding, R. E., Harmon, R. J., & Morgan, G. A. (1990). Maternal depression and infants' mastery behaviors. *Infant Behavior and Development, 13,* 391-396.

Skodak., M., & Skeels, H. M. (1949). A final follow-up of one hundred adopted children. *Journal of Genetic Psychology, 75*, 85-125.

Snow, C. E. (1989). Understanding social interaction and language acquisition: Sentences are not enough. In M. Bornstein & J. Bruner (Eds.), *Interaction in human development* (pp. 83-104). Hillsdale, NJ: Erlhaum.

Spencer, P. E., & Gutfreund, M. K. (1990). Directiveness in mother-infant interactions. In D. F. Moores & K. P. Meadow-Orlans (Eds.), *Educational and developmental aspects of deafness* (pp. 350-365). Washington, DC: Gallaudet University Press.

Spitz, R. (1945). Hospitalism. *Psychoanalytic Study of the Child, 1*, 53-74.

Sroufe, L. A. (1983). Infant-caregiver attachment and patterns of adaption in preschool: The roots of maladaptation and competence. In M. Perlmutter (Ed.), *Minnesota symposium in child psychology* (Vol. 16, pp. 41-81). Hillsdale, NJ: Erlbaum.

Sroufe, L. A., & Waters, E. (1977). Attachment as an organizational construct. *Child Development, 48*, 1184-1199.

Stevenson, M. B., Roach, M. A., Ver Hoeve, J. N., & Leavitt, L. A. (1990). Rhythms in the dialogue of infant feeding: Preterm and term infants. *Infant Behavior and Development, 13*, 51-70.

Tronick, E. Z., Als, H., & Brazelton, T. B. (1980). Monadic phases: A structural descriptive analysis of infant-mother face-to-face interaction. *Merrill-Palmer Quarterly, 62*, 3-24.

Tronick, E. Z., Als, H., Adamson, L., Wise, S., & Brazelton, T. (1978). The infant's response to entrapment between contradictory messages in face-to-face interaction. *Journal of the American Academy of Child Psychiatry 17*, 1-13.

Tukey, J. (1977). *Exploratory data analysis*. Reading, MA: Addison-Wesley.

Wachs, T. D., & Gruen, D. (1982). *Early experience and human development*. New York: Plenum.

Watson, J. S. (1972). Smiling, cooing, and "The Game." *Merrill-Palmer Quarterly, 18*, 323-339.

Watson, J. S., & Ramey, C. T. (1972). Reactions to response-contingent stimulation in early infancy. *Merrill-Palmer Quarterly, 18*, 219-227.

Weinraub, M., & Wolf, B. M. (1983). Effects of stress and social supports on mother-child interactions in single- and two-parent families. *Child Development, 54*, 1297-1311.

Wood, D. J. (1982). The linguistic experiences of the pre-lingually hearing-impaired child. *Journal of the British Association of Teachers of the Deaf, 6*, 86-93.

Yarrow, L. J. (1961). Maternal deprivation: Toward an empirical and conceptual re-evaluation. *Psychological Bulletin, 58*, 459-490.

Yarrow, L. J., McQuiston, S., MacTurk, R. H., McCarthy, M. E., Klein, R. P., & Vietze, P. M. (1983). Assessment of mastery motivation in the first year of life: Contemporaneous and cross-age relationships. *Developmental Psychology, 19*, 159-171.

Hearing-Impaired Children in Black and Hispanic Families

Joseph E. Fischgrund
Oscar P. Cohen
Richard L. Clarkson

Abstract: *At present, nearly one third of hearing-impaired children in the United States are either Black or Hispanic. The changing demographics of deafness require special skills and sensitivities on the part of professionals working with parents. This chapter presents basic sociocultural information about Black and Hispanic families and the implications for parent intervention programs and specialists.*

The United States of America is a nation of over 240 million people, about 50 million (21%) of whom are Black, Hispanic, and Asian. Federal and private projections estimate that soon after the turn of the century one of every three Americans will be non-White. Currently most of the non-White student population is concentrated in a band of states that begins in New York, stretches south along the Atlantic coast, and then turns west-ending in California. California now has a "majority of minorities" in its elementary schools; 46% of students in Texas are Black and Hispanic. In the 25 largest urban school systems, the majority of students belong to racial, ethnic, or linguistic minorities (Cohen, 1987).

These changing demographics continue to have profound impact on programs for hearing-impaired children. Specifically, the parents of minority hearing-impaired children and programs designed to serve them will be increasingly affected. This chapter examines some of the social realities of Black and Hispanic families, the parenting of minority hearing-impaired children, and the implications of minority status for deafness and parent education programs.

Hispanic Families

Hispanic families are predominantly poor, often recently immigrated, and culturally diverse. These larger issues and their implications need to be studied before professionals can work successfully with Hispanic children and their families.

Economic Status. A high percentage of female-headed households with several young children contributes to low income levels among Hispanics because participation in the workforce is generally discouraged in such families. The 1980 median household income for the entire population of New York City was $14,000 (Rodriguez, 1985). Hispanics (who made up 20% of that population) had a median household income of $11,700.

The Puerto Rican portion of this Hispanic population (12% of the total and 60% of Hispanics) had a median household income of $8,000 (Rodriguez, 1985). Families living at this level of poverty face struggles of daily survival, and thus are much less likely to participate in services related to their children's education.

Immigrant Status. The young immigrant parent can be isolated from American culture, often seeing the school as just one more alien institution— not unlike the courts, police, and municipal government—that is sometimes puzzling, often difficult to deal with, and possibly even feared. Immigration is a process of acculturation—the learning of new ways of behaving. It is a slow, anxiety-producing process that unfolds over a lifetime and places great strains on families. Often being torn in different directions by the teacher and the immigrant parent, children are at a pivotal point in this process. Already pressured by the stress and anxiety of immigration, the immigrant parents of a deaf child require special skills, sensitivities, and approaches on the part of the parent intervention specialist.

Cultural Life. The Hispanic family generally has a pronounced sexual division of labor. The father is considered the main source of authority and the final arbiter; the mother is the chief executive, conducting the daily business of running the family. As the primary broker of services to the family, she conducts relations with institutions, including the school. A parent specialist who wishes to discuss either a problem or special programs with a parent must usually deal with the mother. However, any major decision requires the father's approval. To communicate with the family, a professional must understand this subtle distinction

There is also a gender difference with respect to children, with different expectations held for females and males. Females, viewed by traditional Hispanic parents as helpless and needing protection, are often disciplined by parents in ways teachers consider unnecessary and out of proportion. The opposite happens with males: When the parenting specialist may believe it is time to impose more discipline on a male child, the parent may believe that the behavior is acceptable in accordance with traditional belief that Hispanic males are naturally driven by innate malice and sexual energies. Further, in the traditional Hispanic context, children are viewed as being dependent on the parents far beyond the age commonly considered appropriate by Americans. Often, an unspoken conflict arises between a parent specialist and a Hispanic parent about the age a child should become independent.

It is also important for the parent specialist to present him or herself less as a professional educator and more as a person with qualities attractive to the Hispanic parent. The educator/administrator must show that he or she is interested in the parent as a human being—not simply as the parent of his or her student. The interaction between socioeconomic status, immigration status, and cultural status must be recognized. For example, much of what is known about Hispanic families is really about *traditional* Hispanic families. A family may be Hispanic but neither immigrant nor traditional. Thus generalizations about the effects of immigration status or cultural values and beliefs cannot be indiscriminately applied if the professional is to understand the individual child, family, or parenting practices.

Black Families

In America, Blacks are a diverse group representing Caribbean culture, African cultures, and the American Black experience. The Black population from the Caribbean islands is growing rapidly in many areas. This may also involve a language difference, as in the case of Haitians. In addition Caribbean Blacks most often come from islands where Blacks are the majority, possibly even holding political power. Thus, they are not accustomed to seeing themselves as minorities in the sense that the White America majority views them. This will certainly influence the way they respond to a White parent specialist or a predominantly White-administered program. Much of our knowledge about Black Americans, whether based on research or part of the general body of knowledge available since the initiation of the Civil Rights movement, deals primarily with Blacks of either Southern or urban American origin. Much of this may be irrelevant to our understanding of Caribbean Blacks.

However, it is necessary to understand the social realities of life for Black families, no matter what their origin. The following profile is provided by the Children's Defense Fund (1985):
   • Eight out of every 10 White children live in two-parent families; only 4 out of 10 Black children do.

• Black children are 3½ times more likely than White children to live in female-headed households. Half the Black children in America now live in female-headed households compared to one-fourth in 1960.

• Almost 10% of America's Black children are in families supervised by a child welfare agency—4 times the supervision rate for White children.

• Black children are about twice as likely as White children to be living in institutions and are 4 times more likely to be living in correctional institutions.

• Regardless of family type, Black families earn significantly less (60%) than White families. Half of all Black families had incomes below $14,500 in 1983.

• Almost half of all Black children are poor compared to 1 of 6 White children. Children make up 36.6% of the White population living in poverty and 44% of the Black population living in poverty.

Within the context of this rather dismal social profile, it is also important to understand some fundamental issues in childbearing and child-rearing in Black families.

Black females have a strong motherhood orientation. Girls are given substantial household responsibility. Black females also consider bearing children a validation of their femaleness. Consequently, a positive attitude is shown toward childbearing. This validation may provide an explanation for the disproportionate number of births by Black females in their teens; however, the impact of the birth and rearing of a child may not be thoroughly considered, especially by young, single, and often uneducated mothers.

Black childbearing practices are generally more authoritarian in nature, having as their objective the development of toughness and self-sufficiency, valued attributes when seen as responses to the conditions faced by many Black Americans. These practices may result in cultural dissonance when teachers behave differently from the way Black children expect authority figures to behave, and when the children display attributes that are not so highly valued in the particular culture of the classroom. Black mothers tend to be more firm and physical in their discipline than White mothers. Consequently, when the child encounters a White professional in a parent program who is demonstrating traditional parent techniques acquired through training or practice, the children "run all over" him or her and then are labeled discipline problems (Hale-Benson, 1982).

Henderson and Washington (1975) conclude that many school practices are inappropriate for treating the educational needs of Black children because their unique cultural attributes are not taken into account. Black communities often evolve a network of significant adults who firmly correct undesirable behavior in neighborhood children and report it to the parent. The significant feature of this system is that it appears to operate externally to the child, with the child developing an external locus of control. In most school situations, however, adults act as if locus of social control exists within the child. They do not behave in ways consistent with the Black child's expectations of how adults should act toward them in situations requiring the enforcement of social controls.

Henderson and Washington also report that parents and teachers of Black children studied almost never communicated with each other and few parents participated in the school's parent association. In short, the school's social control apparatus functioned quite differently than that of the community, and parents were not included in its operation (Henderson & Washington, 1975).

As with Hispanic populations, there is great diversity among Black families. Among the variables are origin, economic status, and the nature of their interactions with various communities, institutions, and individuals. Once again, the professional must view the preceding generalizations and findings in the context of an individual family's functioning.

The preceding discussions touch upon just a very few of the salient issues professionals working with hearing-impaired children from Black and Hispanic homes must understand and address with families. Lack of consideration and understanding of how the social realities of life in Black and Hispanic communities affect parenting will hamper the effectiveness of parent intervention programs.

Deaf Children in Minority Families

Deaf children from minority families represent a significant percentage of hearing-impaired children and youth. Out of the 48,720 students surveyed in the 1985-1986 Annual National Survey of Hearing-Impaired Children and Youth (Center for Assessment and Demographic Studies, 1985-1986), 62.2% are White, 17.5% are Black, and 11.7% are Hispanic Americans.

Black and Hispanic students thus represent nearly a third of the hearing-impaired children and youth in this country. Many programs for the deaf are minority-majority programs, where children from racial, linguistic, and ethnic minority backgrounds make up the majority of the students. Given the current demographic trends, the numbers of Black, Hispanic, and other minority hearing-impaired children will continue to grow, requiring appropriate parent-oriented programs that are sensitive to the unique needs of these children and their families.

The process by which a family discovers, adjusts to, and eventually accepts a significant hearing loss in one of its young members is complex and difficult, varying considerably from family to family. Naturally, this variability is due to a wide range of responses among families reflecting psychological, socioeconomic, educational, cultural, and religious differences. Yet despite this diversity, there may be certain predictable stages most parents go through as they attempt to deal with the possibility that their young child has a significant hearing impairment. The following discussion reviews those common responses, at the same time raising questions about factors affecting families characterized as "non-mainstream," that is, those whose home language is not English, whose cultural orientation is not middle class American, or who are of minority standing or low socioeconomic status.

The first major commonality among parents with hearing-impaired children involves the long, anxious process of identifying and confirming the hearing loss. There are several reasons for this prolonged identification period relative to other handicaps, not the least of which is the low incidence of severe hearing impairment in the general population. The invisible nature of hearing impairment also increases the chances of its being a surprise to the parents. This is further complicated by surprisingly poor knowledge about etiology and detection of hearing impairment among members of the medical profession—as well as the lack of early identification programs. In fact, one study shows nearly half of the involved pediatricians resisting recognition of hearing loss when specifically questioned by suspecting parents (Luterman & Chasin, 1970).

For minority families this process is often slower and more anxiety-producing for several reasons. First, attitudes toward professionals, including the degree of trust in medical and educational bureaucracies, are not consistent across subcultures in the United States. While the typical American family demonstrates considerable respect for the medical profession and readily accepts its services, this is not the case with all groups. When accessibility is reduced by cultural and linguistic barriers, it is not surprising that families resist using health care resources, thus delaying identification. For example, the typical American family often equates quality of service with prestige or size of the facility. Conversely, the immigrant Hispanic family, accustomed to the *"clinica"* or *"centro"* (neighborhood or community health center), may find audiological services in a large hospital threatening and inaccessible and so avoids the service. In addition, medical contact for these families often involves more than a single physician, resulting in less continuity of medical services and a greater chance of misdiagnosing the hearing-impaired child. Further, many Hispanic and Black families of Caribbean origin look to nonmedical and noneducational networks rather than to hospitals and schools for advice, support, and information. Such networks may include a person or organization in the community who is of their national, racial, or ethnic origin. Finally, public awareness programs about hearing loss seldom reach into non-English speaking communities.

It is important to remember that using and participating in community and ethnic support systems and networks does not preclude the use of mainstream services. The parent specialist must recognize and encourage family participation in culturally relevant and accessible systems while also helping them to use new service delivery systems. Professionals involved in the identification and confirmation process, who naturally perceive themselves as helpers and service providers, may not be welcomed because they come from what is perceived as an alien agency. This may make the professional feel unwanted, unappreciated, and even angry. Clearly, the helping professional who understands these issues and can accept a less than enthusiastic response is more likely to keep open the possibility of building a positive relationship with the family.

When anxious parents finally receive a diagnosis of severe hearing loss, reconfirmation is psychologically necessary; however, it may be postponed due to elevated anxiety levels and reinforced denial. In families without established or readily available support networks, this period of anxiety or doubt may be significantly extended. Factors that help delay the realization that the child has a hearing loss also reinforce the parent's denial of the existence of a problem. Parents may search for any support that will attribute their child's apparent hearing loss to slow development, stubbornness, shyness, or any other terms well-meaning friends, relatives, and doctors attempt to use to console the anxious parents. Eventually, realization begins to close in on the already distressed family. At this point many view the situation as a common stage in psychological reaction to crisis (Shontz, 1967). Luterman (1979) even suggests that parental reaction to discovery of their child's handicap is similar to the emotional reaction documented by Kubler-Ross (1969) of terminally ill patients; that is, when parents are finally told their child has a hearing loss, they begin to actively mourn a monumental loss. Moses (1985) describes this response as the parent's loss of a dream and their expectation that their child will lead a normal life. He suggests that because something "very bad" has happened to their child, the parents feel powerless to change what has happened; they have lost their feeling of invulnerability.

This process of beginning to accept the hearing loss, Luterman concludes, involves the stages of shock, recognition, denial, acknowledgment, and constructive action. Although the term stage connotes fixed parameters and the idea that once a stage is completed the parent no longer has to deal with problems associated with it, this may not be the case. Moses (1985) suggests that a state theory is more tenable because it allows for movement back and forth among various psychological reactions. Regardless of one's viewpoint, certain behaviors appear to be common to parents' reactions at the time of diagnosis and recognition.

The initial shock reaction is necessary in most cases since it provides a short-term defense mechanism for getting through the initial period of time. It is equally important to understand that the way a family responds to what is perceived as a loss also depends on culturally determined factors and socioeconomic realities. There is no normal response to loss, thus one should not be expected. For the poor, poorly educated, or non-English speaking family, information presented by a professional during this time may be misunderstood or misconstrued, possibly becoming the basis for responses that are misinterpreted by the professional.

As the shock begins to wear off, the parents must deal with the disparity of their situation. Because they know so little about deafness, they are initially overwhelmed. As their anxiety level rapidly increases, they are often bombarded with a deluge of information they have little capacity for assimilating. For non-English-speaking families, the lack of English proficiency—and in some cases of formal education—considerably exacerbates the situation.

The intensity involved in actually recognizing the problem often requires that parents seek someone to blame. If they cannot hold a doctor responsible, they may hold themselves or their spouse (or spouse's family) responsible. It is not uncommon for parents to go through a bargaining process, often with God, in which they make grandiose promises and seek to trade their ears for their children's ears. Their feelings of guilt, anger, and dismay during this time place a tremendous strain on the family. Occasionally, a family never fully recovers from this strain, especially when it is added to the stresses caused by poverty, immigration, and persistent inequalities that exist for Black and Hispanic Americans.

Because recognizing the problem requires so much energy, it cannot continue for a long period of time. The anxiety needs to be reduced, and this happens during a period of denial. This defensive retreat is sometimes characterized in middle class families by wishful thinking (waking up hoping it was a dream), shopping (looking around at other diagnostic centers, programs, etc., of which the "better" programs are those that communicate to the parents things they want to hear), and activism (becoming involved in public issues associated with the hearing impaired rather than becoming closely involved with their own child). Parents need to be guided gently yet firmly through this stage. At a time when middle class parents are discussing topics such as total communication vs. oralism, cochlear implants, speech therapy, and public awareness, they may need to refocus on the status of the individual hearing-impaired child and his or her personal needs.

For many minority families, particularly immigrant families, this wishful thinking and shopping might include increased religious activity or consideration of a return to the homeland. Overt activism, on the other hand, is generally not observed because fluency in English and familiarity with the special education system are prerequisites for such activity. It is important that the professional does not view these behaviors as deviant or inappropriate, but rather as culturally determined and acceptable responses.

Finally, a parent needs to reach the point of constructive action. Parents can decide to restructure certain aspects of their lifestyle in order to accommodate the communicative and educational needs of their hearing-impaired child. Unfortunately, this is not usually a once-and-for-all stage, since each time a major change occurs in a family more restructuring may follow.

For minority families, particularly those of Hispanic heritage, the gap between acknowledgment and constructive action is often influenced by the cultural perception that a handicapped child is given to a family by God, perhaps as a cross to be born. This orientation is quite antithetical to ideas about constructive action and involvement, often presenting programmatic and attitudinal barriers for the professional. While there is no easy solution to this situation, extreme cultural sensitivity is necessary. In many instances it has been helpful to have Hispanic parents of older hearing-impaired children share their experiences, conflicts, and successes with families of younger children during these times.

Conclusion

Minority families bring with them their belief systems, including what they have been taught to believe about handicaps, illnesses, and related responsibilities. In many situations it is the extended family's sole responsibility to attend to the needs of a handicapped person (Ross, 1974). In other cultures the community assumes care for the person as they wander through the village or countryside. Seldom are they entrusted to an institution for their care. Beyond the custodial or protective care of the individual, the belief system also provides answers to the question: Why did this happen to my family? It is important for professionals to realize that while these belief systems may cause inconveniences during intervention, they also provide a source of strength for the family. Conversely, professionals must recognize that they too, like the minority family, act out of a set of beliefs, values, and practices determined by their own cultural milieu.

Despite the fact that the culturally determined format for intervention among some groups may not go beyond basic domestic care, it is often difficult for American educators and other service providers to see beyond the letter of Public Law 94-142 or their agencies' policies and procedures. When families do not keep appointments for IEP (Individualized Educational Plan) meetings or hearing evaluations, agency personnel can become quite disturbed and insensitive to different intervention formats. Or it may be considered culturally improper or embarrassing for parents to go to a school or institution for a particular type of service, and therefore the parent does not receive the necessary help. Communication in the appropriate language and cultural style greatly increases the possibility of successful service delivery. In many cases home or community-based services are more appropriate and less threatening.

For many immigrant and poor families there may be other pressing anxieties—such as survival in a new or alienating culture—that replace or alter typical anxiety patterns. Priorities are not always determined in a manner consistent with those of American professionals' thinking. Consequently, missing an appointment can be seen by an institution as reason enough to terminate a family's services when perhaps it is actually an expression of need or cultural difference.

In summary, there is considerable intrapersonal and intrafamily stress during the time when a child's hearing loss is suspected and immediately after it is detected. A child born with significant hearing loss is often not diagnosed until 12 to 18 months of age or greater. While this time period is characterized by considerable stress, it is not until the hearing loss is confirmed that parents enter an active mourning process by which they can come to accept their child's handicap. A family's status—whether it be non-English speaking, low-income, culturally different, or a member of a racial minority group—affects its responses to a deaf child. To the extent knowledge permits, these responses are described in the preceding sections. However, while many of these stages and processes appear to be somewhat universal, it is not altogether clear how the stages are manifested in Black and Hispanic families. The influence of associated socioeconomic and cultural factors on families attempting to deal with the discovery of a hearing loss is likewise poorly understood. Both of these areas are in need of new research and greater attention and understanding if parent programs for Black and Hispanic families are to be truly effective.

Some factors that should be considered by professionals working with these families include: attitudes toward professionals and bureaucracies, accessibility of professional services, use of various nonmedical networks for support, belief systems about handicaps, intervention formats, and anxieties related to survival or adjustment to a new or alien culture. Professional sensitivity to such cultural variables is necessary for the family during this stressful time and will ultimately allow for more appropriate and effective programming for minority hearing-impaired children and their families.

References

Center for Assessment and Demographic Studies (1985-1986). *The Annual Survey of Hearing-Impaired Children and Youth, 1985-1986 School Year* (unpublished report). Gallaudet University, Washington, DC.

Children's Defense Fund (1985). *Black and White children in America: Key facts.* Children's Defense Fund, Washington, DC.

Cohen, O. (1987). *Current and future needs of minority hearing-impaired children and youth.* Testimony before the Commission on the Education of the Deaf, Washington, DC.

Garrison, V. (1972). *Social networks, social change, and mental health among migrants in a New York City slum.* Unpublished dissertation, Columbia University, New York, NY.

Hale-Benson, J. E. (1982). *Black children: Their roots, culture and learning styles* (rev. ed.). Baltimore, MD: John Hopkins University Press.

Henderson, D. H., & Washington, A. B. (1975). Cultural differences and the education of Black children: An alternate model for program development. *Journal of Negro Education, 44,* 353-360.

Kubler-Ross, E. (1969). *On death and dying.* New York, NY: Macmillan.

Luterman, D. (1979). *Counseling parents of hearing-impaired children.* Boston, MA: Little, Brown.

Luterman, D., & Chasin, J. (1970). The pediatrician and the parent of the deaf child. *Pediatrics, 45,* 115-116.

Moses, K. L. (1985). Infant deafness and parental grief: Psychosocial early intervention. In E. Powell, J. Finitzo-Hieken, S. Friel-Patti, & D. Henderson (Eds.). *Education of the hearing-impaired child.* San Diego, CA: College-Hill Press.

Rodriguez, O. (1985). Hispanic families and children. Presentation at the Urban Minority Deaf Child Conference, Teachers College, Columbia University, New York, NY.

Ross, C. (1974). *Identification of cultural characteristics of young Puerto Rican children in mainland schools: A survey of the reference literature and a study and analysis of teachers' perceptions.* Unpublished dissertation, Rutgers University, New Brunswick, NJ.

Shontz, F. (1967). Reactions to crisis. *The Volta Review, 69,* 405-411.

Parenting Stress and Social Support in Hearing Mothers of Deaf and Hearing Children: A Longitudinal Study

Amy R. Lederberg
Traci Golbach

Abstract: *This longitudinal study investigated the impact of child deafness on mothers' stress, size of social networks, and satisfaction with social support. Twenty-three hearing mothers of deaf children and 23 hearing mothers of hearing children completed a series of self-report questionnaires when their children were 22 months, 3, and 4 years old. When children were 22 months, more mothers of deaf children reported pessimism about their children's achieving self-sufficiency and concerns about their children's communication abilities than did mothers of hearing children. When their children were 3 and 4 years old, mothers of deaf and hearing children did not differ in their reports of general parenting stress, as measured by the Parenting Stress Index (PSI). Likewise, mothers' ratings of satisfaction with social support were not affected by child deafness, nor did they change developmentally. Mothers of deaf and hearing children did differ in the types of support networks utilized. Mothers of deaf 22-month-olds reported larger professional support networks, while mothers of hearing children reported larger general support networks across all child ages. Mothers' feelings of stress and satisfaction with social support were very stable across the 2 years examined. The results suggest that most mothers of deaf children do not feel a high level of general parenting stress or dissatisfaction with their lives and support networks. However, mothers of deaf children are likely to feel stress in areas specific to deafness. In addition, because parenting stress was highly stable, special efforts should be made to intervene when mothers of deaf children are expressing high levels of stress.*

> In raising a deaf child, parents are faced with a number of chronic stresses. These include frequent visits to speech therapists, controversies about oral versus manual communication, and decisions about educational placement. . . . These chronic stresses may substantially drain parents' energy, time, and financial resources, potentially leading to emotional reactions of frustration, depression, and social isolation. (Quittner,1991, pp. 206-207)

This view, that hearing parents are stressed by the difficulties they face while parenting a deaf child, has been repeated frequently throughout the last 30 years (e.g., Moses, 1985; Quittner, Glueckauf, & Jackson, 1990; Schlesinger, 1985) and has intuitive appeal. Although the diagnosis of deafness clearly has to be a stressful experience for hearing parents, does parenting young deaf children cause parents to experience more stress than parenting a young hearing child? Professionals have frequently assumed that the answer to this question is yes (see Moses, 1985). However, empirical research examining the level of parenting stress experienced by hearing mothers of deaf infants and preschoolers suggests that a high level of stress may not be inevitable. Out of three recent studies that examined this question, Quittner and her colleagues (1990,1991) found that hearing parents of deaf children felt more stressed than parents of hearing children, while Meadow-Orlans (1994) and Pipp-Siegel, Sedey, and Yoshinaga-Itano (2001) did not.

These contradictory findings are especially surprising because these three studies defined stress similarly, using versions of the Parenting Stress Index (PSI; Abidin, 1990). This instrument measures parenting stress in both the Child and Parent Domains. Specifically, scores obtained on the Child Domain scale reflect parents' perceptions of the degree to which their children are difficult to parent because of socio-emotional problems, such as distractibility, adaptability, and moodiness. Scores obtained on the Parent Domain scale reflect the degree the parent feels affected by factors related to the parental role, such as attachment to the child, feelings of parenting competence, depression, and social isolation.

The differences found in the impact of child deafness on parental stress seemed to be true differences between the studies, not consequences of sample size or inappropriate control groups. The mothers studied by Quittner et al. (1990) evidenced a high level of stress. The average stress level among the mothers of the children with hearing loss was at the 90th percentile of norms established for the PSI Child Domain. On the other hand, the well-matched control sample of mothers of hearing children scored at the 50th percentile. In contrast, the mothers of deaf infants studied by Meadow-Orlans (1994) had an average stress score at the 50th percentile of the normative sample. These mothers also did not differ in their stress level compared to a matched group of mothers of hearing infants. Similarly, using a short form of the PSI (Abidin, 1995; as cited in Pipp-Siegel et al., 2001), Pipp-Siegel et al. found that a large sample of hearing mothers of children with hearing loss did not differ significantly from the normative sample of mothers with hearing children on the Difficult Child and Dysfunctional Parent-Child Interaction subscales. In fact, on a third scale (Parental Distress) mothers of children with hearing loss were less stressed than mothers of hearing children.

Although any number of factors may have caused child hearing loss to be a stressor in the Quittner et al. study (1990) and not the other two, two explanations seem to be the most likely. First, the studies differed in the chronological age of the children studied. Quittner et al. examined the stress level of mothers whose children had an average age of 4 years (range = 2 to 5 years). The other studies examined children who were considerably younger. Meadow-Orlans (1994) studied only 9-month-old infants. Pipp-Siegel et al. (2001) included children whose average age was 2 years (range = 6 months to 5 years). It may be that the functioning of the family of the deaf child is not static, but changes as the child grows and develops. In infancy, when language is not integral to communication, the impact of a hearing loss may be qualitatively different than when the infant reaches early childhood. The family may experience a sense of grief or loss without an increase in parenting stress. However, as the child gets older and the impact of the hearing loss becomes more apparent, parenting stress may increase. Thus, Meadow-Orlans speculated "that the full impact of early deafness is felt by parents only in the preschool years when the communication gap between children who are deaf and those who are hearing becomes more evident" (p. 98).

Alternatively, parenting stress may be related to the amount of educational support children and parents receive during infancy and toddlerhood. All of Meadow-Orlans' (1994) sample and the majority of Pipp-Siegel et al.'s (2001) families were identified and enrolled in intervention programs before age 2. In contrast, Quittner et al. (1990) examined stress among a large sample of children in the province of Ontario during a time when early identification and intervention were less frequent and intensive. Although Quittner et al. do not specify age of identification and intervention in their research report, they indicated that their sample was similar to the children included in another study (Musselman, Wilson, & Lindsay, 1988). In Musselman et al.'s study, only half of the children were enrolled in intervention programs before 2 years of age. In addition, many children lived in rural areas of Ontario and received less intensive intervention. Mothers of deaf children in Meadow-Orlans' and Pipp-Siegel et al.'s studies may have experienced less stress than those studied by Quittner et al. because most had been receiving appropriate intervention services from the time their children were infants or toddlers.

The major purpose of this study was to examine if parenting stress changes developmentally by examining parenting stress longitudinally when children were 22 months, 3 years, and 4 years of age. All deaf children in this study were identified prior to 2 years of age, with the majority identified and enrolled in an intervention program during infancy. Therefore, we can test whether parental stress increased during preschool among families who have had educational support during their deaf children's early development. Because of the longitudinal design, we also can determine the long-term stability of stress over the 2-year period.

A second purpose of this study was to examine developmental changes in the influence of child deafness on the size of social networks and on the satisfaction mothers feel for the social support they receive from family, friends, community, and professionals. Social support plays a critical role in parents' ability to cope with stress (Feher-Prout, 1996; Hintermair, 2000; Koester & Meadow-Orlans, 1990). Child deafness may affect maternal social networks in several ways. Quittner et al. (1990) found that mothers of deaf children reported smaller social networks and less frequent contact with family and friends than mothers of hearing children. In addition, mothers of deaf and hearing children differed in terms of the actual providers of support. The mothers of the deaf children were more likely to name health care providers as sources of support, whereas mothers of hearing children were more likely to name family and friends. Surprisingly, despite differences in the size and nature of these networks, mothers of deaf and hearing infants and children seem equally satisfied with their social support (Meadow-Orlans, 1994; Quittner et al., 1990). Thus, these smaller networks may be serving the needs of these parents.

A third purpose of this study was to examine how a mother's feelings of stress and her social support affect her overall feelings of well-being. For mothers of both deaf and hearing children, parenting stress is likely to influence both their feelings of satisfaction with social support and their own psychological functioning. Quittner et al. (1990) found that stress had both a direct and an indirect effect on parents' psychological functioning. Mothers who reported having children who were moody, distractible, and demanding also reported having more psychological distress. Furthermore, Quittner et al. suggested that ability to cope with stress is mediated by satisfaction with social support. Mothers who experienced high levels of parent- and child-related stress felt less satisfied with their social support. Dissatisfaction with social support, in turn, related to mothers' poorer psychological functioning.

This longitudinal study investigated maternal perceptions of stress and social support at 22 months, 3 years, and 4 years of age. By looking longitudinally at perceptions of hearing mothers with deaf and hearing children, we hoped to begin to address the contradictions and fill in the gaps created by the existing research and to examine developmental changes in the impact of child deafness on parenting stress and social support in the course of the family's early growth.

Based on past research, four hypotheses were tested: (1) the influence of child deafness on parenting stress will increase with child age; (2) mothers of deaf children will have smaller social support networks and will rely more heavily on professional and educational support than will mothers of hearing children; (3) there will be no differences in perceived satisfaction with social support for mothers of deaf and hearing children; and (4) mothers' general life satisfaction will be related to parenting stress. This relation will be mediated by satisfaction with social support. A fifth issue investigated was the stability or predictability of maternal perceptions from child-age 22 months through 4 years of age. Because this study was the first longitudinal study of maternal perceptions of deaf children, it was uniquely suited to determine if maternal perceptions remain stable across the preschool years. This information should be of particular interest to professionals working in early intervention.

Method

Participants

This study was part of a larger longitudinal investigation (that occurred from 1985 to 1993) of parent-child interaction, language, and adjustment in mothers of deaf and hearing children (Lederberg, 1993; Lederberg & Everhart, 1998; Lederberg & Mobley, 1990; Lederberg & Prezbindowski, 2000). The sample for the study consisted of 23 hearing mothers of children with severe to profound hearing loss and 23 hearing mothers of hearing children. Mothers of the deaf children were recruited through five parent intervention programs for children with hearing loss in a major metropolitan area. Children whose hearing loss was identified before the age of 22 months, who did not have multiple handicaps, and who had hearing parents were eligible for inclusion in the larger study. Mothers of the hearing children were recruited through referrals from the mothers of deaf toddlers participating in this study, church groups, and personal contacts. Only those children who remained in the longitudinal investigation for all 3 years were included in this study. Seven children with a severe-profound loss who were assessed at 22 months were not assessed at 3 years or 4 years (two children moved away and five children's parents declined to participate).

A samplewise matching approach was used to obtain matched samples of deaf and hearing children. Mothers of the deaf and hearing children were matched as closely as possible (±1 for categorical demographic characteristics) on maternal age, marital status, years of education, child gender, and ethnicity (see Table 1). Prestige scores for maternal and paternal occupations were assigned using the Hodge-Siegel-Rossi Index (Hodge, Siegel, & Rossi, 1972). The two groups did not differ significantly for maternal age (t[44] = 1.55, p =.13), maternal occupation (t[44] = .91, p = .37), paternal education (t[44] = .27, p = .79), paternal occupation (t[44] = .87, p = .39), or child-age at the first data collection (t[44] = 1.55, p = .13) or second data collection (t[44] = 1.36,

Table 1   Demographic Information for the Mother-Child Dyads

Variables	Deaf Children	Hearing Children
Child gender		
Girls	13	13
Boys	10	10
Ethnicity		
Caucasian	19	19
African American	3	3
Hispanic	1	1
Maternal education		
High school or less	8	8
Some college	8	7
College graduate or beyond	7	8
Marital status at 22 months		
Married	21	22
Single/divorced	2	1
Maternal work status at 22 months		
Full-time out of home	13	11
Part-time out of home	1	2
Homemaker	9	10

$p = .18$). The groups differed on age at the third data collection ($t[37] = 2.13$, $p = .04$). The deaf children were, on average, one month older ($M = 51.4$ months, $SD = 2.7$, range = 48-57) than the hearing children ($M = 50.0$ months, $SD = 1.7$, range = 48-53). It is unlikely that the variables measured in this study would be affected by this age difference, especially given the lack of developmental change in these variables (see below).

All of the deaf children were classified as having a severe to profound hearing loss. The average age of identification of hearing loss was 9 months ($SD = 5.26$, range = 1-21 months); average age of intervention was 12 months ($SD = 4.99$, range = 3-22 months); and the average time between the two was 2.65 months ($SD = 2.87$, range = 0-11 months). Early intervention followed the SKI*HI model, with parent advisors visiting families weekly. Deaf children in this sample began center-based, all-day educational programming when they were 36 months old.

Parents and school programs used a variety of different language approaches. At the first assessment, 15 mothers had taken at least one sign language class, with 1 also learning cued speech. Three mothers were trained to use an auditory-verbal approach with their toddlers, and five additional mothers used an oral (speech only) approach. The latter five had started taking sign language classes by child-age 3 years. At both 3 and 4 years of age, 20 children (including the child whose mother used cued speech) were enrolled in Simultaneous Communication (SC) classes, (i.e., where an English-based sign system and speech were used), and three children continued to be in the auditory-verbal training program. None of the mothers was using American Sign Language (ASL).

Nineteen of the 23 hearing mother-deaf child dyads were included in an intensive study of communication at child ages 22 months and 3 years (see Lederberg & Everhart, 1998, 2000, for complete report). The majority of the deaf children were severely language-delayed. At 22 months, 50% of the deaf children used no spoken or signed words in 10 minutes of free play; an additional 30% used fewer than nine one-word utterances. At 3 years of age, the language of 70% of the deaf children was still restricted to one-word utterances and was similar to that of the hearing 22-month-olds. Although the majority of parents were learning to sign, most parents primarily communicated through speech that was only occasionally accompanied by signs. At 22 months, less than 15% of the SC mothers' communications contained signs. By 3 years, 30% of the communications contained signs.

Procedure

As part of the larger research project, all hearing and deaf children with their hearing mothers visited the early intervention center four times. When children were approximately 22 months old (M age in months = 21.7, SD = 2.2, range = 18-26), each dyad was scheduled for two visits approximately 1 week apart. To obtain background and demographic information, mothers were interviewed twice, once at the start of the first visit and again at the end of the second visit. Each dyad visited the early intervention center two more times; when the children were 3 years old (M age in months = 38.4, SD = 2.2, range = 36-44) and again at 4 years old (M age in months = 50.7, SD = 2.4, range = 48-57). Mothers were interviewed to update demographic information at the beginning of each visit. In addition, at all three ages, two self-report questionnaires were given. One questionnaire measured parenting stress. The second measured maternal perceptions of social support and life satisfaction. The questionnaires were completed either during the visits or shortly after the visit at home.

Instruments

Questionnaire on Resources and Stress-Short Form (QRS-F). During the first phase of data collection, when the children were 22 months of age, parenting stress was measured using the short form of the Questionnaire on Resources and Stress (QRS-F; Friedrich, Greenberg, & Crnic, 1983). The QRS-F is a 52-item self-report questionnaire specifically designed to measure stress in families of children with disabilities (including children with hearing loss). Friedrich et al. report a KR-20 reliability coefficient for the QRS-F of .95.

The items on the short form were selected from the longer QRS to create an assessment that concentrated on issues that concern families of children with disabilities (Friedrich et al., 1983). Respondents are asked to judge whether each of 52 items is true or false. Blanks in the items are to be filled in with the child's name. The items are divided into four scales.

1. The Parent and Family Problems scale, consisting of 20 items, measures problems in the self, family members, or the family as a whole. Two exemplars are "Other members of the family have to do without things because of _____." and "I can go visit with friends whenever I want."

2. The Pessimism scale, consisting of 11 items, measures both immediate and future pessimism about the child's achieving self-sufficiency. An exemplar: "I worry about what will happen to _____ when I can no longer take care of him/her."

3. The Child Characteristics scale, consisting of 15 items, measures communication, behavioral, and attitudinal difficulties of the child. An exemplar: "I feel tense when I take _____ out in public."

4. Finally, the Physical Incapacitation scale consists of 6 items and measures physical limitations and self-help skills of the child. An exemplar: "_____ can walk without help."

Parenting Stress Index. We replaced the QRS-F with the PSI-Version 6 (Abidin, 1990) during the second and third phase of data collection (i.e., when children were 3 and 4 years old) because it had become the most commonly used instrument to measure parenting stress. The PSI is a 101-item clinical and research self-report questionnaire designed to identify sources of stress and dysfunction in parent-child relationships and was used by both Quittner et al. (1990) and Meadow-Orlans (1994). Parents are asked to rate items on 5-point Likert scales that range from *strongly agree to strongly disagree*. The PSI yields two scores that reflect the levels of child-related and parent-related stress. The Child Domain consists of six subscales: Acceptability of the child to the mother, Adaptability, Demandingness, Moodiness, and Distractibility/Hyperactivity of the child, and the degree to which the Child Reinforces Parent. The Parent Domain consists of seven subscales measuring

Depression, Parental Attachment, Restrictions of Role, Parental Sense of Competence in the Parenting Role, Social Isolation, Relations with Spouse, and Parental Health.

Scores from the Child Domain and the Parent Domain may be combined to create a single score, or Total Stress Score, measuring overall parenting stress. The two domain scores and the total score can be converted to percentile ranks based on a normed sample of 2,633 parents. With these norms, parents can be identified as those who need professional intervention (defined as scores at the 90th percentile or above; Abidin, 1990).

Alpha reliability coefficients for the individual subscales of the PSI range from .71 to .97 for the Child Domain and from .79 to .99 for the Parent Domain (Abidin, 1990). The PSI has also demonstrated good test-retest reliability, ranging from .70 to .82 for a 3-4 week interval (Abidin).

Social Support Questionnaire. Mothers completed a second questionnaire compiled by Crnic, Greenberg, Ragozin, Robinson, and Basham (1983) that measures parents' size of social network, satisfaction with social support, and general life satisfaction. This questionnaire included multiple-choice questions that addressed the following areas:

1. Size of parents' social networks is measured by four questions. Two items measure the size of the mothers' professional network ("How many medically [educationally]-related professionals do/could you talk to about your child?"). Two items measure the size of the mothers' general social network. ("If sometime you were to have bad or angry feelings about your child, how many people do you talk to about this?" "If you were to have a minor problem with your child, how many people [friends or family] would you talk to, whose advice you trust?")

2. Satisfaction with support is measured with 18 questions concerning available support at four ecological levels: spouse/partner, friends, community, and professionals. Questions address the frequency of and satisfaction with support given by partners/ spouses, friends, community/neighborhood organizations, and medical and educational professionals.

3. Life satisfaction was measured by one question: "When you take everything into consideration—the child, your adult life, etc.,— how would you describe your current life situation?"). Parents respond to this question using a 5-point Likert scale that ranges from *very bad to very good.*

Results: Developmental Change and Group Differences

Did mothers of deaf children differ from mothers of hearing children in their feelings/perceptions of stress and social support? Did they differ in how those feelings changed developmentally from 22 months to 4 years of age? To address these questions, we examined the effect of child deafness on stress, social support, and life satisfaction, as well as developmental changes in these areas. Multiple Analyses of Variance (MANOVAs) were used to analyze related dependent variables. Stress at 22 months was analyzed separately from stress at 3 and 4 years because different instruments were used at these ages. Whenever there were significant main or interaction effects, analyses of variance (ANOVAs) were conducted for individual scales. Size of networks, satisfaction with support, and life satisfaction analyses included scores from all three ages.

Parenting Stress at 22 Months

One-way (hearing status) MANOVA and subsequent ANOVAs revealed group differences for two of the four individual subscales of the QRS-F (see Table 2). Mothers of deaf children reported greater pessimism about their child's achieving self-sufficiency (t[43] = 2.76, p < .01) and greater stress because of child characteristics (t[43] = 4.55, p < .001) than did mothers of hearing children. Mothers of deaf and hearing children did not differ in their reports of the level of physical incapacitation of their children (t[43] =.68,p = .5) or in their reports of the amount of parent and family problems (t[43] = 1.22,p < .2).

Table 2   Mean Scores (Standard Deviations) on Four Qrs-f Scales for Mothers of Deaf and Hearing 22-Month-Olds

Type of scale	Mothers of deaf children	Mothers of hearing children
Child Characteristics	.30 (.21)	.14[a] (.15)
Pessimism	.23 (.21)	.00[a] (.15)
Parent and family problems	.16 (.15)	.11 (.13)
Physical incapacitation	.32 (.11)	.34 (.11)

Means can vary from 1.00 (all of the mothers' answers to the questions indicate stress) to 0 (the mother never selected an answer that indicates stress).
[a] Means of the mothers of deaf and hearing children are significantly different at p < .001.

To further explore the sources of stress for mothers of deaf 22-month-olds, 2 (hearing status) x 2 (type of answer) chi-square analyses were conducted on the QRS-F items contained in the two scales that showed group differences. Of the 15 items in the Child Characteristics scale, 4 items showed significant group differences (see Table 3). Three of the items specifically refer to children's ability to communicate with people in their environment. The last item addresses concerns about restrictions to their children's future employment. The two items on the Pessimism Scale that showed significant group differences seem to reflect concerns by some mothers about deaf children's ability to lead a normal life. Thus, the increased stress expressed by mothers of deaf children seems to be primarily due to the children's communication difficulties and to maternal concerns about the future.

Parenting Stress at 3 and 4 Years

Parent Domain Stress. As is evident in Table 4, the Parent Domain stress scores of mothers of deaf and hearing children were similar at both ages. The seven subscales of the Parent Domain of the PSI were analyzed using a 2 (age) x 2 (hearing status) repeated measures MANOVA. Parent Domain stress did not differ significantly for the deaf and hearing groups ($F[1, 44] = .72$, $p = .63$) or by child age ($F[1, 44] = 1.03$, $p = .42$) nor was there a significant interaction between age and hearing status, ($F[1, 44] = 1.02$, $p = .43$).

Child Domain Stress. Mothers of deaf and hearing children were also similar in the amount of child-related stress at both ages (see Table 4). A 2 (age) x 2 (hearing status) repeated measures MANOVA analyzing the six individual Child Domain subscales revealed no significant main effects, $F(1, 44) = 1.69$, $p = .16$; $F(1, 44) = .67$, $p = .65$; or interaction, $F(1, 44) = .32$, $p = .90$.

Normative Comparisons. Because of the relatively small sample size, the power to detect group differences was low in this study and therefore the above analyses must be viewed with caution. However, normative comparisons further indicate an "average" level of stress among mothers of deaf children. PSI (but not the QRS-F) allowed comparison with the norms provided for the scale (Abidin, 1990). Analyses of percentile ranks of mothers of deaf children confirm that only a very few of these mothers expressed a high stress level. The average total, parent-domain, and child-domain stress levels of the mothers of deaf and hearing children at child-age 3 and 4 years were between the 40th and 65th percentile on Abidin's norms (see Table 4). Thus, this sample is similar to the normed sample, and a series of one-sample t tests confirms that there were no significant differences between stress levels of these mothers of deaf children and Abidin's (1990) normative levels.

Table 3   Items that differentiated mothers of deaf and hearing toddlers on the QRS-F

| | Mothers | | |
Scale and item	Deaf children	Hearing children	Chi square
Child Characteristics Scale			
"It is difficult to communicate with_____ because he/she has difficulty understanding what is being said to him/her."	50%	0%	15.21***
"It is easy to communicate with_____."	41%	9%	6.32**
"People can't understand what ___tries to say."	73%	44%	3.94*
"_____ is limited in the kind of work he/she can do to make a living."	27%	0%	7.23**
Pessimism Scale			
"It bothers me that ___will always be this way."	50%	4%	11.98***
"I worry about what will happen to _____ when I no longer take care of him/her."	41%	13%	4.47*

Percentage of mothers in the sample who chose the answer (true/false) that indicated stress.

*$p < .05$.

**$p < .01$.

***$p < .001$.

Table 4   Mean scores (standard deviations) on the PSI scales for mothers of deaf and hearing children

| | Deaf children | | Hearing children | |
PSI Scale	3 years	4 years	3 years	4 years
Child Domain	105.9[c] (17.3)	101.1[c] (18.8)	100.2[b] (16.5)	97.7[b] (13.7)
Parent Domain	125.1[c] (26.6)	115.17[a] (24.0)	112.9[a] (19.1)	114.1[a] (20.6)
Total	221.7[b] (37.4)	214.0[b] (35.7)	213.1[a] (33.0)	211.7[a] (32.2)

Superscripts denote the percentile ranks on the PSI norms.

[c] 35–45.

[b] 46–55.

[a] 56–65.

For comparison, 50th percentile scores from the normative sample for each scale are Child Domain = 99; Parent Domain = 121. Total Stress = 221.

Abidin (1990) suggested that anyone with a stress score above the 90th percentile should be referred for clinical treatment. At 3 years of age, slightly more mothers of deaf children (17%, n = 4) and fewer mothers of hearing children (4%; n = 1) were highly stressed compared to the normed sample (which by definition had 10% of respondents scoring above the clinical cut-off). At 4 years, similar proportions of mothers of deaf and hearing children (9%, n = 2; 13%, n = 3, respectively) appeared highly stressed and these proportions are similar to the normed sample. Chi-square analyses indicated no significant differences in the number of highly stressed mothers of deaf and hearing children.

There was considerable stability in which mothers of deaf and hearing children were highly stressed at child-age 3 and 4 years of age. All but two mothers who were below the cut-off at 3 years remained below the cut-off at 4 years. Of the five mothers who were highly stressed at 3, three were still highly stressed at 4.

In summary, mothers of deaf children expressed more stress than mothers of hearing children at child-age 22 months as measured by the QRS-F, but not at child-ages 3 and 4 years as measured by the PSI. Because different instruments were used, these findings could be due to age effects or to the fact that different aspects of stress were measured at the different ages. Content analyses of the QRS-F supports the latter interpretation; the higher levels of stress expressed by mothers of deaf 22-month-olds seemed to be primarily due to the children's communication difficulties and maternal concerns about the future, which are sources of stress not measured on the PSI.

Results: Social Networks, Support, and Life Satisfaction

Size of General and Professional Networks

The 2 (hearing status) x 3 (age) repeated measures MANOVA that analyzed the two subscales for size of networks showed a significant main effect for hearing status, $F(1, 44) = 13.6$, $p < .01$, and a significant interaction between hearing status and age, $F(1, 44) = 2.67$, $p < .05$.

The follow-up ANOVA analyzing size of general networks revealed only a significant main effect for hearing status, $F(1, 44) = 8.51$, $p < .01$. Mothers of hearing children had significantly larger social networks ($M = 2.8$, $SD = .64$) than mothers of deaf children ($M = 2.4$, $SD=.61$).

The ANOVA analyzing size of professional networks showed only a significant interaction for hearing status and age, $F(1, 44) = 7.90$, $p <.001$. Mothers of deaf children had significantly more professionals available to them than mothers of hearing children at child-age 22 months (t [44] = 4.74, $p < .001$). At this age, mothers of deaf children, on average, had more than four medical and two educational professionals for support; whereas mothers of hearing toddlers averaged two medical and one educational professionals. By the time their children reached 3 years of age, however, the size of the professional network for the mothers of hearing children had increased significantly to, on average, three medical and two educational professionals.

Satisfaction with Social Support

The next MANOVA analyzed the four subscales of the Social Support Questionnaire that measured maternal satisfaction with support from partners, friends, community, and medical/educational personnel. Satisfaction with social support did not differ significantly for the deaf and hearing groups, $F(1, 44) =$

1.75, p = .16, or by child age F(1, 44) = .412, p = .91, nor was there a significant interaction, F(1, 44) =.434, p = .89. Despite differences in size of networks, mothers of deaf and hearing children were equally satisfied with social support. On average, mothers rated themselves between "somewhat satisfied" and "very satisfied" with the amount of support provided them by their partners, friends, and professional personnel. While, on average, mothers were satisfied with the social support they received from partners and friends, there was a substantial dissatisfied minority. Dissatisfaction with support by partners, friends, and professionals ranged from 10% to 33% of mothers, depending on age and child hearing status. Satisfaction with their community/neighborhood support was lower than other sources of support, averaging between "somewhat dissatisfied" and "somewhat satisfied."

Life Satisfaction

A 2 (hearing status) x 3 (age) ANOVA revealed no significant main or interaction effects for general life satisfaction. For both groups, the majority of mothers were satisfied with their lives. Over 70% of mothers of deaf and hearing children at all 3 ages said things in their lives were either "fairly good" or "very good" ("4" or "5" on the 5-point scale). With the exception of one or two at each age, the rest of the mothers said "things are OK-not bad or not good."

Results: Stability of Maternal Perceptions for Mothers of Deaf Children

Do maternal perceptions and concerns about their deaf toddler predict their general parenting stress when their children are 4 years of age? Does size of social networks and satisfaction with social supports show stability from 22 months to 4 years of age? This series of analyses examined the stability or long-term predictability of stress, size of networks, satisfaction with social support, and general life satisfaction over the toddler-preschool years. We were specifically interested in the predictability of these perceptions of mothers of deaf children, so mothers of hearing children were not included in these analyses.

Stability or predictability was assessed using hierarchical multiple regression. Each dependent variable at age 4 was first regressed on the related dependent variable at 22 months (to assess long-term predictability) and then on the related dependent variable at 3 years. If a variable was completely predictable from 22 months to 4 years, then the addition of the 3 year-old variable to the equation will not account for any additional variance.

Parenting Stress

The two QRS-F subscales (Parent and Family Problem scale and Child Characteristics scale) whose items were similar in content to the items on the PSI Parent Domain and Child Domain scales were used to predict stress at 4 years old (see Table 5). Parent-related stress was very predictable over this two-year age span (adjusted $R^2 = .74$). The 22-month Parent and Family Problem Scale accounted for almost half of the variance (49%) of the 4-year Parent Domain PSI scores. The 3 year Parent-Domain PSI scale accounted for an additional 25% of the variance.

Child-related stress was also highly predictable (adjusted $R^2 = .71$). The 22-month Child Characteristics subscale of the QRS-F predicted 34% of the variance of the 4-year Child-Domain PSI scores. The 3-year Child Domain PSI scores accounted for an additional 38% of the variance at 4. For both types of stress, scores at 22 months and at 3 years uniquely predicted stress at 4 years (see βs and t tests in Table 5). Thus, it appears that expressing concerns and

Table 5 Summary of series of hierarchical multiple regression analysis for predicting mothers of deaf children's stress, size of network, and satisfaction with social support at 4 years of age

	df	R^2	R^2 change	F change	β	t
Parent domain stress: 4 years						
QRS-F parent: 22 months	1, 18	.49		17.41***	.35	2.33***
PSI parent: 3 years	1, 17	.74	.25	16.06***	.61	4.01***
Child domain stress: 4 years						
QRS-F child: 22 months	1, 18	.34		9.16**	.42	3.17**
PSI child: 3 years	1, 17	.71	.38	22.36***	.63	4.73***
Size of social network: 4 years						
Size: 22 months	1, 19	.12		2.62	.13	.71
Size: 3 years	1, 18	.50	.38	13.71**	.66	3.70***
Size of professional network: 4 years						
Size: 22 months	1, 19	.00		0.04	.23	0.34
Size: 3 years	1, 18	.26	.26	6.18***	.59	2.92**
Satisfaction with intimate social support: 4 years						
Satisfaction: 22 months	1, 18	.58		25.20***	.38	2.28*
Satisfaction: 3 years	1, 17	.74	.16	10.31***	.55	3.21***
Satisfaction with friends' social support: 4 years						
Satisfaction: 22 months	1, 19	.14		2.96	.07	0.34
Satisfaction: 3 years	1, 18	.42	.29	9.08**	.62	3.01**

Each variable at 4 years of age was first regressed on related variable at 22 months and then the variable at 3 years. R^2 and F tests are for the two steps. βs and t tests are reported only for the last step.

*$p < .05$.

**$p < .01$.

***$p < .001$.

worries about a toddler's disability and feelings of general parenting stress at
3 years have an additive effect on parenting stress at 4 years.

Size of Social Networks

Size of the mothers' general social networks showed significant stability
(adjusted $R^2 = .50$), with most of the variance accounted for by the size of social
networks at 3 years (38%). The size of the mothers' network of medical and
educational professionals was much less stable over time (adjusted $R^2 = .26$).

Satisfaction with Social Support and Life Satisfaction

Satisfaction with the intimate support was extremely stable across the preschool
years (adjusted $R^2 = .74$). Twenty-two-month intimate social support scores
predicted more than half (59%) of the 4-year satisfaction scores and 3-year
scores predicted an additional 16%. Satisfaction with support provided by
friends was moderately stable (adjusted $R^2 = .43$). Satisfaction with
professional and community support did not show stability during the preschool
years (professional, adjusted $R^2 = .12$; community, adjusted $R^2 = .11$).

In summary, hearing mothers' concerns about, and satisfaction with,
their deaf toddlers, partners, and family life strongly predicted their degree of
stress and satisfaction with their family at 4 years of age. Size of general social
networks and satisfaction with friends was also moderately stable. Satisfaction
with other sources of support showed much less stability.

Effects of Parenting Stress and Satisfaction of
Social Support on Life Satisfaction

How does parent-related and child-related stress relate to mothers' feelings of
satisfaction with their lives? Direct and indirect effects of parenting stress on
general life satisfaction were tested by three path analyses. Satisfaction with
social support was included in the analyses to determine if it mediated the
relation between parenting stress and general life satisfaction (Quittner et al.,
1990). The three path analyses were conducted once at each age to test the
robustness of the pattern of relations between stress, satisfaction with social
support, and general life satisfaction. As Quittner et al. (1990) did, these path
analyses included data from mothers of both hearing and deaf children. Because
of our sample size and issues of power, we were not able to examine how child

deafness affected these relations. Although there is no past research that suggests that child deafness or other child characteristics affect these relations, generalizing to the subsample of hearing mothers of deaf children should be viewed as tentative.

For purposes of these analyses, computing the mean of Intimate and Friend Social Support subscales created a combined variable: satisfaction with social support. The Community and Professional Social Support subscales were not significantly correlated with these subscales and were therefore not included in the combined social support variable.

22 months old. The first path analysis examined relations between the three subscales of the QRS-F (Parent and Family Problems, Pessimism, and Child Characteristics), satisfaction with social support, and general life satisfaction. Results revealed that only the Parent and Family Problems factor was significantly directly related to general life satisfaction (see Figure 1, Table 6). Mothers who reported greater stress related to parenting and family problems reported significantly less general life satisfaction. The relation between parent-related stress and life satisfaction was not mediated through social support satisfaction.

The two child-related stress scales had no direct effect on general life satisfaction. In addition, the relation between these scales and life satisfaction was not mediated by social support. On the other hand, both childrelated stress scales were significantly correlated with the parent-related scale. Therefore, child-related stress seems to have an indirect effect on life satisfaction through parent-related stress.

3 years old. Results of a similar path analysis investigating the direct and indirect effects of parent and child stress on life satisfaction at age 3 indicated again that only parent-related stress was directly related to life satisfaction. Mothers with greater parent-related stress reported less life satisfaction. In addition, at 3, the relation between parent-related stress and life satisfaction was mediated by satisfaction with social support (see Figure 2, Table 7). Mothers who reported greater parent-related stress reported significantly less satisfaction with social support. Mothers who reported less satisfaction with social support reported significantly less life satisfaction. Therefore, parent-related stress was negatively related to general life satisfaction both directly and indirectly through its negative effect on satisfaction with social support. Child stress was highly and significantly correlated with parent stress but did not have a direct relation with life satisfaction. Child stress was only indirectly related to life satisfaction through parent stress, and not through satisfaction with social support.

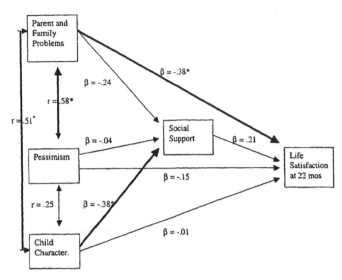

Figure 1. Path diagram of direct and indirect effects of parenting stress at 22 months on life satisfaction at 22 months.

Table 6 Explaining life satisfaction at child age 22 months: Partition into direct and indirect effects

Scales	Direct effect	Total indirect	Total effect	Redundancy	Zero-order (Pearson's r)
Parent and Family Problems	-.38*	-.05	-.43	-.14	-.57*
Pessimism	-.15	-.01	-.16	-.28	-.44*
Child Characteristics	-.01	-.08	-.09	-.26	-.35*
Social Support	.21	.00	.21	.22	.43*

Redundancy is the difference between the zero-order correlation and the total effect. Significance is noted for direct effects and zero-order correlations only.

$N = 46$.

*$p < .05$.

4 years old. The 4-year-old path analysis revealed results similar to the earlier ages (see Figure 3, Table 8). There was a significant direct relationship between parent stress and life satisfaction. Mothers who reported greater parent stress also reported significantly less satisfaction with social support. However, satisfaction with social support was not significantly related to life satisfaction and therefore could not mediate the effects of parent-related stress on general life satisfaction. Child-related stress was again highly correlated with parenting-related stress.

In summary, at all three ages, parent-related stress had a direct link with mothers' feelings of satisfaction with their lives. Child-related stress only had an indirect effect on life satisfaction (through parent-related stress). The mediating effect of satisfaction with social support was not consistent across ages. Thus, how satisfied mothers felt with their lives was most closely related to how they felt about their parenting, and only indirectly related to their assessment of their children's problems.

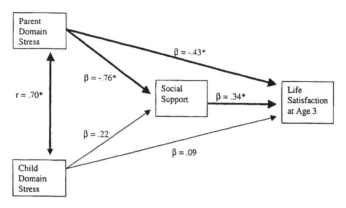

Figure 2. Path diagram of direct and indirect effects of parent and child stress at 3 years on life satisfaction at 3 years.

Table 7 Explaining life satisfaction at child age 3 years: Partition into direct and indirect effects

Scale	Direct effect	Total indirect	Total effect	Redundancy	Zero-order (Pearson's r)
Parent Domain	−.43*	−.26	−.69	.12	−.57*
Child Domain	.09	.07	.16	−.48	−.32*
Social Support	.34*	.00	.34	.23	.57*

Redundancy is the difference between the zero-order correlation and the total effect. Significance is noted for direct effects and zero-order correlations only.

$N = 46.$

*$p < .05.$

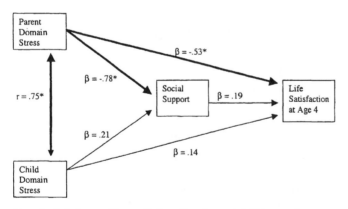

Figure 3. Path diagram of direct and indirect effects of parent and child stress at 4 years on life satisfaction at 4 years.

Table 8 Explaining life satisfaction at 4 years: Partition into direct and indirect effects

Variable	Direct effect	Total indirect	Total effect	Redundancy	Zero-order (Pearson's r)
Parent Domain	−.53*	−.15	−.68	.14	−.54*
Child Domain	.14	.04	.18	−.51	−.33*
Social Support	.19	.00	.19	.25	.44*

Redundancy is the difference between the zero-order correlation and the total effect. Significance is noted for direct effects and zero-order correlations only.

$N = 46.$

*$p < .05.$

Discussion

One of the major goals of this study was to clarify past research on the effect of child deafness on hearing mothers' feelings of stress. Our results suggest that, for families enrolled in early intervention programs, child deafness may increase stress only in specific areas. At child age 22 months, mothers of deaf children expressed more stress, as measured by the QRS-F, than mothers of hearing children. At child-age 3 and 4 years, the amount of stress experienced by mothers of deaf children was comparable to our control group of mothers of hearing children and to the general population as established by the norms of the PSI.

Because different instruments were used to measure stress, these "age effects" could have been due to the instruments or to a decrease in parental stress as deaf children entered preschool. Comparison with past research suggests the latter is unlikely. Both Meadow-Orlans (1994) and Pipp-Siegel et al. (2001) found no differences in stress as measured by the PSI during infancy and toddlerhood, while Quittner et al. (1990) found a high degree of stress on the PSI for mothers of deaf preschoolers. In fact, our original hypothesis (like that of Meadow-Orlans) was that stress would increase in preschool as language becomes more important.

The higher levels of stress experienced by mothers of deaf 22-month-olds was in two areas that were measured on the QRS-F but not the PSI. More mothers of deaf 22-month-olds described their children as having communication difficulties than mothers of hearing 22-month-olds. More mothers of deaf toddlers also expressed concerns about their 22-month-olds' futures than mothers of hearing children. The Parent and Family Problems scale on the QRS-F, which shows the highest content similarity and cross-age correlation with the Parent-Domain PSI, did not show group differences.

It is not surprising that hearing parents of deaf children were concerned with the communication difficulties they and others face with their children. For the mother-child dyads in our study, these difficulties were extensive. Communication breakdowns were common in the interactions between the hearing mothers and their deaf children (Lederberg & Mobley,1990), and the majority of the children were severely language-delayed (Lederberg & Everhart, 1998). Surprisingly, these difficulties did not seem to have a broad impact on stress or these mothers' satisfaction with their lives. Mothers of deaf children did not perceive their children as more difficult, doubt their abilities as parents, or feel more restricted by their children. Path analysis found that feelings of life satisfaction at child age 22 months was not related to mothers' concerns about their children's communication difficulties or pessimism about the future. This group data are consistent with the picture that emerged in an in-depth case study of one hearing family's adjustment to parenting a deaf child from infancy through preschool. Spencer (2000) found that the parents' concerns and stress were centered on communication needs of their child. She notes, "Instead of wanting to talk about feelings of grief and loss, they appreciated opportunities to learn specifics about the potential of various communication systems" (p. 128).

The lack of high levels of parenting stress during preschool in our study may be a measure of success of early intervention programs. Greenberg (1983) found that intensive early intervention decreased stress among mothers of deaf children. All the mothers in the present study, as well as most of those studied by Pipp-Siegel et al. (2001) and Meadow-Orlans (1994), were enrolled in early intervention programs. In contrast, Quittner et al.'s (1990) sample included children who were identified late and lived in rural areas with less intensive intervention services (Musselman et al., 1988). The high level of maternal stress in the latter study can serve as a warning for the importance of early identification and intervention.

It is important to note that, although the level of stress of mothers in our study was similar in both groups and to the PSI's normed sample, a number of mothers in both groups had a stress level high enough to suggest they would benefit from family therapy. The long-term stability of parental stress (both parent- and child-related) over the preschool years suggests that parent stress is frequently not a result of acute crisis but rather a long-term part of some parents' lives that will not change without increased intervention. In addition, the independent contributions of feelings of stress at 22 months and 3 years on perceptions at 4 years suggest that stress is a cumulative, additive process.

Although the extra demands of caring for a deaf child do not seem to cause increased parenting stress, these added demands might restrict the time mothers have to spend with other people. As in Quittner et al. (1990), mothers of deaf children in our study had smaller social networks than mothers of hearing children. Although these networks were smaller, mothers of deaf and hearing children were equally satisfied by the social support they received from their partners, friends, communities, and professionals. Satisfaction with the different types of social support did not change developmentally. Quittner et al. and Meadow-Orlans (1994) also found similar levels of satisfaction with social support among mothers of deaf and hearing children. Thus, the majority of mothers of deaf children feel that their smaller social networks provide the social support that they need. However, a substantial minority (25%-33%) felt dissatisfied with the support they receive from their partners and friends. Because satisfaction with support, especially partner support, was very stable from 22 months to 4 years, family therapy may be an important component of intervention with these mothers. Meadow-Orlans and Steinberg (1993) found that satisfaction with social support was especially important for mothers of deaf children. Specifically, mothers of deaf children who were satisfied with their social support had more positive interactions with their deaf toddlers than those who had less support. Therefore, increasing mothers' satisfaction with their support may improve relations with their deaf children.

Finally, results from path analyses at all three ages consistently indicated that parent-related stress has the most direct and significant effect on how mothers perceive and evaluate their lives. In contrast, Child-Domain stress only had an indirect effect on mothers' life satisfaction, through its strong and significant relation with parent-domain stress. Similarly, satisfaction with social support, although strongly related to Parent-Domain stress, did not have a direct effect on life satisfaction. Thus, mothers' feelings of competence about their abilities to parent, and their acceptance of the changes in their lives derived from being a parent, are the most important predictors of these mothers' satisfaction with their lives. If parents feel they are coping with Child-Domain stressors, these stressors do not seem to affect the mothers' feelings of well-being. This supports the hypothesis advanced by both Lederberg and Prezbindowski (2000) and Spencer (2000), which states that emphasizing the strengths and competencies of hearing parents' abilities to parent their deaf children may be an important component of early intervention with these families.

The importance of parent-domain stressors may be specific to mothers who are not feeling extremely stressed by their children. Quittner et al. (1990) found, in their path analyses, that Child-Domain stress had a strong direct effect on maternal well-being, while Parent-Domain stress were only weakly related to mothers' mental health and was mediated by satisfaction with social support. The differences in the degree of Child Domain stress experienced by parents in the two studies may account for these different findings. The Child Domain stress scores reported by Quittner et al. suggest that the majority of these parents viewed their deaf children as unadaptable, distractible, hyperactive, moody, and not reinforcing. Because many of these children were late-identified and these families did not have the benefits of early intervention, it may be that these mothers were reporting real (rather than just perceived) behavioral difficulties. Such high degree of Child-Domain stress may be so overwhelming, that other factors (e.g., Parent Domain stress and social support) do not affect mothers' mental health.

In summary, this study is the only longitudinal study of the impact of child deafness on hearing mothers' perceptions of stress and social support. Contrary to our hypotheses, we found that, along most dimensions, these perceptions did not change developmentally during the preschool years. In fact, individual differences in parenting stress, size of general social networks, and satisfaction with social support remained very stable across the more than 2 years that were assessed. Mothers of deaf toddlers expressed concern about their children's communication difficulties and ability to be self-sufficient as adults. These concerns did not seem to affect mothers' perceptions and satisfaction with their lives, social support, or other areas of child and parent stress. Because researchers have used instruments that measure general parenting stress, we do not know if the concerns specific to parenting deaf children are experienced as very stressful by parents. Future research should explore the affective impact of these concerns by using instruments more focused on parenting deaf children. Meadow-Orlans (1990) developed a questionnaire, Impact of Childhood Hearing Loss on the Family, which might provide a more in-depth description of stress and coping in families of deaf children than more general measures.

References

Abidin, R. R. (1990). *Parenting stress index manual* (3rd ed.). Charlottesville, VA: Pediatric Psychology Press.

Crnic, K. A., Greenberg, M. T., Ragozin, A. S., Robinson, N. M., & Basham, R. B. (1983). The effects of stress and social support on mothers of premature and full-term infants. *Child Development, 45*, 209-217.

Feher-Prout, T. (1996). Stress and coping in families with deaf children. *Journal of Deaf Studies and Deaf Education, 1*, 155-166.

Friedrich, W. N., Greenberg, M. T., & Crnic, K. (1983). A short form of the questionnaire on resources and stress. *American Journal of Mental Deficiency, 88*, 41-48.

Greenberg, M. T. (1983). Family stress and child competence: The effects of early intervention of families with deaf infants. *American Annals of the Deaf, 128*, 407-417.

Hintermair, M. (2000). Hearing impairment, social networks and coping. *American Annals of the Deaf, 145*, 41-53.

Hodge, R. W., Siegel, P. M., & Rossi, P. (1972). Occupational prestige in the United States. In P. Blaumberg (Ed.), *The impact of social class* (pp. 231-246). New York: Harper & Row.

Koester, L. S., & Meadow-Orlans, K. P. (1990). Parenting a deaf child: Stress, strength, and support. In D. E. Moores & K. P. Meadow-Orlans (Eds.), *Educational and developmental aspects of deafness* (pp. 299-320). Washington, DC: Gallaudet University Press.

Lederberg, A. R. (1993). The impact of deafness on mother-child and peer relationships. In M. Marschark & D. Clark (Eds.), *Psychological perspectives on deafness* (pp. 93-119). Hillsdale, NJ: Lawrence Erlbaum.

Lederberg, A. R., & Everhart, V. S. (1998). Communication between deaf children and their hearing mothers: The role of language, gesture, and vocalizations. *Journal of Speech, Language, and Hearing Research, 41*, 887-899.

Lederberg, A. R., & Everhart, V. S. (2000). Conversations between deaf children and their hearing mothers: Pragmatic and dialogic characteristics. *Journal of Deaf Studies and Deaf Education, 5*, 303-322.

Lederberg, A. R., & Mobley, C. (1990). The effect of hearing impairment on the quality of attachment and mother-toddler interaction. *Child Development, 61*, 1596-1604.

Lederberg, A. R., & Prezbindowski, A. K. (2000). Impact of child deafness on mother-toddler interaction: Strengths and weaknesses. In P. E. Spencer, C. J. Erting, & M. Marschark (Eds.), *The deaf child in the family and at school* (pp. 73-92). Mahwah, NJ: Lawrence Erlbaum.

Meadow-Orlans, K. P. (1990). The impact of childhood hearing loss on the family. In D. E. Moores & K. P. Meadow-Orlans (Eds.), *Educational and developmental aspects of deafness* (pp. 321-338). Washington, DC: Gallaudet University Press.

Meadow-Orlans, K. P. (1994). Stress, support, and deafness: Perceptions of infants' mothers and fathers. *Journal of Early Intervention, 18*, 91-102.

Meadow-Orlans, K. P., & Steinberg, A. G. (1993). Effects of infant hearing loss and maternal support on mother-infant interactions at 18 months. *Journal of Applied Developmental Psychology, 14*, 407-426.

Moses K. (1985). Infant deafness and parental grief: Psychosocial early intervention. In F. Powell, T. Finitzo-Heiber, S. Friel-Patti, & D. Henderson (Eds.), *Education of the hearing impaired child* (pp. 86-102). San Diego, CA: College-Hill Press.

Musselman, C. R., Wilson, A. K., & Lindsay, P. H. (1988). Effects of early intervention on hearing impaired children. *Exceptional Children, 55*, 222-228.

Quittner, A. L. (1991). Coping with a hearing-impaired child. In J. H. Johnson & S. B. Johnson (Eds.), *Advances in child health psychology* (pp. 206-223). Gainesville: University of Florida Press.

Quittner, A. L., Glueckauf, R. L., & Jackson, D. N. (1990). Chronic parenting stress: Moderating versus mediating effects of social support. *Journal of Personality and Social Psychology, 59*, 1266-1278.

Pipp-Siegel, S., Sedey, A. L., & Yoshinaga-Itano, C. (2001). *Parental stress in mothers of young children with hearing loss*. Manuscript submitted for publication.

Schlesinger, H. S. (1985). Deafness, mental health, and language. In F. Powell, T. Finitzo-Heiber, S. Friel-Patti, & D. Henderson (Eds.), *Education of the hearing impaired child* (pp. 103-113). San Diego, CA: College-Hill Press.

Spencer, P. E. (2000). Every opportunity: A case study of hearing parents and their deaf child. In P. E. Spencer, C. J. Erring, & M. Marschark (Eds.), *The deaf child in the family and at school* (pp. 111-132). Mahwah, NJ: Lawrence Erlbaum.

Psychosocial Effects on Parents of Raising a Physically Handicapped Child

J. B. Tavormina, T. J. Boll, N. J. Dunn
R. L. Luscomb, J. R. Taylor

Abstract: *The present study assessed the personality styles, attitudes, perspectives, and coping strategies of 133 mothers and 93 fathers of hearing-impaired, diabetic, asthmatic, and cystic fibrotic children. Across measures, both the essential positive adjustment levels and special problems of the sample were demonstrated, such that they formed a distinct group whose functioning fell between that reported for either "normal" or poorly-adjusted parents. Furthermore, the presence of the ill child served as the primary contributor to these patterns, with types of illness providing a secondary but significant thrust to its exact extent and scope. Mothers consistently reported more problems and more involvement than fathers, which illustrated their differential roles within these particular families as well as their typical modes of response to the stress of the ill child. Without a doubt, the stress was taking its toll on the parents. Even though they still managed to cope, a focus on the parental needs is necessary in the total management program for the physically ill child.*

Although the parental and family functioning of normal and emotionally disturbed children has received considerable experimental attention, parents of physically ill or handicapped children rarely have been evaluated. With the growing emphasis on the "family" as a significant variable in the developmental outcome for the child, it has become important to determine the coping patterns of families attempting to deal with constant stress, such as that presented by a handicapped child.

Hypotheses abound concerning the detrimental effects of the pressures and difficulties in managing and caring for such children, but no data have been presented. Travis (1976) examined a number of potential problem areas, but her conclusions were based on clinical experience and case descriptions. Unfortunately, no systematic data base is available for parents with ill children; no normative data have been collected on this population. Consequently, it is premature to make inferences about this group of parents, but clinical needs often preclude the wait for data: practitioners deal with these families and make decisions about management without a sufficient data base.

Furthermore, the available literature has focused almost exclusively on the mothers; very little is known about the fathers. In addition, many negative conceptions have been developed, even in the absence of systematic data: the over protective mother, the smothered child. Consequently aside from the stereotyping terms like depression, guilt, denial, and rejection, which focus solely on the negative aspects of raising such children, no clear-cut objective delineations of family functioning with this population have been attempted.

The present study provides a first look at this population of parents. It attempts to provide a normative evaluation of personality styles, attitudes, and perceptions of a sample of both mothers and fathers of physically ill children. As an initial study, it was exploratory in nature with the goal of isolating trends and setting the stage for subsequent research. Overall, this study attempted to address the type and quality of the coping strategies these parents used in response to the stress they faced in dealing with their children.

Method

Subjects

In the overall project, 144 families with a hearing-impaired, diabetic, asthmatic, or cystic fibrotic child participated. The child data, with respect to coping style as well as age, sex, race, and family income by illness group, have been presented previously (Tavormina, Kastner, Slater, & Watt, 1976). The overall pool of families contacted was 160, but permission was secured from 144. Children's ages ranged from 5 to 19, with an average of 12. All children were outpatients of the University of Virginia Pediatrics Department; hence all were receiving ambulatory care. A wide range of family income levels was represented: $200 to $4,000 per month, with an average of $1,200. Twelve of the families were black, the others were white.

The specific illness categories were chosen as a function of the large-scale project, which was involved in the evaluation of a summer camp for these physically ill children. In all, 133 mothers and 93 fathers completed the battery of tests.

Procedure

Each family was contacted initially by letter, with a follow-up phone call to explain the project and to secure permission for participation. If permission was granted, a home visit was made by a two-person assessment team to administer the measures. Both parents (if available) were interviewed and tested. The measures were chosen in an attempt to sample areas of parental attitudes, personality functioning, and coping strategies. In addition, most measures had normative data available that would facilitate comparison with the current sample. Clearly, the utility of an actual group of control parents with children who had no chronic illnesses cannot be overlooked; however, it was beyond the scope of this study.

Instruments

A battery of measures was chosen in an attempt to sample areas of personality functioning, parent attitude, and parent reports of problems with the child's behavior.

1. The Hereford Parent Attitude Survey (Hereford, 1963) measures the following areas: (a) confidence in parental role, that is, parental feelings of adequacy or inadequacy; (b) causation of the child's behavior, that is, the extent to which the parent sees himself as a major factor in determining the child's behavior; (c) acceptance; that is, the extent to which the parent is satisfied with the child and is willing to see him as an individual; (d) mutual understanding, that is, parental perception about the degree of reciprocity of feelings between parent and child; and (e) mutual trust, that is, the amount of confidence that the parent feels he and the child have in each other. The sum of the scale scores yields a total attitude score.

2. The Eysenck Personality Inventory (Eysenck & Eysenck, 1963) is a personality scale that taps the dimensions of social desirability (lie scale), stabilily-instability (neuroticism), and sociability (extroversion-introversion).

3. The Missouri Behavior Problem Checklist (Sines, Pauker, Sines, & Owen, 1969) is a yes-no checklist containing 70 statements that have been factor-analyzed into group scores of parent-reported symptoms of children. Scores are tabulated to determine a child's place on the various dimensions of the scale: Aggressiveness, Inhibition, Activity Level, Sleep Disturbance, Somatization, and Sociability. The sum of the first five scales yields a total deviancy score, with high scores indicating deviancy. The Sociability scale is scored in a positive direction.

4. A special problem area checklist was designed to assess the parent's views of problems their family had to face because of the illness. Each parent rated the following areas in terms of frequency of occurrence from (I) "never" to (5) "always": extra demands on time and energy, decreased social life with spouse, tense atmosphere around the house, pressure to do the right thing to

take proper care of the child, life is centered around the child's needs, special problems your family has to cope with (compared to the average family), shortage of friends due to the illness, need to constantly watch over the child's behavior, less time to devote to spouse and other children, and disruptions of family routine and family harmony.

5. The van der Veen Family Unit Inventory (van der Veen, Howard, & Austria, 1970) tapped parental perceptions of the quality of their family functioning. The multiple-choice format was used. The discrepancy between perceived current (real family) and proposed (ideal family) levels of functioning served as a measure of family concept. Three other sets of scores also were used: the factor scales developed by the authors; the family satisfaction score, the correlation between each parent's real and ideal family responses; and the dyadic agreement scores, the correlation between a couple's individual scores on the real (termed *congruence*) and on the ideal (termed *compatibility*) responses.

Analysis

The primary analysis centered on comparisons of mother versus father scores with each other and with the standardization norms developed for each scale, when they were available. Both *z* and *t* tests were used where appropriate for these analyses. In addition, scores were broken down by parent across illness category in order to evaluate parental differences across illnesses. To facilitate this analysis, a two-way analysis of variance was performed on each measure with sex of parent and illness as between-subjects factors.

Results

Hereford Survey

The sample scored lower (Table I) than available norms ($p < .01$), especially in areas of parental confidence ($p < .01$), causation ($p < .01$), and understanding ($p < .01$). These parents also tended toward less acceptance of the child ($p < .05$), but the fathers primarily accounted for this result. Interestingly, the mothers reported significantly more trust ($p < .01$) of the child than either scale norms or the fathers, whose scores approximated the norm on this dimension. In general, the mothers had higher (better) levels of all attitudes than fathers, but most noticeably on the understanding ($p < .01$), acceptance ($p < .01$), and trust ($p < .01$) subscales. Hence, while both mothers and fathers had lowered attitudinal scores, the mothers were typically closer in their scoring patterns to the established norms.

Table I. Parent Scores on the Hereford Survey[a]

	Total sample (219)		Mother (127)		Fathers (92)		Available norms
	$\overline{X}$	SD	$\overline{X}$	SD	$\overline{X}$	SD	$\overline{X}$[b]
Confidence	3.9	6.5	4.0	6.4	3.7	6.6	5.7
Causation	11.4	6.8	11.6	6.2	11.2	7.7	13.6
Acceptance	6.2	6.8	6.6	7.1	5.6	6.4	7.1
Understanding	13.0	6.4	14.1	6.3	11.4	6.3	15.3
Trust	8.7	8.8	9.4	8.3	7.8	9.4	7.6
Total	43.2	27.0	45.3	26.0	40.3	27.0	49.3

[a] Higher scores are in the positive direction.
[b] Norms extrapolated from scores presented by Hereford (1963); no standard deviations available.

Eysenck Inventory

On the Lie scale (Table II), the parents scored significantly higher than the established norms, which illustrated their heightened sense of social desirability, but this result was accounted for primarily by maternal scores, since the paternal scores were not significantly higher than the norms. The mothers also scored as more neurotic (less stable) than both scale norms (p < .01) and fathers (p < .01), who actually were less neurotic (p < .01) than scale norms. Both parents were less extroverted (sociable) than norms (p < .01), but once again mothers scored lower than fathers (p < .05).

Missouri Checklist

On the behavior problem checklist, the mothers reported more overall concerns (p < .05) than did the fathers (Table III). This pattern held across each of the five problem areas and for both boys and girls. Interestingly, the mothers also saw the children (again both boys and girls) as more sociable (p < .01) than did the fathers.

Table II. Parent Scores on the Eysenck Personality Inventory (Form-B)

Scale	Total sample (233)		Mothers (133)		Fathers (90)		Standardization norms	
	$\overline{X}$	SD	$\overline{X}$	SD	$\overline{X}$	SD	$\overline{X}$	SD
Neuroticism	11.5	4.9	12.5	4.9	9.9	4.5	11.4	4.8
Extroversion	13.8	3.6	13.4	3.8	14.4	3.3	15.2	3.5
Lie	1.7	1.4	1.9	1.6	1.3	1.2	1.1	1.2

Table III. Parent Scores on the Missouri Behavior Problem Checklist

Scale		Mothers (N = 131)			Fathers (N = 89)			Available norms boys only[a]	
		Total group	Ms of boys (73)	Ms of girls (58)	Total	Fs of boys (48)	Fs of girls (41)	Normal	Clinic
Aggression	$\overline{X}$	4.6	3.6	3.6	4.0	4.3	3.6	3.2	8.7
	SD	3.6	3.7	3.3	2.8	3.1	3.1	2.6	4.9
Inhibition	$\overline{X}$	3.4	3.1	2.9	3.0	2.6	3.4	2.0	4.0
	SD	2.7	2.4	2.9	2.7	2.1	3.1	2.8	3.1
Activity level	$\overline{X}$	2.6	3.1	2.0	2.3	2.6	1.8	2.5	5.4
	SD	2.4	2.6	2.0	1.9	2.0	1.8	2.0	2.7
Sleep disturbance	$\overline{X}$	1.7	1.8	1.4	1.3	1.6	1.0	.8	1.9
	SD	1.7	1.8	1.7	1.4	1.6	1.2	1.8	2.2
Somatization	$\overline{X}$	1.3	1.4	1.2	.8	.7	.8	.8	1.3
	SD	1.6	1.4	1.7	1.1	.9	1.2	1.0	1.4
Problem total	$\overline{X}$	13.6	14.7	12.0	11.5	11.9	10.7	--	--
	SD	8.0	8.2	7.3	6.6	6.0	7.2	--	--
Sociability[b]	$\overline{X}$	6.7	6.5	6.9	5.9	5.9	5.8	5.9	3.5
	SD	2.0	2.2	1.7	2.1	2.0	2.2	2.1	2.0

[a] Available norms are for a sample of "normal" and "clinic" (referred) boys; none are available for girls.
[b] Larger scores are more positive only on this scale; for all others, large scores indicate more problems.

Boys were seen consistently with more problems than girls. Mothers saw boys as more aggressive (p < .01), more overactive (p < .05), and with more overall problems, whereas fathers saw boys as more overactive (P < .05) and with more overall problems, whereas father saw boys as more overactive (P < .05) and with more sleep disturbances (p < .05). Hence, the data point out that mothers see more behavior problems than fathers, and that both sets of parents see more behavior problems in their physically ill sons than in their daughters.

In contrast to scale norms, which are only available for boys, the parents (both mothers and fathers) showed a strong tendency to report more problems than did parents of normal children, but they reported significantly (p < .01) fewer problems than did parents of children referred for emotional problems. These physically ill children were reported to present more behavior problems than "normal" counterparts, but not nearly as many as emotionally disturbed children.

Problem Area Checklist

The parents reported many special problems (Table IV) as a result of the child's illness: extra demands on their time and energy, tense home atmosphere, pressure to do the right thing to take proper care of the child, their lives were centered around the child's needs, and the need to watch constantly over the child's behavior. The mothers voiced more overall concerns, but especially extra demands on time and energy ($p < .05$); tense home atmosphere ($p < .01$); special family problems ($p < .05$); and a strong tendency ($p < .06$) to feel greater pressure to take proper care of the child It is important to note, however, that in the other areas, both parents voiced similar and significant levels of concern, most noticeably on the factor that they both felt that their lives were centered around their child's needs.

Table IV. Parent Scores on the Problem Area List[a]

Problem areas	Total sample (225)		Mothers (132)		Fathers (93)	
	$\overline{X}$	SD	$\overline{X}$	SD	$\overline{X}$	SD
Extra demands on time	2.5	1.1	2.7	1.1	2.3	1.0
Decreased social life	1.7	1.0	1.8	1.1	1.7	.9
Tense home atmosphere	2.2	1.0	2.3	1.1	2.0	1.0
Pressure to do the right thing to take proper care of the child	2.5	1.3	2.7	1.3	2.3	1.3
Life centered around the child	3.0	1.5	3.0	1.4	3.0	1.6
Special problems the family has	2.5	1.1	2.6	1.1	2.3	1.1
Shortage of family friends	1.3	.8	1.3	.8	1.3	.7
Need to constantly watch the child	2.3	1.2	2.4	1.2	2.1	1.1
Less time to devote to other children	1.7	.9	1.8	1.0	1.6	.9
Discruptions of family routine	1.9	.9	1.9	1.0	1.8	.9
Problem total	21.7	7.7	22.5	7.9	20.6	7.3

[a] No standardization norms are available; the scales are ranked from 1 (never) to 5 (always).

Family Unit Inventory

Significant differences (Table V) were found between the parents' perceptions of their present level of family functioning (real) and their projected (ideal) mode of functioning ($p < .01$). In addition, although no specific analyses could be performed because of the different test forms used, sample scores of couple satisfaction, congruence, and compatibility fell approximately midway between the scores previously reported for low versus high adjusted families. Hence, in terms of family concept, the parents strongly agreed with each other in terms of their appraisal of their current family status.

In spite of these major mother-father agreements, they did differ in their scoring patterns on three of the factor scores. Mothers reported higher levels of open personal communication (p < .01), viewed the family as more sociable (p < .05), and had lowered family ambition (p < .01) than did fathers. No differences emerged on the other six factors.

Across-Illness Comparisons

One critical intervening variable that affects parental coping style is the type of handicap or illness of the child. Even though the scope of the present study did not allow for systematic comparisons, trends in scoring across the four separate illness categories will be reported as directions for subsequent work. Caution must be taken in interpreting these results.

On the Hereford and Eysenck scales, the mothers of asthmatic children consistently scored in more positive directions that did any other groups of mothers. Fathers of asthmatic and cystic fibrotic children had higher parent attitudes and were more sociable (extroverted) than the other fathers. On both these scales, mothers and fathers of hearing-impaired youngsters had the most problematic scoring patterns.

Table V. Parent Scores on the Family Unit Inventory

	Total parent N = 221		Mothers N = 123		Fathers N = 88		Available norms[a]	
							Low adjusted family	High adjusted family
	$\bar{X}$	SD	$\bar{X}$	SD	$\bar{X}$	SD		
Total adjustment score, real	36.4	7.8	36.1	8.5	36.9	6.6		
Total adjustment score, ideal	40.9	6.7	40.5	7.4	41.4	5.4		
Factor scores								
1. Consideration vs. conflict	5.0	1.2	5.0	1.2	5.0	1.2		
2. Enjoyment vs. concern with problems	4.8	1.1	4.8	1.2	4.9	1.0		
3. Open personal communications	4.8	1.6	5.1	1.6	4.5	1.5		
4. Extrafamily sociability	5.7	1.3	5.9	1.3	5.5	1.2		
5. Family ambition	4.1	1.8	3.8	1.9	3.6	1.5		
6. Acceptance vs. rejection of responsibility	5.9	1.1	6.0	1.1	5.8	1.2		
7. Togetherness vs. separateness	5.5	1.4	5.5	1.4	5.5	1.3		
8. Importance of family	6.8	1.1	6.7	1.2	6.8	1.0		
9. Trust vs. alienation	5.7	1.3	5.7	1.4	5.7	1.3		
Satisfaction score (r)	.65	.2	.64	.2	.65	.2	.48 to .59	.78
Mother/father dyad congruence								
real (r); N = 74 pairs	.50	.3					.43	.66
(compatibility) ideal (r); N = 74 pairs	.63	.4					.60	.67

[a] Norms were determined with Q-Sort format; since this study used the multiple-choice format, no statistical comparisons can be made. The figures are reported for illustrative purposes.

The parents (again both mothers and fathers) of hearing-impaired children reported the most behavior problems, especially in areas of aggression and activity level, while parents of cystic fibrosis youngsters recorded the least. On the other hand, the parents of cystic fibrosis children reported the most special problem areas, especially that their lives were centered around the child. Hence, the parents with hearing-impaired children reported more behavior management issues, while those with cystic fibrosis children voiced more consuming caretaking needs.

Finally, the parents of asthmatics reported more open family communication and more acceptance of family responsibility, while the parents of cystic fibrosis children reported the highest levels of family importance. However, on the other scales of the Family Unit Inventory, parental attitudes showed similar profiles across the four illness categories.

Discussion

Across measures, both the ability to cope and the stress and strain on these parents was illustrated. Their scoring patterns were different from either normative or clinical groups; i.e., their scores tended to fall midway between those of normal and those of psychiatric clinic samples. Hence, they formed a separate entity, such that they were adjusting but had to face moderate stress with which they had some but not insurmountable difficulties. In addition, the mothers reported more deleterious effects from the stress of daily management than did fathers, which may suggest either a heightened concomitant of what are traditionally normative parenting styles or a degree of emotional divorce by the fathers.

The overall scoring patterns made it very difficult to categorize these parents simply as either well or poorly adjusted. The most appropriate classification seems to be that of an essentially normal group with special problems and with special needs for support and interventions geared to help them deal with the extra stresses they must face. For example, as a group these parents emphasized their social desirability, a characteristic that illustrated their need for approval as "good parents" and their desire to project as good an image as possible. They did not appear secure in their parental roles and had doubts about their abilities as parents. Nevertheless, such phenomena very likely can be accounted for by the realistically difficult job these parents face in their day-to-day struggles in raising their physically ill children. Most work with "normal" groups of parents assumes that their children will be physically healthy, and draws conclusions from the premise of physical health. Those assumptions do not hold for these parents who face realistic, tension-raising issues as a result of the physical condition of the child. Clearly, these parents were showing the effects of that tension. The fact that they were able to handle it does not obviate their need for support and professional and personal acceptance and understanding of the magnitude and duration of their task as parents. It is the realistic cost of this coping effort and not internally mediated psychologic failure to adjust that characterizes the less positive descriptors used by this group, and we should consider that any parents, no matter how psychologically adjusted, would face such doubt, insecurity, and considerable tension if they had to manage a physically ill child.

References

Eysenck, H. J., & Eysenck, S. B. G. *Eysenck Personality Inventory*. San Diego: Educational and Industrial Testing Service, 1963.

Hereford, C. F. *Changing parental attitude through group discussion*. Austin: University of Texas Press, 1963.

Sines, J. O., Pauker, J. D., Sines, L. K., & Owen, D. R. Identification of clinically relevant dimensions of children's behavior. *Journal of Consulting and Clinical Psychology*, 1969, *33*, 728-734.

Tavormina, J. B., Kastner, L. S., Slater, P., & Watt, S. Chronic illness in children. *Journal of Abnormal Child Psychology*, 1976, *4*, 99-110.

Travis, G. *Chronic illness in children, its impact on child and family*. Stanford: Stanford University Press, 1976.

van der Veen, F., Howard, K. I., & Austria, A. M. Stability and equivalence of scores based on three different response formats. *Proceedings of the 78th APA Convention*, 1970.

Decisions Hispanic Families Make After the Identification of Deafness

Annie Steinberg, Lisa Bain, Yuelin Li
Gilbert Delgado, Vivian Ruperto

Abstract: *This study examines the decision-making process for Hispanic families living in the United States who have a child with a hearing loss. Twenty-nine families in four geographical areas shared their experiences in searching for appropriate interventions and making choices regarding communication and education. We explored the impact of language, culture, minority status, and access to information and services on the decision-making process. The results indicate that the deliberations of Hispanic parents are often complicated by language and cultural barriers and by limited access to information, resources, and a full range of options. The communication method chosen tended to be the one recommended by professionals, usually a combination of spoken English and sign language. Parents frequently expressed the hope that their child would learn Spanish as well. These subjects displayed a higher degree of assertiveness in obtaining services for their children than other studies have suggested.*

The diagnosis of a chronic condition in an infant or child can have a profound impact on the family. In the case of deafness, the experience of identification and the period immediately following has been described as one of grief, anger, guilt, helplessness, denial, and above all, confusion (Mindel & Vernon, 1971; Schlesinger, 1972; Steinberg, 1991). Although identification of a child's deafness is inevitably a highly charged emotional experience, not all families respond in the same way, nor are responses necessarily consistent with the previous description. One factor influencing the response by a family to a child's disability is the family's cultural background. Cultural elements such as language, family structure, gender roles, beliefs about health and healing, and acculturative stress play significant roles in the family's decisions about rehabilitation and treatment of disabilities (Arnold, 1987).

Individuals of Hispanic descent constitute the largest minority group in the United States, accounting for 12.5% of the total population (U.S. Census Bureau, 2001). This rapidly growing U.S. minority group is a heterogeneous community of Americans and immigrants who derive their cultural identity from Mexico, Puerto Rico, Cuba, and Central and South America. Individuals in these groups share certain cultural traits such as the Spanish language, emphasis on the importance of family, and many unique cultural traditions but differ in other characteristics (Becerra & Zambrana, 1985; Seligman & Darling, 1989). Among individuals of Hispanic descent living in the United States in 1990 to 1991, 4.2%, or over 900,000 individuals, had hearing impairments (Ries, 1994).

The extent to which culture influences decision making has not been adequately studied. In one study of Hispanic families with children who are deaf, many families expressed difficulty dealing with their community's stigmatization and lack of understanding about their children's deafness and deafness in general, and most identified some problems with communicating with their children. Most families were keenly aware of and valued the higher quality of specialized services generally provided at no cost to families in the United States, compared with the vastly different quality and cost of services to deaf children in their countries of origin, yet they experienced additional stress as a result of separation from familial and community supports (Steinberg, Davila, Collazo, Loew, & Fischgrund, 1997). In another recent study, Hispanics living in the United States were found to experience additional stress originating from a difficulty in communicating with their physicians (Collins et al., 2002).

The process of decision making is a complicated one, influenced by emotions, beliefs, values, and expectations (Eleweke & Rodda, 2000; Steinberg & Bain, 2001; Steinberg, Brainsky, Bain, & Montoya, 1999). In the United States, the majority of parents of newly identified deaf children share the same language as the professionals from whom they seek help. Parents from minority cultures, particularly those whose primary language is not English, may have additional difficulty in coping with and successfully navigating through the decision-making process for their deaf children. Janis and Mann (1977) proposed a decision-making model that requires appraising the challenges and surveying the alternatives as initial steps. These steps require that parents have access to complete and accurate information in order to make decisions for their children.

Even when parents and professionals speak the same language, the information presented may be misunderstood. A difference in the language spoken by professionals rendering care and families receiving the information may exacerbate the chances for misunderstanding, difficulty, and stress. Interpreters may mitigate the communication barrier to some extent but may also introduce additional complications if interpreters are poorly trained (Vasquez & Javier, 1991).

For Hispanic families, the choice of communication mode may become even more difficult if the spoken language used in the home is different from the spoken language used in school. Families in this situation face the prospect of learning two new languages: English and sign language. In addition, the issue of educational mainstreaming takes on added complexity when the family itself does not communicate in the language of the majority culture (Cohen, Fischgrund, & Redding, 1990). Several studies suggest that Hispanic families underutilize support services that are available in the school system (Bennett, 1989). Furthermore, older studies suggest that parents of Hispanic heritage seldom participate in the development of their children's individual educational plans (Delgado, 1984; Stein, 1983).

In this study, we explored the decisions that Hispanic parents make for their deaf children regarding medical interventions, language, and children's use of early intervention services and entry into preschool and elementary school. The author's (A. S.'s) clinical experience with both Hispanic and non-Hispanic families suggests that parents make choices at transitional points that impact long-term outcome. A recent study of non-Hispanic families examined the extent to which the following factors influence choices after identification: accessibility of resources and information; quality and content of professional guidance; the family's hopes, expectations, and religious beliefs; and the parents' decision-making style (Li, Bain, & Steinberg, 2002). This study expands this previous work to address the decision-making process of Hispanic families.

Methods

Subject Recruitment

To sample a variety of cultural backgrounds, 29 families of Hispanic descent were recruited from four distinct geographical areas in the United States: Pennsylvania, Texas, central Florida, and northern California. Members of each community were hired to assist in recruitment of subjects, data collection, and translation of interviews. Each of the four communities had one community facilitator and one interviewer. In general, the facilitators knew the subject families prior to the study and thus did not conduct the interviews themselves. The researchers traveled to each of the four sites to train the community facilitators and interviewers in topics such as recruiting and eliminating bias from interviews. The community facilitators were all connected with deaf education in their respective communities and were in charge of recruiting Hispanic families with hearing-impaired children between the ages of 3 and 13.

Instruments

Families who volunteered to participate were asked to complete a questionnaire and participate in a 1- to 2-hour semi-structured interview. The questionnaire was developed in consultation with Kay Meadow-Orlans (Meadow-Orlans, Mertens, SassLehrer, & Scott Olson, 1997). The semistructured, open-ended interview was designed to allow informants to discuss issues of importance to them with guidance from the interviewer but few directed questions that would have elicited yes or no answers. Thus, issues emerged somewhat spontaneously, and not all informants directly addressed the topics we subsequently chose to analyze. This process allows analysis of the study subjects' experiences as well as their insights, cultural beliefs, and language.

Interviewers and community facilitators assisted families in filling out questionnaires when necessary. Interviews were conducted in either English or Spanish, according to the subject's preference. With subject's consent, interviews were audiotaped, videotaped, or both. Interviews that were conducted in Spanish were translated into English. Twenty-seven of 29 interviews were fully translated and transcribed. The translators were native Spanish speakers who were also fluent in English and who had prior translation experience. To the extent possible, translators were also matched to subjects according to dialect of Spanish spoken. Two interviews, both from families in the Texas subgroup, were not translated or transcribed due to technical problems. Thus, the sample size of interviews was reduced from 29 to 27 families, whereas the sample size of the data from the survey questionnaire remained at 29 families. A survey questionnaire gathered basic demographic information (age, gender, family composition, education, ethnic identification, etc.) as well as specific information about the child's hearing loss, interventions that had been used, the child's progress, communication methods used, sources of support and information, parental attitudes about deafness, family stress, and parental satisfaction with options available and guidance received. All instruments used in this study were approved by the institutional review board of the Children's Hospital of Philadelphia. The institutional review boards of several of the cooperating schools also reviewed and approved the instruments.

Analysis

Demographic items from the survey questionnaire were summarized by tables of frequency counts and percentages (see Table 1). Answers to questions regarding support, utilization of resources, and attitudes and beliefs about deafness were dichotomized, and the percentage of affirmative responses was calculated (e.g., "somewhat supportive" and "very supportive" vs. "not very supportive" and "unsupportive"). Responses to questions regarding the use of resources were dichotomized into "used, found helpful" (coded affirmative) versus "did not use" and "used, did not find helpful" (coded negative). These data are presented in bar graph form (see Figure 1). Analysis of the interviews used qualitative methods (Miles & Huberman, 1994.) Translations of interviews were fully transcribed from audiotapes. Transcripts were coded for themes of interest according to a coding schema developed by the research team. Themes were grouped in five categories of potential influence on parental decision making: guidance provided by professionals (including whether information was available in Spanish), internal factors (e.g., parental expectations, values), external factors (e.g., availability of resources), decisions made, and satisfaction. The codes were then applied to the transcripts using a computer

Table 1   Child demographics $(N = 29)^a$

Demographic variable	Demographic category	n	Percentage
Who child lives with			
	Mother and father	17	(59%)
	Mother only	6	(21%)
	Mother and stepfather	2	(7%)
	Other	4	(14%)
Gender of child with hearing loss			
	Male	14	(48%)
	Female	15	(52%)
Level of hearing loss			
	Profound	15	(52%)
	Severe	8	(28%)
	Moderate	3	(10%)
	Mild	1	(3%)
	Don't know	2	(7%)
Cause of hearing loss			
	Unknown	15	(52%)
	Heredity	3	(10%)
	Prematurity	2	(7%)
	Meningitis	1	(3%)
	Prenatal infections	1	(3%)
	Other	7	(24%)
Age at loss			
	Unknown	9	(32%)
	Birth or earlier	15	(54%)
	No answer	5	(17%)
Other disabilities		8	(28%)
Children with cochlear implant		4	(14%)

[a] Ages of children in the sample ranged from 4 years, 5 months to 13 years, 11 months, with a mean of 8 years, 7 months.

program called Folio Views (Folio VIEWS Infobase Production Kit, 1995), which allows for easy markup of text, followed by compilation of all segments coded with a particular theme. Each interview was coded by at least two researchers. Disagreements between the coders were resolved by the senior research analyst. Through this process, themes emerged that were of particular importance to the respondents in the study, and these themes were further analyzed for this publication.

Results

Respondents

Eighteen of the interviews were conducted with mothers only, one with the father only, and nine with both mother and father. For one of the two interviews not transcribed for technical reasons, it is unclear who participated. Questionnaires were filled out by 28 mothers and one father.

All parents had at least some high school education, and about a third also had some college education. Eleven mothers (39%) and 14 fathers (58%) did not complete high school. Seven mothers (25%) and six fathers (25%) graduated from high school, and another nine mothers (32%) and four fathers (16%) attended college. One mother had achieved a bachelor's degree.

Seventeen (59%) of the 29 children in the Hispanic group lived with both parents. Six children (21%) lived with their mothers only; two (7%) lived with mothers and stepfathers. The remaining four (14%) lived with family other than parents. Twenty-one parents (72%) reported that they had other children. Three parents (10%) reported that their deaf children had other deaf siblings: One parent had three children, and two parents had two deaf children each. Four parents (14%) reported that there were extended family members (e.g., cousins, uncles, grandparents) who also had hearing losses.

For most of the families in this study, the identification of hearing loss was obtained in the United States (69%). Many of the families left their countries of origin (usually Puerto Rico or Mexico) either when they suspected a hearing loss or after hearing loss was confirmed, believing that the opportunities, resources, and services for deaf children were superior in the United States and that children would face less discrimination there than at home.

Figure 1

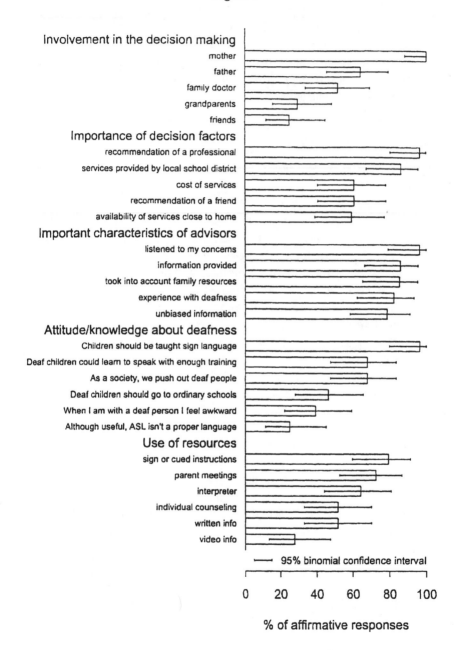

Table 1 summarizes the demographic information of the children in our sample. The children ranged in age from 4 years, 5 months to 13 years, 12 months. The mean age was 8 years, 7 months. The majority of children (23, or 79%) had profound or severe hearing loss. Three children had hereditary deafness, and about half of the parents (n = 15) did not know the etiology of their children's deafness. The average age that hearing loss was confirmed was 24 months (SD = 16), and the average age that the parents suspected that their children had hearing loss was at 14 months. (SD = 10.7). Twelve parents (41%) considered the cochlear implant as an option for their children. Of these twelve, six parents had their children evaluated for the implant. Four children (14%), two in Texas and one each in Florida and Pennsylvania, underwent cochlear implant surgery. Of those four parents, three reported that their insurance covered more than 75% of the cost for the cochlear implant. The fourth parent did not answer this question. All four parents reported that they are very satisfied with the cochlear implant.

Preferred Language in Family

Spanish is the primary language used in most of the homes of the participants (n = 16, 55%). Three parents (10%) cited Spanish and some sign language as their primary means of communication. Two parents (7%) stated that they communicate through a combination of Spanish, English, and signing or gestures. One parent (3%) responded that the children speak English and the parents speak Spanish. Four parents (17%) use English and some sign language to communicate with their children. One parent (3%) cites English as the family's primary means of communication. One parent uses Signed English as the primary means of communication, and another parent states that American Sign Language (ASL) is the primary language used in the home. Further exploration of preferred language occurred during the interviews with respondents and is discussed later in this article.

Decision Factors

Figure 1 summarizes the data about factors that influenced the decisions made by respondents. The factors analyzed include: the amount of involvement in decision making for parents, grandparents, friends, and the family doctor; the importance of five decision factors; which characteristics of influential people were most important; attitudes and knowledge about deafness; and the use of resources.

     The results showed that mothers were most involved (100%) in decision making. Fathers were somewhat less involved (64%), followed by the family doctor, grand parents, and friends. The most important factors in the parents' deliberations were the recommendations of professionals (96%) and the services provided by the local school district (86%). The parents thought that the most important characteristic of influential people was that they "listened to my concerns." The availability of services close to home, cost of services, and recommendations of friends were somewhat less important.

Attitudes and beliefs about deafness were assessed by asking respondents about their agreement with six statements. Ninety-six percent of the Hispanic families agreed (strongly agreed or agreed somewhat) with the statement, "Children should be taught sign language so they can talk to deaf people."

At the same time, only 25% agreed with the statement, "Although sign language may be useful, it isn't really a proper language." This positive attitude toward sign language was also accompanied by the belief that "All deaf children can learn to speak if enough time and effort were put into teaching them" and that "As a society, we push out deaf people." Less than half (46%) agreed with the statement that "Deaf children should go to ordinary schools."

We studied six aspects of resource utilization: whether the parents had been given written and videotaped information about different approaches or instructions for sign language or cued speech, whether they participated in parent meetings or individual counseling, and whether they had used interpreters. Sign instruction was the most widely used resource, followed by parent meetings and use of interpreters. We did not distinguish Spanish language from sign language interpreters; however, the interviews suggest that parents were referring to Spanish language interpreters. Individual counseling was used by more than half of respondents. Somewhat surprising was the finding that only 52% of the Hispanic families were given written materials about different options. Videotaped information was even less widely used.

Results

Interview Data

Two interviews were not translated and transcribed because of technical problems. Therefore, the analysis of the interview data includes only 27 subjects. We refer to the subjects as "families" although as we noted earlier, in some cases only one parent was interviewed. In the semistructured interview, we examined how parents go about making important decisions for their children. When a child has a hearing loss, parents need to decide how they will communicate with their child, how the child and parent both will learn to communicate effectively in the chosen modality, whether the child will use hearing aids or other assistive devices, whether the child will get early intervention services, and where the child will go to school. Early intervention and school decisions also often require collaboration between parents and the state, county, or local school system.

We found that the decision-making process for children with hearing loss is a complex one, affected by information and resource availability, including the quality of the information imparted by professionals and other sources; the parents' ability to acquire information and services; the parents' personal preferences and values; their decision-making style; and their beliefs about the causes and consequences of deafness. Although shared decision making between parents and professionals is often seen as the desired model (Charles, Gafni, & Whelan, 1997), we found that there were barriers that sometimes prevented parents from participating fully in the decision-making process. We explored the extent to which access to information that is a requirement for shared decision making is blocked in the Hispanic community by language and cultural factors as well as by the limited availability of resources and knowledge of legal rights. The interviews demonstrate the uniqueness of each individual case and the diversity of experiences among Hispanic parents of deaf children in the United States. Several common themes emerged in the interviews, including language differences, language preferences, choice of communication method, decision-making style, and religious beliefs.

Language Differences

Eight families reported that they experienced language difficulties that interfered with their acquisition of complete information. Four of these families reported that language differences presented barriers in some situations but that in other situations, interpreters, Spanish-speaking professionals, or the parents' own English-speaking ability mitigated these problems. It is especially noteworthy that 19 families, a majority of our respondents, reported that language differences were not a barrier to information access because interpreters were available and effective, Spanish-speaking professionals were available, one or both parents spoke English, or a combination of the above factors.

One Florida mother who felt language was a barrier said, "If it had been in Spanish, although it was hard to accept . . . one is free, one can ask the questions one wants to ask as he or she wishes. But it is hard when one feels trapped [by the language]. In a foreign language, the words don't come out."

Only one parent (in California) reported a problem with getting interpreters. She said, "Usually it was because the interpreter took a long time to arrive. We would have to wait one or two hours . . . so we finally decided that it was just easier for us to go in to the appointment on our own and talk to the doctor."

Three families said interpreters were available but ineffective. In one case, the audiologist provided information in English to the teacher and the mother; when the teacher and mother returned to school, the teacher would tell the interpreter what had been said, and the interpreter would translate for the mother. As a result, the mother was unable to pose questions directly to the audiologist. Parents also reported that the translations were not good or that the interpreter was difficult for the parent to understand. One parent stated that

> One of the terms that he used was used in a wrong way, and that made the whole translation different. . . . when they had the interpreter that was Puerto Rican, I understood a lot better. . . . It was not convenient for me to have Mexican interpreters because they do not interpret the same.... We have the same culture, but we don't have the same language.

Twelve families said that written materials were provided in both Spanish and English. Four families said they were available in English only, and the remaining 11 families did not address this issue. Most of the Spanish written materials appear to have been translations from English. Many of the parents said that written documents were provided with English on one side of the sheet and Spanish on the other. One parent said:

> They send them to me in English, also in Spanish, but I prefer in English, because the Spanish, they really kill it. I feel bad but I have told them that when they send something to me, send it to me in English because you have a problem with translations, that they kill my Spanish, oh my God! And it's better understood in English, because of the terminology and the translations are incoherent.

Language Preferences

Of the 27 families included in this analysis, 17 (63%) expressed the hope that their children would be bilingual (English and Spanish) or trilingual (English, Spanish, and sign language). Of the ten families (37%) who did not express a preference for bi- or trilingualism, four indicated that English was the most important language, five indicated that sign language was most important, and one indicated no preference.

Parents who expressed a preference for trilingualism cited the importance of access to Hispanic culture. Said a mother in Florida, "We are trying to avoid the error we made with the older boy, so that later he will have access to his culture and language which is Spanish, and also that he has complete use of English." Another mother said, "I want her to know both . . . because I do want her to know her background."

Retaining the ability to communicate with extended family members was frequently mentioned as a primary reason for learning Spanish. A mother in Texas said, "I believe that all three languages are important. Because the family speaks Spanish, at schools she needs to communicate in English, and she needs the sign language if she is not able to speak."

Parents who expressed a preference for sign language often hoped that their children would also learn English, Spanish, or both but indicated that sign language was the more accessible and useful language. A mother in California said, "Well I really think the best thing would be that she learned to communicate in English, but she can't speak so I guess she's going to have to use sign language. I think that would be for the rest of her life." Many of the parents who cited the importance of sign language nonetheless said they hoped their children would eventually learn Spanish as well. Said a mother in Pennsylvania, "The loss of hearing that my son has makes me think that it's more important for me that he knows how to communicate with people that use sign languages. Now culturally . . . I would like that he would be able to speak Spanish, but we live in the United States."

Parents who expressed a preference for English cited the use of English in the schools as a determining factor. A mother in Texas said, "I think it's more important that he learns and understands English because at the school where he is, the teachers speak only English. It is better for him to understand English than Spanish." Parents who stressed the importance of English also often hoped for Spanish fluency as well. Said a mother in Florida,

> I wish he could learn both, but it's very hard for him, and the most important thing is that he learns how to sign in English in order to communicate. That's the reason that we are here. That is the option that we made and he can learn English now, and maybe later he will be able to do sign language in Spanish.

Choice of Communication Method

According to 17 of the 27 families included in this analysis (63%), the only communication option offered by the school or county in which they live was total communication; these families accepted that option without exploring other methods. Five families (19%), all of them from Pennsylvania, were offered multiple options, and all of these families chose total communication. Another five families (19%) sought alternatives beyond those initially presented to them and made choices that differed from professional recommendations.

Parents indicated that different communication modes were rarely discussed or presented as possible options. For example, one parent said, "They didn't really . . . tell me much about communication, just that she needs to learn sign language." Another said, "They told me that he had to go to a special school and learn sign language." In one case, the parent was told about two options: "The only option they did give me was oral versus total communication, but it was mostly total communication because of the quality of my child's hearing, because what my child could hear, it wasn't enough for them to be put in an oral program."

Only in Pennsylvania were the different options presented. Said one mother, "They gave me two options, sign language only or sign language with voice." Another mother said, "They gave me a list of, you know, different places to call, different people to meet, make interviews, see the different schools and everything." All of the families in the Pennsylvania cohort spoke highly of the guidance they received from early intervention specialists at the school for the deaf. Said one mother, "I love that school because they helped him a lot since he was little."

Decision-Making Style

Previous studies (e.g., Young & Klingle, 1996) have indicated cultural differences for assertiveness in the medical encounter. We explored the extent to which parents played an active or passive role in seeking medical, audiological, or educational services for their children. Of the 27 families included in this analysis, 14 (52%) were rated "active" and 10 (37%) "passive" (Table 2). We were unable to classify the decision-making style of three families. Families were rated active when they described their efforts in words such as inquire, explore, investigate, challenge, fight, and organize. Families were rated passive when they made statements indicating acceptance of guidance without question or followup. Table 2 summarizes the statements of these two groups.

Religious Beliefs and Faith

Seventeen of the 27 families (63%) indicated that their religious beliefs and faith influenced their decisionmaking process. Seven families (26%) said their decisions were not influenced by religious beliefs, faith, or the Church. One mother answered, "I don't know, I don't know if that's anything that has helped us." Two families did not address the questions.

For some families, faith and prayer were cited as key factors in the decision-making process. For example, a mother in Florida said, "I put everything in God's hands. . . . I ask God to give me the wisdom to make proper decisions for him." A father in Pennsylvania said, "We were praying to God that everything would be okay, and God listened to our prayers."

Several parents (4; 15%) attributed improvements in the children's hearing to God or indicated a belief that God would cure their children's hearing impairment in the future. A mother in Florida said, "I am sure that God helped his ears, even though he needs the hearing aids. In time God will be restoring his hearing." A mother in California described an experience of praying to Santo Niño about her child, who was born with multiple problems, including deafness. "My husband and I knelt down to pray and at that moment I felt that that saint had helped me to save my child and ever since she has been better off." Another mother in Pennsylvania remembered, "They told me that there was nothing impossible that could not be done with God's help, and that's the way it has been and thanks to God's help is that the child has improved a lot and I have seen how he is better now"

Discussion

Upon learning that a child has a hearing loss, parents face a host of confusing options and must quickly evaluate the numerous choices in communication, education, and habilitation in the absence of an evidence base and with only limited information about the expected outcomes of the interventions. This decision-making process is challenging, regardless of cultural background. In this study, we sought to determine the degree to which Hispanic parents who live in the United States and who have children with hearing loss are at a disadvantage relative to their non-Hispanic counterparts in the same situation. The findings we discuss below suggest that Hispanic parents of children who are deaf often make their decisions in the context of language and cultural barriers, and limited access to information, resources, and the full range of options. Special issues such as trilingualism are rarely addressed by professionals, leaving parents to grapple with their questions alone.

Language Barriers Scaled by Hispanic or
Bilingual Professionals

Language differences presented significant obstacles to less than a third of our families. The availability of Hispanic or bilingual professionals (counselors, audiologists, nurses, and teachers) reduced the impact of language differences to a great extent in some areas. When bilingual professionals were not available, interpreters were also useful, although parents seemed to benefit from clearer communication with professionals who spoke the same language. Even parents who spoke English relatively well described how the presence of a Hispanic professional added to their comfort and ability to integrate and respond to the information. When interpreters were necessary and available, parents expressed a preference for those with whom they shared the same dialect of Spanish.

Table 2   Parenting style

Active (n = 14)

DHF03 I made them change. I communicated with people that helped me. I'm the type of mother who shows up unexpectedly to see what they are doing. I'm in the process of organizing a support group for the parents. I need to investigate more and know someone who knows more and gain more information.

DHF04 I was very involved, every situation. I talk to some more people and see what they get out of it . . . see what decisions they made and why they made that decision. I do think about it, I don't just jump into it.

DHF06 We went to talk with the county and the board and she [lawyer] prepared with a binder with all the laws . . . and she underlined very clearly all the rights that the child had . . . so then finally they transferred us.

DHT15 I told them if you're putting a barrier or a limit, I am very sorry but I am going to remove my kids from the school and the next day we start terminating all the paperwork. We look for the best school and we try to really get into the school to try and to help. You have to grab the bull by the horns and otherwise you're going to be wasting your time. We never just stay in one place and don't do anything.

DHT16 We went totally against what the school wanted.

DHC20 We discuss the options and what we think is best and he [husband] helps me make the decisions. . . . I had done some research about these different schools. We're just looking into other resources right now.

DHC21 I always try to get help somewhere to help me with the decision. I always ask questions. I make sure I go visit the school first and get information about the school.

DHC22 I decided to get her out of that school so then I transferred her to a regular school and I started to notice that she progressed a lot and that she started to do things right.

DHC23 The thing I learned most was my rights. I would start to notice these other women and mothers that were in these meetings and you know, the American women, they were very aggressive and would ask a lot of questions and I would watch them and study them and think that that's how I should be behaving. I had to get a lawyer and everything. I also feel that it is my responsibility to get more information about the things they are not telling me.

DHC24 I called an agency for the deaf and I asked them to please send me any information, any paperwork that they had. I sent out about 40 letters to different agencies. I'm a person with a very strong character. I really don't let anybody tell me anything.

DHP26 Started to analyze and to think that no, I should look for other specialists and that I should look for other tools to give to him. I have always been a person that I never give up.

DHP28 My questions were very hard questions. Other professionals that were around me also said that they didn't expect that I would be so strong, so strong in my questions, because they thought that it was going to be a lot easier with me.

DHP30 When we found out that she didn't hear anything, that's when we make decision. That's when we call over there and then, when there was no more options in Puerto Rico. So we said if she was born like that, we have to look for her progress.

DHP31 So I woke up and I'm like, all right, this is what I got to do for him and I called them up and I went to their office and they scheduled a lot of appointments. I was very involved in it.

Passive (n = 10)

DHF02 I don't think that here I have enough information, and also I don't have enough time.

DHT09 They give us the only option and we just follow up.

DHT10 I did not inquire about any other.

DHT11 I never told them what I had decided. They gave me the information and I went to the school and that was all.

DHT12 We only looked at the school program that we were told about.

DHT13 They would give us options and we knew that if they recommended it to us it was for the well-being of our daughter. We always agreed with what they told us.

DHT14 I have never been a person of asking too many questions. So whatever they say, it's okay.

DHC16 It [the program child attends] was just given to me. I really didn't

choose it.They really didn't give me much options.
DHC19 It was their decision. They tell me it's very important for me to go to
be able to communicate with her, but I've never gone, and they sent me a notice
and I told them that I couldn't go because I have no form of transportation.
Then after that they never said anything.
DHP25 They decided. I accepted them.

Information Unavailable or Incomplete

Despite the best intentions of professionals who serve the Hispanic community,
there remains a significant divide in access to information. Most parents relied
on the professionals who were treating their children to provide information and
guidance about not only hearing loss but also available services, medical
assistance, and children's and parents' rights. The survey results indicate that
written materials were used by only slightly more than half of respondents.
Materials written in Spanish were frequently offered but appear limited to
general pamphlets that have been translated from English, rather than materials
written to be culturally relevant to Hispanic people. As a result, some Hispanic
parents preferred to receive materials written in English because they felt that
the quality of the information they received was compromised by the translation
process. Moreover, although English-speaking parents frequently can obtain
materials from numerous sources, including popular books, magazines,
professional literature, videos, and the Internet, Hispanic parents appear to have
far fewer resources at their disposal. Thus, although Hispanic families in this
study appeared to be more inclined than non-Hispanic families to heed the
advice of the professionals treating their children without seeking multiple
sources of information, this may be attributable to the paucity of appropriate
materials as well as to language and cultural factors that influence
information-seeking behavior.

The author's (A. S.'s) clinical experience suggests that non-Hispanic
parents of deaf children often use and appreciate information and support
provided by other parents of deaf children. The data in Figure 1 suggest that
Hispanic parents also benefit from parent meetings; however in the interviews,
parents rarely brought up parent meetings as a valued resource. It may be that
in translation the question on the survey took on a meaning different from that
which was intended. The interviews suggest that Hispanic parents, particularly
those living in communities with small Hispanic populations, may not have
access to the type of parent support afforded by structured or unstructured
parent meetings. Further investigation is needed to determine whether this is
true and whether parent meetings would be helpful to this community.

Communication Choices Limited

The finding that the recommendation of a professional was the most important decision factor considered corresponds with the results obtained in the interview study. The communication method chosen tended to be the one recommended by the professionals consulted, with little consideration of alternative approaches. Usually the only option presented was a combination of sign language and speech; the option of oral communication was presented but discouraged. The subjects' attitudes and knowledge about deafness suggest that sign language is presented as a positive alternative. Approaches such as bilingual/bicultural, which uses ASL as the main form of communication; auditory/verbal, which emphasizes optimization of residual hearing; or cued speech, which uses handshapes to provide a visual form of phonemes, did not appear to be offered as options. It is not clear whether the professionals guiding the parents presented only those options that were available in the geographical area or whether they simply lacked knowledge and information about alternative approaches. However, it does appear that the Hispanic families in this study were rarely confronted with the "oral-manual controversy" that in other studies appears to frustrate and confuse so many parents. Interestingly, none of the families mentioned residential schools for the deaf, which historically have played a significant role in reinforcing Deaf culture in the United States. In part, the lack of knowledge or interest in residential schools may be due to the fact that most parents are receiving information from educators in the public school system. Another factor, however, is that traditionally and culturally, Hispanic parents do not wish to have their children living away from home, especially in the early years. Hence, this population tends to be enrolled in public school systems.

Retaining Native Language and Culture

Although most parents cited English, sign language, or both as the language that was most important for their children to learn, they also expressed a strong desire for their deaf children to learn and retain Spanish and its related culture. The task before these parents seems daunting, particularly in light of the fact that professionals often recommended a single language or bilingual approach and fail to highlight options that might allow them to achieve their goal of trilingualism.

Moreover, maintaining a connection to the Spanish language is difficult even for Hispanic citizens with normal hearing. In a recent article about the possible disappearance of Spanish in the United States, Rumbaut (2000) stated that "the hope of fluid bilingualism in the third and fourth generations is slight if not nonexistent." If this is true, deaf children of Hispanic parents have even less chance of learning, let alone retaining Spanish. Counteracting the diminution of Spanish in the United States are several factors: Spanish is still the dominant language in a very large part of the world and is tightly integrated with the cognition, literature, conversation, music, foods, and traditions of people who use it. Additionally, immigration from Spanish-speaking countries to the United States continues to be high, with population forecasts indicating that by 2025, 25% of the U.S. population will be Hispanic.

Decision-Making Style in the Hispanic Community

In contrast to previous studies that have cited minimal involvement of Hispanic parents with educational support services (Bennett, 1989; Cohen et al., 1990), the families in this study indicated a remarkably high degree of effort in obtaining appropriate services for their children, particularly those whose parenting style was rated as active (see Table 2).

Conclusions

Although decision-making literature demonstrates that parents have a strong desire for information and involvement in medical decisions, making informed choices involves access to culturally relevant information and resources. A shared language between parents and medical professionals is also necessary to optimize the discussion and exploration of treatment options. This study demonstrated that various factors impact on the decision-making process for Hispanic families living in the United States who have children with hearing loss, including religious beliefs and faith in God as the ultimate guide to the best options and outcome for the children and complications resulting from language and cultural barriers. Included in the latter category are the following factors: paucity of appropriate Spanish language materials about deafness, little offering or consideration of communication options, absence of shared language with professionals with whom decisions are typically explored, and the failure of professionals to address trilingualism as a feasible family goal. Degrees of assimilation into American culture (including the acceptability of advocating aggressively for one's child) and satisfaction with the United States relative to services and options available in one's country of origin are additional factors recognized by parents who participated in this study.

Limitations of This Study

Although this small sample size limits the generalizability of this study, recruitment from various geographic regions and through different sources minimizes the risk of sampling too narrow a range of respondents. Nevertheless, because of the size and diversity of the Hispanic community, a larger study would be necessary to understand fully the barriers that face this diverse community and the optimal efforts that can be made to overcome these obstacles.

Additionally, because of the voluntary nature of the subjects, we may have gained access to families with a more active decision-making style and resultant higher degree of satisfaction; thus we cannot be sure that our sample is representative of the full range of experience and sentiments. The problem of a small, self-selected sample group is common to many ethnographies, including this one, and is difficult to escape. However, this type of sample group does not necessarily detract from the validity of the study's findings as long as one keeps in mind that the findings should not be overgeneralized.

Translation issues also arose during the translation and transcription of the interviews. Although all of the translations for this study were completed by native Spanish speakers, we originally hoped to utilize translators from within the communities in which the interviews were conducted, but we were unable to realize this goal in all cases. Additionally, although interviewers and community facilitators were instructed not to espouse their own preferences regarding communication modality, school, or other interventions, personal biases or misconceptions may have inadvertently crept into the interview discussions.

One final limitation concerns the relatively broad age range (approximately 4-14 years) of the deaf children whose families we studied. It is likely that parents of the older children may have unintentionally recalled events that occurred early in their children's lives less accurately than parents of the younger children. This problem was unavoidable from our point of view because we aimed for a broad sample within the diverse Hispanic community rather than, for instance, a sample that included only newly identified deaf children.

Implications of This Study

The implications of this study's findings for professionals working with Hispanic families who have children with hearing loss are noteworthy for several areas, including the need for a shared language. Although there is much we don't know about the interplay of language with factors such as client characteristics, acculturation, and fluency levels, the recognition of the importance of culture and respect for language preference applies not only to ASL and Deaf culture but also to Spanish and Hispanic culture. The families we interviewed greatly valued the opportunity to converse in Spanish with a member of the community, suggesting that cultural matching may ultimately prove to be the critical variable in interventions. Trilingual interpreters would be particularly well equipped to address the complexity of translation and interpretation and should be very involved in innovating future linguistic options and intervention trials for the Hispanic family with a child who is deaf.

Informational channels were significantly reduced for many participating families, making the direct service provider communication and relationship even more vital. Although we did not inquire about perceived literacy, significantly fewer Hispanic parents (55%) were given written materials for review than non-Hispanic parents (92%); more globally, access to health care was most likely reduced for this community, given that a third of Hispanic families in America do not have health insurance. Further investigation in the areas of resource material development, building informational telephone networks, and a heightened understanding of computer utilization and utility for Hispanic families with deaf children are clearly needed in order to ensure equal access to information. Hispanic families need all available information regarding communication methods. Our study demonstrated that information provided reliably affected how the families' decisions were made, but in the absence of information, reasoned decisions are not possible, and decision making must rely on other actions, such as an act of faith. Because Hispanic families have significantly less access to other parents of deaf children, they may benefit greatly from peer support. Facilitated parent groups based in the community (e.g., homes, churches, etc.) would best serve to connect families and provide needed support.

Learning a second language is a challenge for many children. Although it is affected by language exposure and positive associated emotions, mastery of two languages requires full and continuous access to rich language. Many hearing children learning English as a second language do not master it, let alone a third language. Hard but realistic choices may need to be made for children who do not receive significant auditory input. Should they be taught in the family's language or should a choice be made to give them primary access to the language of the community with which they will most likely affiliate? Should cochlear implantation be recommended earlier to optimize the auditory input necessary to master several languages? Should a focus be put on a single language, and if so, which one? How much of a role should professionals play in this decision making, and how can their involvement be most helpful? If the decision is made to emphasize the language of the child's presumed future community, how can home communication be supported?

We have learned that Hispanic families are presented with fewer options such as cochlear implantation. It also appears that cued speech is rarely considered as an option, although it is not clear whether this is due to a lack of knowledge within the Hispanic community about cued speech or whether cued speech is not thought to be a good choice for families who are struggling with English in the home. When Hispanic parents are presented with the news that their child is deaf or hard of hearing and can learn a manual representation of their language, parents may wish to select this option to begin offering the child their language. Further elucidation of parental preference of language is indicated on both the individual clinical and community levels. The limitations of the knowledge base should be shared when presenting information to Hispanic families (e.g., we don't know the relative merits of lipreading, auditory training, etc. for children who must negotiate at least two spoken languages daily). Multisite and international collaborations may be helpful in understanding the balance between the added benefits of seeking services in the United States and the challenges of trilingualism for the child who is deaf. Our participating families came to the United States seeking better lives for their children. Would they have achieved the same general well-being (and satisfaction) if they had remained in their country of origin? The issues related to trilingualism complicate literacy enhancement and shared reading programs; reading role models culturally matched for families from different backgrounds would offer the most benefit from the intervention effort.

The findings of this study underscore the need for a significantly greater presence of Hispanic professionals, educators, peer-to-peer support, parent liaisons, and so on. This would assure a higher degree of cultural competence in addressing the needs of this unique community. Finally, the religious beliefs and values of Hispanic Americans have great significance to and deeply affect their caregiving. The heightened understanding of religious values should be an important training component in services programs addressing the needs of Hispanic families with deaf children.

Note

The contents of this report were developed under a cooperative agreement from Gallaudet University. However, the contents herein do not represent the policy of Gallaudet University, and endorsement by Gallaudet or the U.S. Department of Education should not be assumed.

References

Arnold, B. R. (Ed.) (1987). *Disability, rehabilitation and the Mexican American*. Edinburg, TX: Pan American University.

Becerra, R. M., & Zambrana, R. E. (1985) Methodological approaches to research on Hispanics. *Social Work Research and Abstracts, 21*(2), 42-49.

Bennett, A. T. (1989). *Hispanic families and children in the special education intake process*. New York: The Lexington Center.

Charles, C., Gafni, A., & Whelan, T. (1997). Shared decision-making in the medical encounter: What does it mean? (or it takes at least two to tango). *Social Science and Medicine, 44*(5), 681-692.

Cohen, O., Fischgrund, J., & Redding, R. (1990). Deaf children from ethnic, linguistic and racial minority backgrounds: An overview. *American Annals of the Deaf, 135*(2), 67-73.

Collins, K. S., Hughes, D. L., Doty, M. M., Ives, B. L., Edwards, J. N., & Tenney, K. (2002). Diverse communities, common concerns: Assessing health care quality for minority Americans. *The Commonwealth Fund, 8*(1), 9.

Delgado, G. L. (1984). Hearing-impaired children from nonnative-language homes. In *The Hispanic deaf: Issues and challenges for bilingual special education*. Washington DC: Gallaudet College Press.

Eleweke, C., & Rodda, M. (2000). Factors contributing to parent's selection of a communication mode to use with their deaf children. *American Annals of the Deaf, 145*(4),375-383.

Folio VIEWS Infobase Production Kit. Provo, Utah, Folio Corp, 1995.

Janis, I. L., & Mann, L. (1977). *Decision-making: A psychological analysis of conflict, choice, and commitment*. New York: Free Press.

Li, Y., Bain, L., & Steinberg, A. G. (2003). Parental decision making and the choice of communication modality for the child who is deaf. *Archives of Pediatric and Adolescent Medicine, 157*, 162-168.

Meadow-Orlans, K. P., Mertens, D. M., Sass-Lehrer, M. A., & Scott Olson, K. (1997). Support services for parents and their children who are deaf or hard of hearing. A national survey. *American Annals of the Deaf, 142*(4), 278-293.

Miles, M. B., & Huberman, A. M. (1994). *Qualitative data analysis*, 2nd ed. Thousand Oaks, CA: Sage Publications.

Mindel E., & Vernon, M. (1971). *They grow in silence—The deaf child and his family*. Silver Spring, MD: National Association of the Deaf. National Center for Health Statistics. (1994).

Ries, P. W. (1994). Prevalence and characteristics of persons with hearing trouble: United States, 1990-91. *Vital and Health Statistics, 10*(188).

Rumbaut, R. (2000). *Desparecea el español? The Orange County Registrar for the New Mexican.* January, Santa Fe, NM.

Schlesinger H. S. (1972). Diagnostic crisis and its participants. *Deafness Annual, Volume II.* Silver Spring, MD: Professional Rehabilitation Workers with the Adult Deaf.

Seligman, M., & Darling, R. (1989). *Ordinary families: Special children.* New York: Guilford.

Stein, R. C. (1983). Hispanic parents' perspectives and participation in their children's special education program: Comparisons by program and race. *Learning Disability Quarterly, 6,* 432-439.

Steinberg, A. (1991). Issues in providing mental health services to hearing-impaired persons. *Hospital and Community Psychiatry, 42*(4), 380-389.

Steinberg, A., & Bain, L. (2001). Parental decision making for infants with hearing impairment. *International Pediatrics, 16*(1),1-6.

Steinberg, A., Brainsky, A., Bain, L., & Montoya, L. (1999, June). Assessment of quality of life and preferences of parents with children who are deaf. Abstract presented at the Meeting of the Academy for Health Services Research and Health Policy, Chicago, IL.

Steinberg, A., Davila, J., Collazo, J., Loew, R. C., & Fischgrund, J. E. (1997). "A little sign and a lot of love . . .": Attitudes, perceptions, and beliefs of Hispanic families with Deaf children. *Qualitative Health Research, 7*(2), 202-222.

U.S. Census Bureau. Census 2000 Summary File 1 (United States), prepared by the U.S. Census Bureau.

Vasquez, C., & Javier, R. A. (1991). The problem with interpreters: Communication with Spanish-speaking patients. *Hospital and Community Psychiatry, 42*(2), 163-165.

Young, M., & Klingle, R. S. (1996). Silent partners in medical care: A cross-cultural study of patient participation. *Health Communication, 8*(1), 29-53.

Psychodynamics Surrounding the Diagnosis of a Child's Deafness

McCay Vernon

Abstract: The psychodynamics that surround the diagnosis of deafness in a child have important, long-lasting effects on both the deaf child and his family. In this process, coping is critical; and there are several key variables that affect coping procedures, including the character structure of the parents, the counseling the parents receive, the parents's attitudes toward having a child, the degree to which the parents use denial in coping, and the stress that results from communication problems between parents associated with deafness. The degree of denial about the implications of deafness by professionals in the field and parents is a major block to successfully coping with deafness, for both the parents and the child. Part of the problem of communication centers around the ambiguity of lipreading and amplified sound to deaf children, and the limitations of the speech of deaf children. A practical way to cope with this part of the problem is the use of fingerspelling and sign language in conjunction with oral communication. Counselors must be prepared to overcome both their denial of the implications of deafness and the providing of parents with realistic recommendations for coping, especially with the communication problem of deafness.

The psychodynamics which occur when parents discover their child is deaf is of vital, often permanent, consequences to the family and to the deaf child. These crucial processes which have their actual beginnings at the time of pregnancy and even before, gradually evolve within the family as the deaf child approaches adulthood.

The impact on parents of the diagnosis of deafness in their child and the counseling of these families is a little-understood, almost universally mishandled, process. The lack of knowledge and the errors have serious effects which often are irreversible (Grinker, 1969, p. 81-82; Mindel and Vernon, 1972). These errors and omissions in counseling tend to be more devastating to the child and family than the deafness itself.

Thus, competent parent counseling is one of the most important services an audiological or otological clinic can offer a deaf child and his parents. Paradixically, it is the rarest service offered. Instead, parents generally get well-intended misinformation about psycho-social aspects of deafness which creates false hopes leading to problems and maladjustment.

What follows is a discussion, starting at the time of pregnancy, of the psychodynamics surrounding the diagnosis of deafness in a child. The author's perspective, based in part on research (Meadow, 1968; Grinker, 1969, p. 81-84) and in part on twenty years of clinical experience, is that effective family communication is basic to coping with deafness. Corollary to this perspective is the belief that, for such communication to be established, the use of fingerspelling and sign language are required along with speech, lipreading, and amplification.

Pregnancy

Often pregnancies occur at times when they were not planned and in many cases were not wanted. Even in couples with whom a pregnancy is desired and comes at a convenient time, there is ambivalence. On the one hand are high expectations and hopes. Feelings of fulfillment and family closeness may develop. There also are hostile attitudes due to the added responsibility, disfigurement, or demands. Sometimes there is a blaming of one spouse by the other for the carelessness that led to conception.

These mixed feelings about the pregnancy inevitably result in some wishful fantasies that the pregnancy may end prematurely. There also may be deliberate violations of clearly understood rules of prenatal care, violations such as taking very hot baths. More direct attempts to abort, e.g., involving quinine or drinking turpentine, while rarely mentioned in professional literature, are well known by obstetricians and psychotherapists who work with young parents.

The point to be made is that it is important to be aware of how widespread these kinds of feelings and fantasies are on the part of normal parents. They have tremendous implications relative to the feelings of guilt and denial which occur later if their child is deaf.

Early Years

Generally it is one to three years after birth before deafness is discovered. Part of the reason for delayed diagnosis is that few infants have total hearing losses. Most respond to the gross sounds of airplanes roaring overhead, motors backfiring, and pots and pans banging. The inability to understand speech sounds is masked. It is this inability to hear speech well eoungh to understand it which is what deafness is.

Even though there is a delay in the actual discovery of deafness, parents generally sense something is wrong long before a diagnosis has been made. For example, they miss the subtle responses and reactions to sound which are basic to the mothering process. Parental expectations often are unfulfilled because of a lack of responsiveness and because of developmental slowness in some areas. Gradually anxiety develops, as the mother wonders if the child is retarded. Some of these expressions are rather common manifestations of the anxieties of many mothers of normal children. Therefore, they often are passed off by physicians and others.

While these responses may temporarily, albeit falsely, allay concern, before long they arouse increasing frustration, confusion, and anxiety in the family. The parents realize something is drastically wrong, yet their communication about this is essentially ignored, and often they are given contrary-to-fact information.

Failure to make the diagnosis of deafness has two serious impacts. First, it delays habilitation past a period some believe is crucial in the psychological and educational development of the child. Second, it causes confusion, anxiety, fear, anger, and guilt feelings in the parents, partly because such feelings cannot be channeled constructively toward the resolution of the child's problem until the family is told what the problem is.

While a failure to detect deafness is bad enough, far worse are the misdiagnoses which occur in at least one-third of parents of deaf children (Mindel and Vernon, 1971, p. 31-32). Some of these misdiagnoses grow out of the complex problem of the differential diagnoses between brain damage, aphasia, delayed speech, autism, childhood schizophrenia, mental retardation and deafness (Hefferman, 1955, p. 274).

The most gross of these misdiagnoses usually are made in cases cf multiple handicapped deaf children: those who have profound hearing losses and cerebral palsy, vestibular pathology, or some other additional disability.

While multiple handicaps may make diagnostic errors more understandable, the errors are more destructive as they compound the difficulties of a child already handicapped. However, to imply that all, or even most of the one-third of deaf children misdiagnosed or undiagnosed are multiply handicapped would be incorrect. While physicians most often are to blame, some of the grossest errors are made by psychologists who give verbal tests to nonverbal deaf children. A major point to be derived from this discussion is that delayed speech or apparent failure to respond to sound should never be ignored, nor should a diagnosis be made in such cases until hearing has been thoroughly tested audiologically.

Parents may be a long time in taking the possibility of deafness seriously, especially the more accepting parent. This delayed awareness can be the first manifestations of the unconscious denial of deafness. Often in interviews parents who can recall the symptoms of the deafness they observed in their child claim never to have associated these with hearing loss. For example, the mother may say, "Mary did not respond to my voice," "Ann was disobedient," "Frank slept with the vacuum cleaner on" or "He slept right through the fireworks, on the Fourth of July."

The Diagnosis of Deafness

By the time deafness is finally diagnosed, the child is usually in his second or third year. For some parents, the finding of deafness results in an initial feeling of relief due to having been told previously that the child was retarded, autistic, or had some other problem perceived to be worse than deafness. However, to most families the discovery of deafness is a traumatic blow, the full depth of which is rarely sensed by the professional making the diagnosis. It is common for parents to say, "I do not remember a thing the doctor said after I was told my child was deaf."

There has been some excellent research on how families cope with the discovery that they have a child with a serious irreversible disability. The work by Hamburg (1953), Cholden (1958, p. 241), and others (Grinker, 1969, p. 63; Siller, 1969) establishes several general principles crucial to making and communicating to the family the diagnosis of deafness.

The first of these principles is that constructive and effective coping with a permanent disability begins only after the patient and family are fully, aware of the irreversibility of the condition and of its total implications. As the ramifications of the disability can be overcome, patients and their families do not adjust to the reality of deafness and the resulting new life circumstance.

When and if a person realizes exactly what changes will have to be made in his life, then the kinds of adaptations that are effective become possible. This generalization holds true across disability groups and is a fundamental premis upon which all rehabilitation must begin (Siller, 1969). It places tremendous responsibility upon the person who informs parents that their child is deaf, a responsibility for which most are unprepared.

The second principle deriving from research on reaction to disability is that certain defenses or coping procedures are almost universal. The most important of these is an initial denial of the defect or at least a denial of implications.

Denial and Deafness

Denial is a normal coping mechanism through which human beings initially protect themselves at a time of trauma. Studies of parents of leukemic children and of blind persons illustrate the process (Cholden, 1958, p. 182; Hamburg, 1953). It is when denial becomes chronic that it is pathological and prevents constructive adjustment to disability.

At the time a child is discovered to be deaf, the deafness is initially denied. For example, parents who have previous children usually sense something different in the deaf child within the first year, but this awareness is rarely dealt with directly. Sometimes it is the grandparents, relatives, or neighbors of the child who finally force the parent to face the fact that their child is deaf. Even when parents identify and acknowledge deafness and want to do something about it, often they are told by the doctor that the child will grow out of it or that everything is going to be all right. Thus, there is a denial of the deafness on the part of parents and the professional community (Mindel and Vernon, 1971, p. 22-24).

When the diagnosis is finally made, the power of denial becomes more vivid. No longer is it the blatant denial of the deafness per se, but the more subtle and destructive denial of the implications of profound hearing loss.

Generally the full implications of deafness are not explained to the parents (Grinker, 1969, p. 81-84; Mindel and Vernon, 1971, p. 22-24). In some cases almost nothing is said about what deafness means in the life of the child and his family. Parents may be told only that the child is deaf and that they should go home and wait until he is old enough to attend school.

On occasion the professional who makes the diagnosis (the audiologist, or the physician) informs the parent that their child is deaf, but that a hearing aid, speech lessons, and lipreading instruction will be provided. This can be painful. The danger is that parents often are led to believe that although the child is deaf, prostheses and training are going to enable him to function as though he were not deaf. Rarely when parents are informed of the deafness are they given time to really sit down and talk about it and to work through the very intense feelings that occur at this time and persist over the weeks and months that follow.

Thus, there are several crucially important occurrences that take place around the diagnosis of deafness and in the period that follows. First is the frequent denial of the full implications of deafness by the professional with whom the parent is in contact. This denial is subtle and usually unintentional. It occurs in the form of inaccurate statements about the speech potential of children and the ultimate functional value of the speech deaf persons are able to develop. Overly optimistic statements, implied or explicit, about the values of hearing aids and the effectiveness of lipreading further compound the problem. Euphemisms blur the very real differences between being prelingually deaf and having normal hearing—a distinction glossed over by many who counsel parents.

The second penomenon, related to diagnosis, is that mourning over loss of hearing is rarely fully experienced as an intense grief which is worked through psychologically (Grinker, 1969, p. 61). In a gesture of false kindness professionals, physicians, and educators often help the parent deny the loss. The mourning which should be experienced is chronically repressed. It becomes a grief that the parents and the deaf persons live with indefinitely. In psychological interviews parents of deaf children, discussing the deafness of fully grown sons and daughters, frequently are brought to tears by grief which has never been fully worked through psychologically. Chronic denial has been substituted.

Relationship of Denial and Family Stress

A breakdown in communication between family members is one of the severest of psychological stresses. The denial of the communication problems of deafness creates in the families of deaf children this kind of stress. The problem grows out of the following difficulties and limitations posed by lipreading and speech for persons deafened prelingually:

> Two-thirds of the forty two sounds that make up the English language are either invisible or else they look just like some other sound on the lips (Hardy, 1970, p. 337). Furthermore, among the most difficult sounds to lip read are the most important ones, for example, the vowels. The few sounds that are visible for speechreading must be grasped in the fleeting instant that they are on the lips (Hardy, 1970, p. 337).
>
> As a consequence of this ambiguity the world's best lipreaders get about one fourth of what is said and they are not deaf (Lowell, 1957-1958). One reason they are not deaf is that in order to lipread for comprehension one must have an adequate command of language (Hardy, 1970, p. 336). Children prelingually deafened do not have this command of language (Mindel and Vernon, 1971, p. 86-97). In fact they are expected to learn language through a process which presupposes that they already have language skill. Thus the average deaf child, consequently, gets about five percent of what is said when he depends upon lipreading (Lowell, 1957-1958; Mindel and Vernon, 1971, p. 86-97; Vernon, 1970) .

> Speech for a person born deaf will never be normal and much of it will not be intelligible. In addition to speech problems, learning language is difficult for a person born deaf because he does not hear it and thereby gets little exposure to it. If he is forced to try to learn language just through lipreading, his task is almost impossible: Over 30 percent of deaf school leavers are functionally illiterate, and only 5 percent achieve a tenth grade achievement level. Most of the latter are actually hard of hearing or adventitiously deaf (McClure, 1966).

These facts are not presented to parents in part because they are not known by many of those who diagnose deafness. If the facts were presented it would be painful, but it would also be reality. Until the reality of deafness is known, the parent and child cannot cope constructively. Consequently there is a communication breakdown and a huge discrepency which creates intense frustration, between parents expectations and the child's attainment.

The frustration leads to an underlying stress and anger for which parents are given no constructive outlet. The result is pervasive and destructive not only to the mother and father but to the child. One manifestation is the avoidance of child-parent interaction because the interaction when attempted is so stressful and frustrating that both the child and the parent understandably want to escape it. Thus, the deaf child often is an isolate in his own home, losing the emotional and educational benefits he needs from close parental contact.The parents in turn miss the satisfactions from their child that they have the right to expect. In extreme cases, when the deaf child comes home from school for the weekend, parents give him money and tell him to go to the movies:, and stay until bedtime. More common, however, is a gradual subtle withdrawal of interaction between the parent and the child.

Another result of the denial of the communication implications of deafness and the accompanying stress is under-education. Deaf children have the same IQ distribution as hearing children yet, as indicated earlier, 30 percent are functionally illiterate when they leave school (Mindel and Vernon, 1971, p. 91); 60 percent test at fifth grade or below. An obvious corollary of under-education is unemployment and under-employment.

Even more tragic is the deaf person's tendency to be emotionally separated from his family. Many deaf adults are extremely bitter about their treatment by their family. They are hurt by being excluded from activities such as mealtime conversation and the planning of family activities.

Constructive Coping

Total communication, which involves the use of fingerspelling and the language of signs in conjunction with speech, lipreading and amplification, offers a reasonable resolution of communication problems faced by the family with a deaf child. The addition of manual communication (fingerspelling and the language of sign) in no way impedes the development of oral communication skills (Meadow, 1968; Vernon and Koh, 1970 and 1971). Its value is that it does not have the ambiquity inherent in speech and lipreading. Thus, full communication between the deaf child and his parents is possible, eliminating much of the stress, frustration, and anger growing out of a limitation to oral communication.

It is only recently that a few parents of young deaf children have begun to be counseled to use both manual and oral communication simultaneously with their deaf children. While certainly not a panacea, this approach of total communication is a step forward. In fact, its potential is so great that the National Association of the Deaf, the world's largest organization for the deaf, has officially endorsed the approach.

Summary

The psychodynamics which surround the diagnosis of deafness have crucial long lasting effects on the deaf child and his family. Key variables affecting coping procedures are the character structure of the parents, the counseling, they receive, their attitudes toward having a child, the degree to which denial is used in coping, and the stress resulting from communication problems concomitant to deafness.

The degree of denial of the implications of deafness by professionals in the field and by parents is a major block to successful coping with deafness for both the parents and the child. Part of the communicational aspect of the problem centers around the ambiguity of lipreading and amplified sound to the deaf child and the limitations of the speech of deaf children. The use of fingerspelling and sign language in conjunction with oral communication is a practical way to cope with this part of the problem. Counseling needs to he geared to overcoming the denial of the implications of deafness and the providing of parents with realistic recomendations for coping especially with the mmunication problem of deafness.

References

Cholden, L. S. *A psychiatrist works with blindness*. New York: American Foundation for the Blind, 1958.

Grinker, R. G. (Ed.) Psychiatric diagnosis, therapy, and research on the psychotic deaf. Final Report Grant #RD-2407-9, Social Rehabilitation Service Department, H.E.W. (Available from Dr. Grinker, Michael Reese Hospital, 2959 S. Ellis, Chicago, Illinois), 1969.

Hamburg, D. A. Psychological adaptive processes in life threatening injuries. Paper presented March 18, 1953 to Symposium on Stress, Walter Reed Medical Center, Washington, D.C.

Hardy, M. Speechreading. In Davis H. and Silverman, S.R., (Eds.), *Hearing and deafness*. New York: Holt, Rinehart and Winston, 1970, 335-345.

Hefferman, Angela. A psychiatric study of fifty children referred to hospital for suspected deafness. In Caplan, Gerald (Ed.), *Emotional problems of childhood*. New York: Basic Books, 1955.

Lowell, E. L. Research in speechreading: Some relationships to language development and implications for the classroom teacher. *Report of the Proceedings of the 39th Meeting of the Convention of American Instructors of the Deaf,* 1959, 68-73.

McClure, W. J. Current problems and trends in the education of the deaf. *Deaf American*, 8-14, *Vol. 18*, 1966.

Meadow, K. P. Early manual communication in relation to the deaf child's intellectual, social, and communicative function. *American Annals of the Deaf, 113*, 1968, 29-41.

Mindel, E. D. and Vernon, M. *They grow in silence*, Silver Spring, Maryland: National Association for Deaf Press, 1971.

Mindel, E. D. and Vernon, M. Out of the shadows and the silence. *J.A.M.A., 220*, 1972, 1127-1128.

Siller, J. Psychological situation of the disabled with spinal cord injuries. *Rehabilitation Literature, 30*, 1969; 290-296.

Vernon, M. Mind over mouth: A rationale for total communication. *Volta Review* (in press).

Vernon, M. Potential, achievement, and rehabilitation in the deaf population. *Rehabilitation Literature, 31*, 1970, 258-267.

Vernon, M. and Koh, S. D. Early manual communication and deaf children's achievement. *American Annals of the Deaf, 115*, 1970, 527-536.

Blackness, Deafness, IQ, and g

William P. Isham
Leon J. Kamin

Abstract: *The authors explain why deaf children should not be treated as a single population with regard to "deprivation." Deaf children of deaf parents outperform children with hearing parents on almost any measure of intelligence or academic achievement investigated in studies. This finding implies different levels of stress and coping strategies for hearing and deaf parents of deaf children. In addition, the authors analyze how Jensen (1985) and Braden (1984, 1989) employed IQ data from deaf children to support their interpretation of "Spearman's hypothesis." They reported, correctly, that positive correlations have been obtained between mean black-white differences on IQ subtests and the subtests' g loadings. They also claimed that the analogous correlation between mean hearing-deaf differences and subtest g loadings is negative. They assumed that the deaf have suffered environmental (linguistic) deprivation, and argued that the different correlations indicate that black-white differences (unlike hearing-deaf differences) are not likely the result of environmental deprivation. The authors demonstrate that the deaf data they employed have been defectively and inconsistently reported, and can provide no support to the claim that black-white differences are not environmental in origin.*

The IQ test scores of deaf children are said to be relevant to the interpretation of black-white differences in psychometric intelligence (Braden, 1984, 1989; Jensen, 1985). The claimed relevance derives from consideration of "Spearman's hypothesis," a term applied by Jensen to Spearman's supposition (1927) that the magnitudes of the mean differences between American blacks and whites on various cognitive measures would be directly related to the loadings of those measures on the hypothetical general factor in intelligence, g. Spearman was aware that blacks had lower average cognitive tests scores than whites. His hypothesis was that the degree of black deficit on a given test depended on the degree to which that test tapped a general intelligence factor.

To provide empirical support for Spearman's hypothesis, Jensen (1985) reviewed several sets of published data on black-white differences. For each data set, Jensen calculated the correlation between the magnitude of the black deficit (expressed in standard deviation units) on a particular test or subtest and the loading of that test or subtest on a "g factor" extracted from the battery of tests employed in the particular study. The g factor was identified with the first principal factor; because different studies employed different tests, the so-called general intelligence factor was not the same from study to study. In any event, Jensen maintained that the typical within-study correlation between the magnitude of the black deficit and a test's g loading was about .59 (Table 3, p. 207).

Taken by itself, the positive correlation between black-white mean differences and g loadings says nothing about the origin of the black-white difference. The IQ scores of deaf children enter the argument at this point. Jensen assumed that deaf children experience grave "linguistic deprivation," and that, as a consequence, their measured IQs may be lower than the hearing norm. It, thus, is of interest to see whether the magnitude of the "deaf deficit" on various subtests will be, as is the case with blacks, correlated with the subtests' g loadings. If not, one might argue that the lower test scores of blacks, relative to whites, are not the result of linguistic or cultural deprivation. Jensen expressed the argument in the following language:

> It should not be assumed, however, that any two groups that differ because of cultural or linguistic deprivation of one group relative to the other will, of mathematical necessity, show a correlation between the g-loadedness of various tests and the magnitudes of the group differences. Quite different results emerge in a comparison of congenitally or preverbally deaf children and normal-hearing children on the WISC-R. . . . average differences between hearing and deaf children [on five Performance subtests of the WISC-R] can be compared with . . . average differences between black and white children in the WISC-R national standardization sample. . . .
>
> The Pearson correlation between g-loadings [of the five subtests] and the mean black-white differences is +0.97. . . . The Pearson correlation between the g loadings and the mean hearing-deaf differences is negative, -.82. . . . the Spearman hypothesis holds for the black-white differences but not for the differences between hearing and deaf children. . . . The language deprivation caused by deafness evidently takes its toll mostly on common factors other than g, or on the tests' specificities. . . . (Jensen, 1985, pp. 204-206).

The Jensen quotation suggests that the deaf IQ scores were also being used as an empirical rebuttal to an argument (Humphreys, 1985; Jensen, 1987; Schonemann, 1983, 1985; Shockley, 1987) about whether correlations between any group mean differences and g loadings might be a statistical artifact. However, Jensen particularly selected blacks and the deaf for comparative study, and clearly implied that for those two groups a case might be made that each had suffered "cultural or linguistic deprivation."

We wish, in this article, first to demonstrate that crucial data from deaf children, used both by Jensen (1985) and by Braden (1984, 1989) in support of their position, are gravely flawed in their presentation, and thus cannot sustain any argument. We shall then call attention to a fact of which many psychologists who regard deaf children as "linguistically deprived" may be unaware: With regard to linguistic experience, deaf children fall into two quite distinct populations. Combining data across those populations can lead to serious error.

The Data on Deaf Children

The data on hearing-deaf differences utilized in Jensen's (1985) calculations are "based on data from Braden 1984" (p. 205), but Jensen indicated that Braden had, in turn, taken the data from a deaf WISC-R standardization sample described by Anderson and Sisco (1977) and by Sisco (1982). Though Jensen wrote of the "toll" caused by deafness, examination of Braden's (1984, p. 405) Table 1 provides little evidence for any substantial "deaf deficit." Braden indicated that the mean Performance IQ of the deaf children was 96.89, suggesting a deficit of .21 SD. For one subtest (Object Assembly) the deaf children were actually .10 SD superior to hearing children. For the remaining subtests, hearing children were superior by margins ranging from .16 SD (Picture Completion) to .63 SD (Coding). Black-white differences in the WISC-R standardization sample were very much larger. Whites had a mean PIQ 1.07 SD higher than blacks, and were superior on all five subtests by margins ranging from .47 to .93 SD.

There are, however, grounds on which to question the validity of the deaf data upon which Jensen (1985) and Braden (1984) depended. The empirical support for a claim can obviously be no stronger than the quality of the data on which it is based, and detailed examination of the Anderson and Sisco (1977) data on deaf test scores reveal insufficiencies and ambiguities that negate, or even reverse, claims made by Jensen and by Braden.

There are, in fact, three separate reports by Anderson and/or Sisco presenting data from the standardization of the WISC-R Performance scale for deaf children (Anderson & Sisco, 1977; Sisco, 1982; Sisco & Anderson, 1980). Mean scores for all subtests are given in Anderson and Sisco (1977) for 1,202 deaf children. These subtest scores were reproduced in Braden (1984) and were utilized by Jensen (1985). However, as indicated in our own Table 1, the Anderson and Sisco (1977) subtest means are radically inconsistent with data provided by Sisco and Anderson (1980, p. 925) for the very same children in their Tables 3 and 4. In those tables, subtest means and mean PIQs are presented separately for 100 children whose parents were deaf, and 1,100 children whose parents were hearing. It is, thus, easy to compute weighted means for the full sample, and these are given in our Table 1. Note that according to Anderson and Sisco (1977), the deaf children do worst in the Coding subtest (standard score 8.03, .63 SD less than hearing children). However, the Sisco and Anderson (1980) data for the same sample indicate that deaf children do best on the Coding subtest (standard score 9.75, .08 SD less than hearing children). Both sets of g-loading values used by Jensen and by Braden (reproduced in our Table 1) to calculate correlations indicate that the Coding subtest is the least g-loaded of the five. Thus, it is of considerable consequence whether one uses the Sisco and Anderson (1980) or the Anderson and Sisco (1977) version of the deaf sample data. Had Jensen used the Sisco and Anderson (1980) means, rather than Anderson and Sisco's (1977), he would have reported a correlation of +.73 (not -.82) between hearing-deaf differences and subtest g loadings. Similarly, the correlation of -.79 reported by Braden (who used a different set of g-loading values) becomes +.67, when employing the Sisco and Anderson (1980) means.[1]

TABLE 1

Mean WISC-R Scores for the Same Sample of Deaf Children and the Subtests' g Loadings

| | Mean Test Scores | | | g Loadings[a] (from Braden, 1984) | |
Subtest	Anderson and Sisco (1977)	Sisco and Anderson (1980)	Sisco (1982)[b]	Hearing	Deaf
Picture Completion	9.51	9.50[c]	9.47	.64	.68
Picture Arrangement	8.71	9.54[c]	9.54	.59	.73
Block Design	9.48	9.54[c]	9.48	.82	.76
Object Assembly	10.32	9.61[c]	9.62	.72	.77
Coding	8.03	9.75[c]	9.69	.36	.58
PIQ	95.70	96.89[d]	96.64	—	—

[a]To report their correlations, Jensen (1985) used the g loadings from the hearing sample; Braden (1984) used those from the deaf sample.
[b]All means from Sisco (1982) derived by Isham and Kamin.
[c]Derived by Isham and Kamin from Sisco and Anderson (1980, Table 4, p. 925).
[d]Derived by Braden (1984) from Sisco and Anderson (1980, Table 3, p. 925).

This choice made between the two discrepant presentations of the same data set drastically affects theoretical interpretations. The correlations of .73 and .67 are, in fact, somewhat higher than the .59 typically found by Jensen (1985) in black-white studies, so Jensen would not have been able to conclude that Spearman's hypothesis holds only for black-white, and not for hearing-deaf, differences. Nor, of course, could Braden (1984, p. 403) have concluded that "the results contradict theories which propose linguistic bias as the cause of the white-black difference in Performance IQ."

There is, as earlier indicated, still a third presentation of data (from the same deaf standardization sample) in Sisco's (1982) unpublished doctoral dissertation. The treatment of data in the dissertation is both more detailed and more sophisticated than in the earlier reports. Sisco's Tables 3 and 4 (pp. 55-56) present subtest means and mean PIQs separately for the 669 males and 536 females in the sample. Thus, it is again easy to calculate weighted means for the entire sample: But this time from a breakdown of data orthogonal to the breakdown employed by Sisco and Anderson (1980). The means calculated from Sisco (1982) are also presented in our Table 1. They agree quite closely (within rounding error?) with means calculated from Sisco and Anderson, and are inconsistent with the means given by Anderson and Sisco (1977). For Sisco, as for Sisco and Anderson, deaf children do best on Coding; had Sisco's data been used, the correlation between hearing-deaf differences and g loadings would have been +.69.

It should be noted that both the Sisco and Anderson (1980) and the Sisco (1982) data were easily available to Braden (1984), and to Jensen (1985). In fact, Braden cited Sisco and Anderson's Table 3 as one of two sources of "deaf metrics." Braden's Table 1 (p. 405) gives the mean deaf PIQ as 96.89 (SD = 15.45). These values were not taken from Braden's other source (Anderson & Sisco, 1977), who reported a deaf mean of 95.70 (SD = 17.55; Table 5, p. 3). The values given by Braden match exactly those that can be calculated by weighting the data for 100 children of deaf, and 1,100 children of hearing parents given in Sisco and Anderson's Table 3 (1980, p. 925). Why did Braden use weighted data from Sisco and Anderson for PIQs, while using unweighted data from Anderson and Sisco (1977) for subtest means? We have noted that Braden's reliance on Anderson and Sisco for subtest means led him to a theoretical conclusion entirely opposite to one that would have followed from the use of Sisco and Anderson's data, a conclusion that appears to lend support to the notion that not all "environmentally deprived" groups will conform to Spearman's hypothesis.

Braden (1989) recently returned to an examination of hearing-deaf differences as related to Spearman's hypothesis about black-white differences. Braden summarized data from six studies of deaf children. Each study provided information about hearing-deaf differences on a set of tests or subtests, plus a matrix of correlations from which g loadings could be calculated. Placing the data from all studies into a single analysis, Braden reported that for 37 observations, the correlation between the deaf-hearing score differences in standard deviation units and the subtests' g loadings was a nonsignificant -.14. This was said to differ significantly from the positive correlation of .59 earlier reported by Jensen (1985) for black-white studies. The 37 observations described by Braden, like Jensen's black-white observations, often involve precisely the same tests or subtests used by different investigators. Braden failed to explain the rationale behind testing correlations based on such observations for significance. Furthermore, in at least two of the six studies summarized by Braden, the deaf children actually had *higher* IQ scores than the hearing children. Nevertheless, Braden concluded that his failure to find a positive correlation between deaf-hearing score differences and g loadings constituted an empirical refutation of the idea that the positive correlation reported for black-white differences is a statistical artifact. It is not clear why or how a positive correlation between a nonexistent deaf deficit and g loadings should appear. Deaf children, in fact, score about the same as hearing children in the various subtests.

Logical objections aside, Braden's (1989) article is seriously marred by several errors. To begin with, as in Braden's (1984) article, the Anderson and Sisco (1977) subtest means are used, paired with g loadings derived from subtest correlations from Sisco (1982). We have already indicated that these two reports of the same data set are mutually inconsistent.

The deaf standardization sample described by Sisco (1982) and by Anderson and Sisco (1977) is by far the largest sample of deaf children to appear in Braden's (1989) summary. The second largest sample comes from a British standardization of the WISC Performance scale (L. J. Murphy, 1957). Braden incorrectly reported that the mean PIQ of this sample of 300 English deaf children was 93.37, a reasonably substantial deficit. But L.J. Murphy clearly and repeatedly indicated (1957, pp. 228, 230, 236) that their mean IQ was in fact 98.79, suggesting that "this sample of deaf children does not differ significantly in respect of intelligence from ordinary children" (p. 229).

Personal communication from Braden (February 8, 1990) has established that Braden (1989) estimated PIQs from a table of subtest standard scores, for a sample of unspecified size, from an entirely different study of 12-year-old deaf children performed by K. P. Murphy (1957), which appeared in the same volume and used the adult Wechsler scale. The standardization study was performed by L.J. Murphy (1957), using the WISC on children ranging from ages 6 to 10.

Braden (1989) appears to have confused the two Murphys. He took some mean subtest scores from K.P. Murphy (1957) and incorrectly paired them with g loadings derived from intercorrelations published by L.J. Murphy (1957). (K.P. Murphy provided no intercorrelations from which g-factor loadings for his study could be derived.) The correct scores from L.J. Murphy

(p. 234) indicate that deaf children had lower scores on two subtests and higher scores on two others, with no perceptible difference on the fifth subtest. The particular subtest scores from K.P. Murphy utilized by Braden indicate a "deaf deficit" of considerable magnitude on each subtest. Despite these deficits, however, K.P. Murphy surprisingly indicated that the mean PIQ was slightly above 100 for the sample as a whole (pp. 260, 261, 266), and that the mean for the deaf children he studied did not differ from that reported by Wechsler (1944) for a similar age group of hearing children.

The most extreme deaf deficit reported in any of the six studies summarized by Braden (1989) came from a small sample of 59 deaf children studied by Hirshoren, Hurley, and Hunt (1977). Their subjects had a mean WISC-R PIQ of only 88.07. Furthermore, within their sample, the correlation between the magnitude of the deaf deficit and subtests' g loading was negative, unlike the positive correlation found for blacks. This finding, however, offers little support for Braden's (1989) or Jensen's (1985) theoretical position. Though Braden did not mention the fact, Hirshoren et al. indicated that 23 of their 59 subjects (39%) were black. The "deaf deficit" in all other studies cited by Braden is either minimal or nonexistent. Presumably, much of the deficit reported by Hirshoren et al. merely reflects the routinely observed lower test performance of blacks. Thus, an alternate interpretation of the Hirshoren et al. data might stress that a sample containing a substantial proportion of blacks does not conform to Spearman's hypothesis. In any event, it is clear that if one wishes to compare hearing-deaf differences to black-white differences, the use of samples within which the racial mix of deaf children differs substantially from the racial mix of the hearing standardization sample is entirely inappropriate.

The Deaf as Two Distinct Populations

We turn now to our second major theme. We suggest that readers interested in issues of intelligence should be cautious when encountering reports using deaf subjects. This is because the term "deaf" encompasses two distinct populations, a fact unknown to many psychologists but widely recognized among those who work with the deaf community. The distinction is made on an initially surprising attribute: the hearing status of the child's parents.

Deaf children with deaf parents constitute a different population than deaf children with hearing parents. The critical difference between these two groups is whether or not the deaf child had the opportunity to acquire a native language (Brill, 1974; Gallaudet Research Institute, 1987; Rodda & Grove, 1987). Deaf children of deaf parents learn American Sign Language in a manner parallel to that of any child learning a natural language (Hoffmeister & Wilbur, 1980, Newport & Meier, 1985): through direct exposure to the language, primarily in the family environment. Thus, deaf children with deaf parents do not have a "language deprivation" any more than do speakers of French.

Deaf children of hearing parents, on the other hand, experience vastly different formative years. The parents do not use American Sign Language and they have little or no contact with the deaf community. Such children do not have natural access to the language around them, or to the information which that language would convey. These are children who may justly be said to suffer from "language deprivation." These facts have been spelled out clearly for those who conduct research employing deaf subjects:

> The justification for studying deaf children of deaf parents separate from deaf children of hearing parents is attributable to the fact children in the two categories typically are born into and develop within quite different linguistic, social and cognitive environments, even though they may attend the same school programs. (Gallaudet Research Institute, 1987, p. 1)

It is clearly incorrect to consider all children with a hearing loss as a single population. A review of studies that group all such children together obtained contradictory findings, ranging from severe deficits in IQ to normal intelligence (Vernon, 1968). Studies that have separated deaf children by their parental hearing status, however, obtain a consistent result: Deaf children of deaf parents outperform children with hearing parents on virtually any measure of intelligence or academic achievement investigated. "The results of numerous studies . . . indicated consistently that deaf children of deaf parents were superior to deaf children of hearing parents in reading, vocabulary, written language, arithmetic, college attendance and social maturity" (Gallaudet Research Institute, 1987, p. 9; for a detailed review of studies comparing these two groups, see pp. 8-34).

The same result is found in intelligence testing. IQs of deaf children with deaf parents are significantly higher than those with hearing parents (Brill, 1974; Rodda & Grove, 1987). More surprisingly, perhaps, researchers have frequently obtained scores from deaf children with deaf parents that are superior even to hearing norms. For example, the Gallaudet Research Institute (1987), searching for predictors of literacy, used the WAIS on two groups of 65 deaf students, one group having deaf parents, the other having hearing parents. They obtained a mean PIQ for the former group of 113.02 (SD = 14.86). This was significantly higher than the hearing norms. The explanation for this may be debated, but the fact that deaf children of deaf parents should be studied separately from those with hearing parents is now accepted as standard procedure at Gallaudet University, a major center of research on the deaf.

Thus, deaf children should not be considered a single population, not even a bimodal one, at least not when they are to be compared with hearing norms. Hearing norms fall between the IQ scores of deaf children with deaf parents and those with hearing parents.

Braden (1984), as already indicated, derived the mean PIQ of deaf children from Sisco and Anderson's (1980, p. 925) Table 3. That table, in fact, presents data separately for 1,100 children of hearing parents and 100 children of deaf parents. As might be expected, Sisco and Anderson obtained mean PIQs from the deaf children of deaf parents that were superior to hearing norms (M = 106.7, SD = 12.3). Deaf children with hearing parents (M = 96.0, SD = 15.7) were, in turn, inferior to the norms for hearing children (both comparisons, p < .01). Braden chose to calculate a correlation between g loadings and deaf-hearing subtest mean differences by employing data from Anderson and Sisco (1977). Those data pooled the two different populations of deaf children. Had Braden employed the subtest means given in Sisco and Anderson's Table 4 (p. 925)—the same article he used to derive a weighted mean PIQ for all deaf children pooled—he would have found correlations between g loadings and hearing-deaf differences of +.65 for children with hearing parents, and of +.47 for children with deaf parents, rather than the -.79 he reported. Those correlations are very similar to the average of .59 reported by Jensen (1985) for black-white differences and g loadings.

We do not suggest that the correlations of .65 and .47 should be taken very seriously; we have already noted the inconsistencies in the Anderson and/or Sisco data sets, and Sisco and Anderson's (1980) Table 4 rounds off subtest means to a single decimal place. We do suggest that readers should be wary of reports that pool the IQ scores of deaf children without regard to parental hearing status. We also conclude that data derived from deaf children do not support the Jensen (1985) and Braden (1984) argument that "deprived" deaf children, unlike blacks, do not conform to Spearman's hypothesis. Positive correlations between mean differences and g loadings are as easily obtained with deaf children as are negative ones. The sign of the correlation obtained depends entirely on selecting from among inconsistent reports of the same data. These data cannot provide adequate support for any theoretical hypothesis.

Notes

[1] Telephone conversations in 1990 with R.J. Anderson and with F.H. Sisco, as well as inquiries to the Gallaudet Research Institute, indicate that the data from

the deaf standardization sample appear to be lost. The ambiguities can therefore not be resolved.

References

Anderson, R. J., & Sisco, F.H. (1977). *Standardization of the WISC-R performance scale for deaf children* (Office of Demographic Studies Publication Series T, No. 1). Washington, DC: Gallaudet College.

Braden, J.P. (1984). The factorial similarity of the WISC-R performance scale in deaf and hearing samples. *Personality and Individual Differences, 5*, 403-409.

Braden, J.P. (1989). Fact or artifact? An empirical test of Spearman's hypothesis. *Intelligence, 13*, 149-155.

Brill, R.G. (1974). The superior IQs of deaf children of deaf parents. In P. J. Fine (Ed.). *Deafness in infancy and early childhood.* New York: Medcom.

Gallaudet Research Institute. (1987). *Factors predictive of literacy in deaf adolescents with deaf parents/Factors predictive of literacy in deaf adolescents in total communication programs* (Report submitted to the National Institute of Neurological and Communicative Disorders and Stroke: Project No. NIH-NINCDS-83-19). Washington, DC: Gallaudet University.

Hirshoren, A., Hurley, O. L., & Hunt, J. T. (1977). The WISC-R and the Hiskey-Nebraska test with deaf children. *American Annals of the Deaf, 122*, 392-394.

Hoffmeister, R., & Wilbur, R. (1980). The acquisition of sign language. In H. Lane & F. Grosjean (Eds.), *Recent perspectives on American Sign Language.* Hillsdale, NJ: Erlbaum.

Humphreys, L.G. (1985). Race differences and the Spearman hypothesis. *Intelligence, 9*, 275-283.

Jensen, A.R. (1985). The nature of the black-white difference on various psychometric tests: Spearman's hypothesis. *Behavioral and Brain Sciences, 8*, 193-219.

Jensen, A.R. (1987). Further evidence for Spearman's hypothesis concerning black-white differences on psychometric tests. *Behavioral and Brain Sciences, 10*, 512-519.

Murphy, K. P. (1957). Tests of abilities and attainments: Pupils in schools for the deaf aged twelve. In A.W.G. Ewing (Ed.), *Educational guidance and the deaf child.* Manchester, England: Manchester University Press.

Murphy, L. J. (1957). Tests of abilities and attainments: Pupils in schools for the deaf aged six to ten. In A.W.G. Ewing (Ed.), *Educational guidance and the deaf child.* Manchester, England: Manchester University Press.

Newport, E. L., & Meier, R. P. *(1985). The acquisition of American Sign Language. In D.I. Slobin (Ed.), The crosslinguistic study of language acquisition: Vol. 1. The data.* Hillsdale, NJ: Erlbaum.

Rodda, M., & Grove, C. (1987). *Language, cognition and deafness.* Hillsdale, NJ: Erlbaum.

Schonemann, P.H. (1983). Do IQ tests really measure intelligence? *Behavioral and Brain Sciences, 6*, 311-313.

Schonemann, P.H. (1985). On artificial intelligence. *Behavioral and Brain Sciences, 8*, 241242.

Shockley, W. (1987). Jensen's data on Spearman's hypothesis: No artifact. *Behavioral and Brain Sciences, 10*, 512.

Sisco, F.H. (1982). *Sex differences in the performance of deaf children on the WISC-R Performance Scale.* Unpublished doctoral dissertation, University of Florida, Tampa. (University Microfilms No. DA82-26,432).

Sisco, F. H., & Anderson, R. J. (1980). Deaf children's performance on the WISC-R relative to hearing status of parents and child-rearing experiences. *American Annals of the Deaf, 125*, 923-930.

Spearman, C. (1927). The abilities of man. New York: MacMillan.

Vernon, M. (1968). Fifty years of research on the intelligence of deaf and hard-of-hearing children: A review of literature and discussion of implications. *Journal of Rehabilitation of the Deaf, 1*, 1-11.

Wechsler, D. (1944). *The measurement of adult intelligence.* Baltimore, MD: Williams & Wilkins.

Permissions

The articles in the anthology appear with the permission of the authors or publishers of the journals in which the articles originally appeared. Original citations are as follows:

Feher-Prout, T. (1996). Stress and coping in families with deaf children. *Journal of Deaf Studies and Deaf Education, 1*(3), 155-166.

Fischgrund, J., Cohen, O. & Clarkson, L. (1992). Hearing-impaired children in Black and Hispanic Families. *Volta Review, 89,* (5), 59-67.

Isham, W. & Kamin, L. (1993). Blackness, deafness, IQ and g. *Intelligence, 17* (1), 37-46.

Kampfe, C. (1989). Parental reaction to a child's hearing impairment. *American Annals of the Deaf, 134*(4), 255-259.

Lederberg, A. & Golbach, T. (2002). Parenting stress and social support in hearing mothers of deaf and hearing children: A longitudinal study. *Journal of Deaf Studies and Deaf Education, 7*(4), 330-345.

MacTurk, R., Meadow-Orlans, K., Koester, L., & Spencer, P. (1993). Social support, motivation, language, and interaction: A longitudinal study of mothers and deaf infants. *American Annals of the Deaf, 138* (1), 19-25.

Mapp, I. (2004). Stress and coping among Black and Hispanic parents of deaf and hearing-impaired children: A Review of the Literature. (Originally written for this volume.)

Moores, D., Jatho, J. & Dunn, Cynthia. (2001). Families with deaf members: *American Annals of the Deaf,* 1996 to 2000. *American Annals of the Deaf, 146* (3), 245-250.

Steinberg, A., Davila, J., Collazo, J., Loew, R. & Fischgrund, J. (1997). "A little sign and a lot of love . . .": Attitudes, perceptions, and beliefs of Hispanic families with deaf children. *Qualitative Health Research, 7* (2), 202–222.

Steinberg, A., Bain, L., Li, Y., Delgado, G. & Ruperto, V. (2003). Decisions Hispanic families make after the identification of deafness. *Journal of Deaf Studies and Deaf Education, 8*(3), 291-314. (Abridged for this volume).

Tavormina, J., Boll, T, Dunn, N., Luscomb, R. & Taylor, J. (1981). Psychosocial effects on parents of raising a physically handicapped child. *Journal of Abnormal Child Psychology, 9*(1), 121-131.

Vernon, M. (1972). Psychodynamics surrounding the diagnosis of a child's deafness (abridged). *Rehabilitation Psychology, 19*(3), 127-134.

Vernon, M. & Wallrabenstein, J. (1984). The diagnosis of deafness in a child. *Journal of Communication Disorders, 17*(1), 1-8.